Austerity and the Remaking of European Education

Also available from Bloomsbury

Digital Governance of Education, Paolo Landri
Education in the European Union: Post-2003 Member States,
edited by Trevor Corner
Education in the European Union: Pre-2003 Member States,
edited by Trevor Corner
Governance of Educational Trajectories in Europe, edited by Andreas Walther,
Marcelo Parreira do Amaral, Morena Cuconato and Roger Dale

Austerity and the Remaking of European Education

Edited by Anna Traianou and Ken Jones

BLOOMSBURY ACADEMIC
LONDON • NEW YORK • OXFORD • NEW DELHI • SYDNEY

BLOOMSBURY ACADEMIC
Bloomsbury Publishing Plc
50 Bedford Square, London, WC1B 3DP, UK
1385 Broadway, New York, NY 10018, USA

BLOOMSBURY, BLOOMSBURY ACADEMIC and the Diana logo are trademarks
of Bloomsbury Publishing Plc

First published in Great Britain 2019

A catalogue record for this book is available from the British Library.

A catalog record for this book is available from the Library of Congress.

ISBN: HB: 978-1-3500-2848-7
ePDF: 978-1-3500-2849-4
eBook: 978-1-3500-2850-0

Typeset by Deanta Global Publishing Services, Chennai, India
Printed and bound in Great Britain

To find out more about our authors and books visit www.bloomsbury.com
and sign up for our newsletters.

Είναι πολλά βράδια
που εκείνο το παλιό τραίνο
μπαίνει αγκομαχώντας στην κάμαρά μου.
Με σφραγισμένα τα βαγόνια
και τα παράθυρα του
μικρές οθόνες του κόσμου.
Θα μεταφέρει τον κύριο Λένιν σκέφτομαι καθώς
σαν από σκοτεινό θάλαμο φωτογράφου το κόκκινο
ξεχύνεται παντού και πλαταγίζουν
λάβαρα και σημαίες. Ανάμεσα στον κόσμο
που χειροκροτά αναγνωρίζω τον εαυτό μου
να καθρεφτίζεται στην απέναντι τζαμαρία...'.

Giorgos Gotis

Contents

Notes on Contributors

Nafsika Alexiadou, Professor, Department of Applied Educational Science, Umeå University, Sweden.

Guy Dreux, Institut de Recherches, Féderation Syndicale Unifiée, Paris.

Ken Jones, Professor, Senior Policy Advisor, National Education Union, UK.

Dr György Mészáros, Assistant Professor, Faculty of Education and Psychology, Eötvös Loránd University, Budapest, Hungary.

Dr Eszter Neumann, Research Fellow, Institute for Minority Studies, Hungarian Academy of Sciences, Hungary.

Dr Linda Rönnberg, Associate Professor, Department of Applied Educational Science, Umeå University, Sweden.

Anna Traianou, Reader in Educational Studies, Department of Educational Studies, Goldsmiths, University of London, UK.

Introduction

Ken Jones and Anna Traianou

The chapters in this book were composed in Europe's long moment of crisis, which followed the crash of 2008, and the decision of national and EU leaders to respond to it with measures of austerity.

In this decade-long period, the expectations of ever-closer convergence which were set in the 1990s were disrupted by processes in which the relative prosperity of some Northern countries was gained at the expense of societies in Southern Europe. At the same time, within national states, social polarization deepened and political conflicts became more acute: the pro-European political centre did not hold, and the relationship between national states and 'Europe' became a contentious question, with national traditions remobilized as the basis of movements of opposition. In these circumstances, argument over the purposes and procedures of education has sharpened: governments may point to rising average levels of achievement, but there is a wide sense of the shortcomings of an educational model focused on the development of human capital for a labour market strongly marked by precarity. Among educational workers, long-term cuts in spending, accompanied by stricter regulation of teachers, have led, across Europe, to concerns about deprofessionalization.

From these contexts arise the book's analytical interests. The various chapters do not share an identical perspective, but they all tend to take education to be a contested field. They register the continuing importance of national pathways in determining the character of national systems. At European level, they address questions of unequal development; they explore the ways in which the place occupied by different national states in European economic hierarchies affect every aspect of social life, education included. They try to convey a sense of educational programmes, national and European, as faltering and uncertain – not the last word on twenty-first-century education, but a set of hopes that may be incapable of realization.

The book has a double focus – on the development of EU education policy, and of the policy of national states, both at the core of Europe, and on its peripheries.

'Education' refers in large part to the policies and practices developed by, or conducted within, nation states. It refers to the systems of primary, secondary and higher education which took shape as part of the neoliberal turn in government policies across Europe in the 1980s and 1990s. We take this turn to be a first remaking of European education, as post-war systems of mass education were given new objectives and reorganized in their ways of working. We suggest that this was followed by a second remaking, prompted by the perception of political leaders that most European education systems fell short of political expectations. They did not resolve problems of unemployment, especially among youth. They did not lead to productivity increases, or a lessening of social inequalities – hence the desire of policy-makers to look for ways of increasing the reach and intensity of neoliberal educational programmes. This second wave of change intersected with, and was intensified by, an austerity deep and prolonged enough to restructure significantly patterns of employment and welfare provision, and in some cases – notably Greece – to set whole countries off in a new and not necessarily productive political direction.

We take these to be common but not uniform processes across European states. It is a major argument of the book that neoliberalism is not an invariant programme, but develops on the basis of national circumstances, and in relation to forces and conditions that differ according to histories, and positionality within the economic geometry of Europe.

This argument is articulated by Anna Traianou and Ken Jones in Chapter 1. It is in this context that the term 'educational formation' is introduced, in an effort to grasp the specificity of national situations. The other chapters of the book focus on various educational formations from different regions, and from different historical experiences. They aim to demonstrate the ways in which neoliberalism combines with or reacts to political tendencies of right and left. They present thus, an account of educational change which grasps both European policy frameworks, and national educational traditions.

In Chapter 2, Nafsika Alexiadou and Ken Jones sketch a history of the educational policies of the European Union as they have moved through boom and crisis.

In Chapter 3, Ken Jones explores the effects of English economic neoliberalism on the development of the English educational formation. He argues that the country's adherence to a market model of education, in school and universities, is especially strong. Yet England's approach to school curriculum, assessment and governance is detached from OECD orthodoxy and makes only occasional, and idiosyncratic, reference to education in other countries and to the EU education policies.

Guy Dreux, in Chapter 4, draws from the 2018 French education reforms to analyse the tensions between the commitment of the country's political elites to EU economic priorities and a long-standing though not unproblematic tradition which has emphasized the need to reduce educational inequalities.

In Chapter 5, Nafsika Alexiadou and Linda Rönnberg draw on empirical evidence from studies about Swedish private school chains and the national education policy for Roma integration to examine the ways in which global discourses about decentralization and marketization and the reform agendas of the OECD and the European Union have remade Swedish social democratic education traditions.

Chapter 6 focuses on Hungary's semi-peripheral position and on how it shaped education policies in the wake of the financial crisis. In their analysis, Eszter Neumann and György Mészáros show how neoconservatism and centralization became instruments of a state-based programme for national economic development. In this context, education reforms – from the establishment of state-maintained primary church schools to the subordination of vocational and tertiary education to the needs of the industry – solidified societal polarization and generated new class ruptures.

Anna Traianou's analysis in Chapter 7 shows how Greece's strong democratic traditions continue to resist the redrawing of the boundaries between the state's obligations to sustain an education system for equality of opportunity and new demands arising largely from supranational organizations. In the concluding chapter, Ken Jones and Anna Traianou survey the themes of critical responses to neoliberalism across Europe and sketch the likely terms of future contestation.

1

Austerity and the Remaking of Education Policy in Europe since 2008

Anna Traianou and Ken Jones

The literature about education policy-making in Europe tends to keep education closely in focus, while education's wider determinations are presented in less precise ways. We don't wish in this chapter to lose sight of the detail of education – but we do intend to locate the emergence of new forms of governance, management and curriculum in broader contexts of policy and social and economic change. The main aim of the chapter is to understand the central features of educational change by analysing the kinds of flow and pressure, originating outside, as well as within, the field of education, which impact on the education systems of European states and on transnational institutions. Acknowledging the accelerating pace of change, we discuss it in terms of such vectors of transformation as adaptation to the wave of financial and economic shock that began in 2008, the commitment of mainstream political parties and transnational institutions to austerity measures and the consolidation of neoliberal paradigms, even after the moment of the 'credit crunch' which was momentarily thought to have destabilized them. Alongside these largely economic dimensions of crisis, conflict and change, we will discuss the significance of other forces and events, especially mass movements of migration into Europe, and the renaissance of nationalism and xenophobia that has accompanied them. In complex ways, which vary across European states, these tendencies act to frame educational debates, and to prompt policy changes.

Before neoliberalism

In post-war European societies, market relations were not unequivocally dominant. This was true not only of the Comecon countries of Eastern Europe but of much of Western Europe too. Hyman (2015: 2) points out that in the latter societies there were 'important limits to the ways in which labour could be bought and sold', often imposed through elaborate employment protection legislation, relating to the length of the working day, holiday entitlements and stipulated levels of pay. Public policy encouraged collective bargaining: agreements negotiated between employers and workers' organizations were a more significant feature of working life than individual employment contracts. These conditions, which strengthened the position of labour and of trade unions, were reinforced by extensive public welfare systems, established at least in part as the result of pressure from labour movements. Esping-Andersen (1990) noted the 'decommodifying' effects of such systems: they removed aspects of social life from the influence of market forces, and reduced the compulsion on populations to remain in the labour market whatever their age, health and family situations. Developments of this sort amounted to an 'institutionalisation of workers' rights' (Hyman 2015) embedded in the world of work. In some national societies in the richer European core, popular rights extended also to the provision of effective systems of social security. The situation was different in peripheral regions. Eastern Europe saw a large-scale expansion of social provision, but in conditions in which the autonomous activity of trade unions was prevented (Mazower 1998). In some countries of the south, where forces of the left had been defeated in the 1930s and 1940s by a militant and reactionary right, welfare systems and trade unionism remained for several decades in an embryonic form; political and social rights were curtailed by dictatorships.

Education, in many countries, was a space in which the influence of labour markets and economic programmes was restrained by other kinds of demand. In countries of the south, the political and social obedience of the population was a more important objective than the training of a skilled workforce (Boyd-Barratt and O'Malley 1995). Thus, although during the 1950s and 1960s global policy organizations placed a strong emphasis on the modernization of vocational education in 'developing' countries such as Greece, these appeals and recommendations did not lead to significant change (see Traianou in this volume). In more developed countries, for different reasons, the priority of economic goals was also challenged. For instance, the Robbins Committee, appointed by the British government to report on higher education, recognized that it was necessary to attune the university to the needs of competition with 'other highly developed countries in an era of rapid technological and social advance' (Robbins 1963: 8). But it noted, at the same time, that 'education ministers to ultimate ends'; higher education was not just about the making of 'good producers but also good men and women' (Robbins 1963: 8). Similarly, in many school systems, practices intended to achieve increased opportunities for working-class students took precedence for both policy-makers and teachers over other, more economically orientated objectives – see Dreux in this volume for the case of France.

It was a sense of the deep-rooted recalcitrance of education to the adoption of an economic logic which, in 1976, at the end of the long boom, impelled civil servants in England to advise their prime minister that 'some teachers and some schools may have over-emphasized the importance of preparing boys and girls for their roles in society compared with the need to prepare them for their economic role', and that in consequence, the time might 'now be ripe for a change (as the national mood and government policies have changed in the face of hard and irreducible economic facts)' (DES 1976: 10). The same kind of critique was set out in one of the first White Papers produced by the post-1992 European Commission. 'The pressure of the market-place [was] spreading and growing' and 'adaptability [to these processes] is becoming a major prerequisite for economic success' (1993: 92). Education and training systems were not sufficiently susceptible to these pressures and this failing was at least in part responsible for the problems of employment policy in Europe. The relay mechanisms between 'education' and 'the economy' needed to be more efficient.

Economic shock and its aftermath

Demands for the adjustment of education to economic requirements have increased not abated; the greater the severity of economic problems, the stronger the requirement that is placed on education to resolve them.

It is over ten years since the crisis of 2008, when the decision by the US financial authorities not to bail out Lehman Brothers triggered a crisis of the financial system, to the point where it appeared for a few months to be on the point of collapse (Gamble 2009). The crisis developed over the following five years into an economic recession that was deep and long-lasting. In the decade since the collapse of Lehman Brothers, European economies and societies have experienced a slump in growth rates – only recently counteracted by an easing of monetary policy (Euromemorandum 2018). In early 2016 the Eurozone's overall real gross domestic product (GDP) was still below its pre-crisis peak.

The Greek economy was 28 per cent smaller, Portugal 6.5 per cent and Spain 4.5 per cent. Industrial production in the Eurozone was down more than 10 per cent compared to the pre-crisis levels. Investment was below 2007 levels in twenty-one of twenty-eight EU countries (Fazi 2016).

Changes provoked or exacerbated by the crisis have become embedded features of societies. The social and economic settlements of earlier decades had already been rendered fragile by globalization and by the policy turn embodied in the Single European Act (1986) and the Maastricht Treaty (1992). After 2008, fragility worsened to the point of break-up. Youth unemployment has not fallen below 20 per cent across the European Union since 2008 (Fazi 2016). In 2014, nearly one in four persons in the European Union (122.3 million people) was at risk of poverty or social exclusion, a figure higher than that of 2008. The percentage of children living in a household 'at risk of poverty or social exclusion' ranged from around 15 per cent in Denmark (14.5 per cent) and Finland (15.6 per cent), to over 35 per cent in six countries: Latvia, Spain, Greece, Hungary, Bulgaria and Romania (European Parliament Think Tank 2016: 6).

The labour market has stopped being a stable source of prosperity for many people (Lopez 2017): a precarious class (Standing 2011) has grown in numbers, lacking secure access to regular employment, long-term housing and other attributes essential to a secure and autonomous existence; the labour force has been flexibilized in its conditions of work, and deprived of many of the legal rights it previously enjoyed. Economic misery has driven mass migration from Southern and Eastern Europe to the more prosperous north. Within states, there has been a 'marked shift in income and wealth away from the majority of citizens dependent on wages and salaries towards those who derive their income from capital' (Euromemorandum 2018: 3). Between EU states, inequalities are stark; between Latvia and Belgium, for instance, there is a fivefold difference in average household wealth (Tiefensee 2018).

Austerity

These embedded features of social and economic life have been kept in place by a policy choice adopted by most national governments, and by European and global institutions – austerity. In organizing large-scale bailouts to avert the collapse of banks, governments in OECD countries had run up significant current account deficits. The banking crisis was transformed for many states into a fiscal crisis, which by 2010 had become a sovereign debt crisis, as the markets began to register that several states had debts they had little hope of repaying (Blackburn 2011). Bond markets, on which governments relied for their borrowing, required plans to cut deficits, through cuts to public spending and long-term adjustments to deal with issues of public debt. In accommodating these demands, governments of the centre-left and centre-right worsened the recession: cuts in the public sector served to weaken aggregate demand, contributing to low rates of growth.

In its plainest form austerity involves the reduction of government deficits through cuts to public spending, often accompanied by tax increases. This is an orientation strongly rooted in the post-1992 European Union: the foundation of the European Monetary Union and the European Union itself was premised on 'austerian' criteria, which stipulated debt and deficit ceilings and low inflation targets (Plehwe, Neujeffski and Krämer 2018). Following the crisis, criteria of this sort were more stringently applied: to a much greater extent, austerity measures have been constitutionalized in laws, pacts and treaties. The 'six pack' of new laws in 2011 tightened EU surveillance procedures over budget-making. In the same year, the 'Fiscal Compact' enabled EU institutions to impose austerity measures on member states with 'structural deficits'. In 2013, the Treaty on Stability, Co-ordination and Governance wrote these procedures into law, while further legislation – the 'Two Pack' imposed stricter requirements for countries in economic difficulties (EU 2012).

Greece, Portugal, Cyprus, Ireland and Spain all felt the impact of this entrenched orthodoxy, in which the bailout of banks by European and global institutions was conditional upon the adoption of austerity policies by national governments, whatever the social costs. However, this policy of extreme constraint is not something that has been implemented only through external intervention. In the Czech Republic, the Nečas government of 2010–13 adopted stringent austerity measures in order to launch an attack on the country's welfare state – pushing the Czech economy into a second recession (Becker 2016). In Britain, the governments of David Cameron and Theresa May adopted austerity policies enthusiastically, and continued to hold fast to them throughout the post-crisis period; for them, austerity meant more than a temporary slowdown in state spending: it signified a long-term attempt to shrink the social state, and to convince the British population that this was both a necessary and a virtuous project (Clarke and Newman 2012). In France, the presidency of Emmanuel Macron was likewise marked by a determination to bring the country's budget into compliance with the European Union's deficit rules – a goal seen as essential to a modernization of social and political relations in which the influence of collectivist traditions would be reduced (Khan 2017).

Austerity at European level is thus more than a temporary or conjunctural measure; it has come to resemble a permanent kind of structural adjustment, involving continuous attritional reforms of the public sector (McBride and Mitrea 2017). Angela Merkel, Europe's most powerful politician in the post-2008 years, never tired of saying that 'Europe has 7% of the world's population, 25% of its GDP and 50% of its social spending'. If the region 'was to prosper in competition with emerging countries', she argued, 'it could not continue to be so generous' in its social provision (Merkel 2013). Speaking from the same perspective, German finance minister Wolfgang Schäuble made clear to Greek politicians seeking relaxation of the financial conditions imposed upon their country by EU institutions that the 'overgenerous' European social model was no longer sustainable; the requirements of economic competitiveness meant that it had to be abandoned (Varoufakis 2018). As Traianou's chapter shows, this was a lesson in which Greece was forcibly instructed. In seven years following the Memorandum of 2010, in which Greece – facing bankruptcy – agreed to implement austerity measures in return for loans to cover public debts, the country lost more than a quarter of GDP. Youth unemployment ran consistently at 45 per cent. The health budget fell from 6.8 per cent to 4.9 per cent of GDP. The combined effects of austerity amounted to a 'disaster without precedent since the 1930s' (Kouvelakis 2018: 23).

The consequences for education of this policy orientation were significant, because they not only involved reductions in funding but also demanded a different rationale for education, orientated towards the ideals of competitiveness evoked by Schäuble, Cameron and many other political leaders. This rationale, and the institutional arrangements associated with it, drew from a repertoire of ideas, policies and strategies that had begun to be compiled three decades earlier, a repertoire characterized as neoliberal.

The meanings of neoliberalism

The meanings attributed to neoliberalism are various. There is a hard core of neoliberal thinking which treats the market as a natural reality; to achieve economic equilibrium, it 'suffices to leave this entity to its own devices' (Dardot and Laval 2013: 2). This is not a theoretical position which is widely supported. Ronald Reagan famously claimed that 'I'm from the government and I'm here to help' were among the most terrifying words in the English language, but neoliberalism as it actually exists is not anti-statist; rather it depends upon state action to bring neoliberal policies into existence and to protect and extend them thereafter. Neoliberalism – in Harvey's 2005 definition – is in the first instance a theory of political economic practices that proposes that human well-being can best be advanced by liberating individual entrepreneurial freedoms and skills. This 'liberation' is secured within an institutional framework characterized by strong private property rights, free markets and free trade. The role of the state is to create and preserve an institutional framework appropriate to such practices. The neoliberal revolution of the late twentieth century, with its emphasis on the privatization of state assets and the marketization of state provision, consisted in large part not of the annihilation of the state but of the reconstruction of state forms and institutions in a way that 'assisted in the production of certain kinds of social relations' (Dardot and Laval 2013: 130). It was states and global organizations, 'in close collusion with private actors' which fashioned rules conducive to the expansion of market finance (2013: 130). Writing, much earlier, of European Union policy Grahl and Teague (1989: 33) make a similar point: the European Community's project to complete a single market in the twelve member states by 1992 entailed not the withdrawal of the state from the economy, but the intensification of its work: to achieve market completion it was necessary to devise 'some three hundred detailed directives aimed at levelling the legal, technical and fiscal barriers to thoroughgoing competition on a continental scale'.

This project entailed efforts to change the political balance of forces and had a strong antagonistic and ideological dimension. It sought to undo collective solidarities – those that existed in the form of trade unionism and those based on the institutions of the post-war welfare state. In a much-noted article, Denis Kessler, deputy president of the French employers' confederation MEDEF, explained that the French social model was the product of a particular historical moment, the aftermath of war, in which the balance of forces had made necessary an alliance with communism around a programme of social reconstruction. Now it was time to find an 'escape route' from 1945 and 'systematically to undo the programme of the National Council of the Resistance'; without such a confrontation it would be difficult to reconnect France to a globalized world (Kessler 2007). This policy of the 'systematic undoing' of reform was pursued across Europe: '[There are] 40 years to be dismantled', wrote Maria Stella Gelmini, Italian minister of education, in 2008 (Gelmini 2008).

In addition to direct political attacks, labour movements were deeply affected by profound changes in economic organization. While labour had played a significant part in the creation of national systems of regulation, organized working-class movements had much less influence when decisions about political economy moved to a European scale; the gains they had made in an earlier period were supplanted by a new legal order in which goods, capital, services and labour were enabled to flow freely across Europe, without comparable attention to workers' rights and social protection (Scharpf 1999). The various economic innovations of neoliberalism should be seen, at least partly, in such a light (Panitch 1987: 136). Financialization, just-in-time production, privatization, a scaled-down public sector operating according to the rules of new public management, a state watchful and repressive towards its own people – all depended on, and further consolidated, a change in the balance of power between classes, to the advantage of capital in general, and finance capital in particular. In place of the solidarities of post-war social democracy, neoliberalism defined 'a certain existential norm' that 'enjoins everyone to live in a world of generalized competition' (Dardot and Laval: 13). Thus the neoliberal project included the formation of subjectivities as much as the rising fortunes of the financial sector. As Foucault suggested in 1979, government became a sort of enterprise whose task it was to universalize competition and invent market-shaped systems of action for individuals, groups and institutions (Lemke 2001). In this context, a new concept of the 'learner' emerged, which focused on the individual and their responsibilities to 'govern' their own development through the life-long accumulation of skills and competencies; qualities of flexibility, creativity and adaptability were repeatedly emphasized.

For these reasons neoliberalism has often presented as a transformative force, which overrides resistance and marginalizes other political projects. For a particular period in the 1990s and early 2000s, this claim was tenable, if not uncontested: Perry Anderson's melancholy judgement at the turn of the century that the 'principal aspect of the past decade' had been 'the virtually uncontested consolidation, and universal diffusion, of neoliberalism' (Anderson 2000: 6) registers the moment of neoliberal triumph. But as every chapter in this present work seeks to demonstrate, 'virtually uncontested consolidation' is not a term which easily applies to neoliberalism in the current period, in which frozen standards of living and increasing inequality have created a constant turbulence and given rise to forms of protest which while they may be politically ambivalent are also posing significant threats to the political and ideological consensus established around neoliberalism.

State authoritarianism, rising populism

Dardot and Laval argue that neoliberalism 'works to reconstruct state forms and institutions' in order to establish the conditions for its reproduction. It is frequently argued that this reconstruction, which affects legal, social and political relations, is inflected in an authoritarian direction. Dominant social groups are now 'less interested in neutralizing resistance and dissent via concessions and forms of compromise that maintain their hegemony, favouring instead the explicit exclusion and marginalization of subordinate social groups' (Bruff 2014: 116). Working to develop this insight, researchers have tracked the punitive nature of new welfare, immigration and penal policies (Wacquant 2009; Clarke and Newman 2012; Fekete 2016), while Gill (1998) traces the ways in which the main features of the neoliberal order have been 'constitutionalized', in an effort to place them beyond the reach of political decisions, in territory where what is allowable in economic programmes is decided by judges rather than parliaments. Greece, again, provides the strongest example of these tendencies. Following the interventions of the Troika, beginning in 2010, 'Greece's sovereignty on economic issues [has] been reduced almost to that of a protectorate' (Keucheyan and Durand 2015: 44). In 2015, resistance to austerity policies from an elected government, led by the left, collapsed within a few months in the face of the intransigence of the European Union.

Concerns about a growing authoritarianism were passed into the mainstream of political analysis. In 2013, the Council of Europe compiled an extensive review of the 'severe human consequences' of the economic crisis and of the austerity measures that accompanied it – stressing that these consequences were as much legal, social and political as they were economic. In terms of social provision, vulnerable and marginal groups had been hit disproportionately hard, in ways that compounded pre-existing inequalities and injustices. In some cases, 'the very capacity of central and local authorities to deliver on the basic promises of a social welfare state' was at risk. Legally enforceable labour market 'reforms' increased precarity, while also holding down levels of pay. Protests against these conditions had been met in several cases by the 'use of excessive force' and 'infringements of the freedoms of expression and peaceful assembly'.

The 'whole spectrum of human rights' had been affected, including 'access to justice' (damaged by cutbacks to legal aid), freedom of expression and rights to 'participation, transparency and accountability', so that those most affected by austerity were denied the means through which to challenge its impacts (Council of Europe 2013: 13–15).

Of course, the character of European societies cannot be reduced to its authoritarian elements. The recognition of fundamental human rights is embedded in a legally binding EU Charter; in the later part of the twentieth century, many countries saw both legal reforms and de facto social changes which expanded personal freedom – in the areas of gender and sexuality, for instance, and also recognized to some extent the rights of minorities and regions. However, it is difficult to deny the increasing prominence of powerful counter-tendencies: the Council of Europe survey is complemented by a number of national studies, which make a similar case in a wealth of detail austerity is an important driver of restrictions on human rights, not least the rights of young people (Williamson 2014). The punitive nature of the state's response to protest has often had little in common with the principles of equity enshrined in Europe's Charter of Fundamental Human Rights (OJEC 2000; Costa-Krivitsky 2018a, b).

The linkage between austerity and authoritarianism is strong enough to have generated a new coinage – austeritarianism (Hyman 2015). But austerity is not the only aspect of the authoritarian turn; it is articulated with another set of issues, in which the response to migration and the European encounter – or re-encounter – with a non-European otherness is an important factor. As a 'theory of political economic practices' (Harvey 2005) neoliberalism is indifferent to cultural difference; it considers human progress to depend on a competitive process which does not *a priori* privilege any particular social group. In practice, things are different. At least in the period of austerity, neoliberalism has been adopted most unequivocally by parties of the right. These parties have operated on the basis that the 'pure doctrine of the free market that is the animating spirit of neo-liberalism is, by itself, too arid and abstract a creed to offer satisfying fare for any mass electorate (Anderson 2001: 2). The 'ideological supplement' which they have combined with neoliberalism has been based upon an attempt to unify a large section of the national population in opposition to minorities presented as undeserving, criminal, terroristic, dangerous – or simply alien. It is this latter kind of contrast – between national states and their opponents, between Europe and its other – which has increasingly informed policy-making; and it is in this context that some of the traditional themes of conservative politics, which centre on questions of authority and allegiance, have found a new life.

The appeal to xenophobic or nationalist themes by those in mainstream of neoliberal politics has been a feature of politics in many European states. As the effects of austerity became more intense, and popular grievances mounted, new parties emerged with agenda which were nativist to the point of racism – Golden Dawn in Greece, the Freedom Party in Austria, AfD in Germany, the Swedish Democrats, the Lega in Italy, the Front National in France and UKIP in Britain: the Lega's Matteo Salvini, interior minister in the Italian coalition government of 2018, pledged to incarcerate and deport 500,000 Roma, 'street by street, piazza by piazza' (Embury-Dennis 2018). Electoral competition with these parties led more established parties of the right to emphasize their own role as advocates of strong borders, and allegiance to the national culture. In Britain, governments set about creating a 'hostile environment' for migrants, denying access to housing and healthcare; following the Brexit vote in the 2016 referendum, Theresa May, the prime minister, denounced 'cosmopolitans' as 'citizens of nowhere'. In France Emmanuel Macron combined an appeal to global rights with policies of deportation (Fassin 2018). The Rajoy government in Spain introduced health care charging for migrants in such a way as to revitalize 'the boundaries between the citizen-worker and the abject migrant' (Fekete 2016). In this context, the decisions of the German and Swedish governments in 2015 to admit significant numbers of Syrian refugees were momentary exceptions, not the general rule. In 2015 several states closed their border to refugees. By 2018, this policy was in practical terms adopted by the European Union as a whole, as it sought to establish holding centres for migrants outside the borders of Europe: there developed a formidable external reinforcement of the European Union's perimeter, protected by fences, guarded by naval forces and linked to an expanded apparatus for the detention and deportation of refugees (Kouvelakis 2018).

It is in this context – in which the many pressures of austerity are combined with a cultural, legal and social politics in which questions of race and religion, nation and identity, loyalty and authority are a forceful presence – that educational institutions continue to experience a reshaping of their purposes, structures, governance and ethos.

Reshaping education

The impact of neoliberalism on education has been described as an aspect of a 'second modernisation' (Seddon et al. 2015). The first modernization addressed the populations of European societies as members of an industrial workforce, and as citizens of a national state. It offered entry to regulated employment, a level of social protection and access to public services, and the expectation of a rising standard of living, underpinned by state policies which prioritized full employment and social cohesion. Modernization in its second form was significantly different. It focused on the requirements of global competition in what was claimed to be a knowledge economy, and emphasized that workforces could safeguard themselves only by adapting to change, committing themselves to a lifetime of continuous reskilling. The 'human capital' to the development of which education and training systems should be orientated was in need of constant renewal.

The knowledge economy was defined as one in which 'production and services [are] based on knowledge-intensive activities that contribute to an accelerated pace of technological and scientific advance as well as equally rapid obsolescence' (Powell and Snellman 2004: 201). Such activities were argued to constitute a large component of economic life in developed countries (Abramovitz and David 1996); they relied more heavily on the general intellect of the workforce than on natural or other resources, and were often combined with efforts to integrate improvements in every stage of the production process: 'from the R&D lab to the factory floor to the interface with customers' (Powell and Snellman 2004: 201). Tony Blair, in 1995, succinctly expressed the premises of the new economy, and their implications for politics:

> Technological change is reducing the capacity of government to control a domestic economy free from external influence. The role of government in this world of change is to represent a national interest, to create a competitive base of physical infrastructure and human skills. The challenge before our party ... is not how to slow down and so get off the world, but to educate and retrain for the next technologies, to prepare our country for new global competition, and to make our country a competitive base from which to produce the goods and services people want to buy. (Blair 1995: 20)

Governments, Blair continued, should focus on 'creating a fully-educated labour force conversant with the skills necessary to implement the new technology'. Education should be lifelong and technologized, and if this was accomplished, then his country would be transformed not only into a country of 'innovative people' but also into the 'electronic capital of the world' (Blair 1996: 93, 98, 127), capable of responding to 'the emergence of the new economy and its increased demands for skills and human capital' (Department for Education and Employment 2001: 8). Blair thus prefigured the Lisbon Declaration of 2000, in which the European Union expressed similar ambitions: Europe should 'become the most competitive and dynamic knowledge-based economy in the world'.

This turn in economic thinking was accompanied by a redesign of education systems, so as to produce the new kinds of human capital, the flexible and creative workers, that the knowledge economy was thought to require. There has been a tendency, unevenly present in the education systems of Europe but endorsed in the policy documents of the OECD and the European Union, for the curriculum to be presented not as a given body of knowledge to be transmitted to students but as a generic set of skills and competences, with a focus on the centrality of the individual learner, supported through active forms of pedagogy and a view of the teacher as a facilitator of 'personalized' learning. Because education systems as they developed in the post-war period were not thought capable of addressing these new priorities, the policy turn has been accompanied by a stronger emphasis on the assessment of learning in relation to the production of closely specified and measurable outcomes, for which institutions from schools to universities are held accountable (Priestley and Sinnema 2014).

Compatible with the focus on measurable performance are other, system-wide, changes, which involve a complex mix of decentralization and recentralization. The UK is sometimes presented (Sahlberg 2009) as the European home of such a programme, seen as a body of ideas generated in the Anglophone world and popularized in the term 'New Public Management' (NPM). As an account of origins, this is broadly true, but it underestimates the extent to which NPM programmes have become a norm across Europe. NPM was introduced in the 1980s initially in the United States, New Zealand, Australia and Britain, as a result of the 'fiscal crisis of the state' (O'Connor 1973) and of consequential demands to control public expenditure by improving the efficiency of the public sector. NPM reforms combined decentralized operational management and detailed central regulation, introducing to the public sector forms of organization which 'approximated to' the 'discipline of the market': 'lean' autonomous organizational forms, devolution of budgets and financial control, outsourcing and other market-type mechanisms such as competitive tendering, and performance-related pay. These decentralizing tendencies were accompanied by recentralizing strategies which favoured a central, stronger executive management, steering sectoral activity through target-setting, evaluation, incentives and sanctions (Hood 1991). NPM required that public funded activities be accountable through the monitoring of performance in the same way private enterprises are believed to be accountable to investors in terms of sales, profits and dividends. Its guiding assumption was that by making institutions responsible in a competitive environment for their own success or failure, standards would be driven up. But what counted as achievement would be determined not only by consumer demand but by government decision. It would be central government that set the criteria for success, measured progress towards them and rewarded or sanctioned institutions accordingly. Market arrangements were thus interwoven with state regulation of a stronger and more intrusive kind.

At the heart of NPM reforms is distrust in the expertise of professionals (e.g. teachers, academics) and an attempt to replace it with 'transparent accountability'. Thus, beyond the establishment of quasi-markets, equally important for NPM is the provision of information, usually to government agencies, about institutional performance: a shift towards measurement and quantification in the public sector in the form of 'performance' indicators and/or explicit 'standards' is claimed to increase competition and improves its effectiveness (Power 1997; Pollitt 2003; Pollitt and Dan 2011). In addition to these effects on the producers of public services, NPM has a wider impact, serving to transform 'citizens' to 'consumers' by steering them towards a position in which they would make responsible choices on the basis of the wealth of information newly supplied by state-funded bodies. The publication of higher education league tables for example or the results of school inspections and audits provides information about the performance of these units which allows the funders of the public sector, both government and citizens, to judge its effectiveness and efficiency (Pollitt 1990; Middlehurst and Kennie 1995; McNay 1995).

In the 1990s a series of publications by the influential Public Management Committee of the OECD suggested that most of the developed world had embarked on an NPM path (OECD 1995). Ten years later the organization insisted that as a result 'most OECD public administrations have become more efficient, more transparent and more customer oriented, more flexible and more focused on performance' (OECD 2005: 10). In the same period funding from the European Commission was directed towards NPM reforms, especially in the accession countries of Eastern Europe as they prepared to join the single market (Pollitt and Dan 2011). As advocated by the OECD (2012b) post-2008 austerity accentuated the emphasis on such reforms, through the European Semester, and presented them as a necessary element in Europe's economic recovery (Asatryan et al. 2016). 'Enhancing the quality of education is central to our efforts to restore long-term economic growth and job creation in Europe', wrote the EU president, Jean-Claude Juncker, in 2015, adding that 'quality needs to be continuously monitored and improved, which calls for effective quality assurance systems covering all education levels' (Eurydice Report 2015: 1–3).

NPM as an education policy construct has thus been worked and reworked through European and international bodies. It is, however, a mistake to assume that there is a high degree of convergence between NPM reforms across European nation states. The labels may be the same, but the underlying story differs all the time from country to country (Pollitt, Thiel and Homburg 2007: 4). At the same time the success of NPM projects varies considerably, with results on the ground being much more mixed than global policy organizations are willing to register. In England, an enduring commitment to NPM led to the establishment of a pervasive machinery composed of markets, metrics and performance management not only in education but also in all aspects of public life (see Jones in this volume): thirty years after its first ventures, it continues to be the matrix of new initiatives. The United Kingdom's 'Office for Students', for instance, established in 2018, affects to evaluate the quality of university teaching, and to identify good and bad performance. It is a programme which involves an intense re-regulation of institutional life, as institutions, seeking to meet performance targets, devise new educational cultures in which everyday practice is opened more closely to management scrutiny and specification (Holmwood 2017). However, in several national cases the gap between 'regulatory aspirations and actual provision' is wide (Verger and Curran 2014: 268): teachers and educational institutions lack the capacity to implement changes for which a national mandate exists. In some countries this appears to be a problem of professional development – which inhibits, for instance, the take-up of formative assessment of learners in the Czech Republic (OECD 2012a). In others such problems may be combined with political hostility. The contrast in this context between different regions of Europe is striking. In Eastern Europe, neoliberal education programmes were boldly advocated and readily accepted. In the post-1989 period of transition towards capitalism, education policy development in Visegrad countries was strongly influenced by the prescriptions and the funding opportunities of the World Bank. Entry to the European Union provided further funding for wide-ranging reform of the education sector. The objectives of education systems were presented in terms of developing the competencies, employability and motivation of the future workforce. Higher education was likewise seen as a driver of competitiveness and was charged with improving the flexibility and competitiveness of graduates (Halasz 2015). In Southern Europe, change has been more controversial. In France, thanks to the impact of the social movement and strike wave of 1995, policies identified as 'neoliberal' were widely rejected, at least until 2010 (Jones 2009; Dreux, this volume). In Catalonia, the implementation of NPM has been 'selective and contested' (Verger and Curran 2014) though NPM accountability increasingly affects the daily work of teachers (Verger and Pages 2018). In Italy, where the Ministry of Education advocated the publication of pupil test results, in order to improve educational quality through inter-school competition, resistance was strong, albeit 'mediated by welfarist legacies, consisting in most cases of the effort to defend the status quo rather than to develop critical alternatives' (Grimaldi and Serpieri 2014: 173). In Greece's centralized education system, NPM reforms continue to be weak (Asatryan et al. 2016): teachers continue to resist the evaluation of their work, making the country one of the few EU states where the gap between regulatory policies and practices is particularly wide.

Neoliberal policies encountered limits of another sort in Nordic countries, which, more strongly than the states of Southern Europe, possessed a model of education in which 'social justice and equality' had a recognized place (Lundahl 2016). The education systems of the five Nordic countries still display 'a number of common inclusive traits, enabled by continued extensive public funding of education: free of charge education and related services at primary, secondary and tertiary levels, well thought-out pre-school education and childcare, integration of students in need of special support in ordinary classrooms'. In addition, all retain nine- or ten-year comprehensive compulsory education with little or no tracking. However, as Lundahl reports, 'decentralization from the state to the local level and various neoliberal policy measures have been applied in all of the Nordic countries, and these changes are undoubtedly undermining the foundations of the Nordic model'. In Sweden private schools were almost non-existent before the early 1990s, but a highly visible commercial school market has developed since then, becoming more pronounced in the 2000s (see Alexiadou and Rönnberg in this volume). Similarly, the marketization of education in Sweden 'affects most aspects of education and schools profoundly – socially, economically, academically and professionally' – and has changed the relationships between actors in school and their pedagogical identities (Lundahl 2016: 10).

Educational formations

It can be argued that despite resistances and uneven development elements of NPM reforms have slowly penetrated national education systems. For example, in 2004, in only a quarter of EU countries did schools use indicators such as students' test results to compare their performance with other similar schools or with national averages. In 2015, the proportion had risen to two-thirds. Many countries have introduced compulsory national testing mechanisms and/or provide individual schools with their aggregated test results (Eurydice 2015). The wider use of standardized tests was seen as an important means of improving educational quality, and thus of raising human capital (OECD 2012b). However, the overall direction of these reforms is ambiguous and, as Pollitt and Bouchart (2017) argued, is shaped by national contexts. There are risks therefore involved in awarding neoliberalism a kind of automatic conceptual primacy in explaining social and policy change, and in treating it as a master concept which holds the key to understanding the character of contemporary education systems. National educational practices and traditions continue to play an important part in shaping education policies, to the extent where the concept of a 'neo-liberal education system' is only in part productive. To be sure, to write of 'neoliberalism' allows the identification of important features of contemporary education systems, in their articulation with political economy. But the term does not in itself point directly towards concrete analysis, and it is useful to think about ways in which it can be revised or elaborated. Althusser, thinking under the influence of Lenin, about similar conceptual problems, proposed 'social formation', as a term which enabled analysis of societies as 'concrete complex totalities', 'comprising economic practice, political practice and ideological practice at a certain place and stage of development'. 'Historical materialism', he added, 'is the science of social formations' (Althusser and Balibar 1970); it is centrally concerned with economic systems, but is not satisfied that social structures can be 'read off' from an analysis of economic foundations. It is not necessary to share Althusser's structural Marxism to see the value of this approach. A perspective similar to his might see us thinking, not of a 'neo-liberal education system', but of an 'educational formation', in which different types of educational practice and ideologies were combined, with neoliberal orientations playing an important but not pre-given role. We might conclude, following the 'concrete analysis of a concrete situation', that some practices and orientations were dominant, and that these reflected particular economic conditions and programmes, but we would not do so prematurely, without fuller exploration of the histories and the social relationships out of which an educational formation was constituted.

'Educational formation' gives us a way of thinking about one of the most striking features of national policy-making in education in Europe. The concern for equity and formal rights which is characteristic of most national policy discourses, and which is encouraged by the European Union and OECD, is combined in practice with measures that work against such commitments, and which orientate education, at school level in particular, towards ideological frameworks which are communalist and ethnocentric. We referred above to a context in which the pressures of austerity are 'combined with a cultural, legal and social politics in which questions of race and religion, nation and identity, loyalty and authority are a forceful presence'. Education has been a central site on which the tensions of this combination have been worked through. Here the question of Islam has been central – the enemy against which governments and parties (mainly) of the right have sought to mobilize. Hungary offers a raucous example of such a strategy – see the chapter by Neumann and Mészáros later in this volume – but there have been striking examples of nativist mobilization in core countries of Europe. In England in 2014 the Conservative-Liberal Democrat coalition government claimed that schools in Birmingham had been subverted by Islamic radicals, and launched a full-scale inquiry, in the course of which the national school inspectorate produced reports on schools designed to support a narrative that an 'enemy within' had infiltrated their governance and management (Holmwood and O'Toole 2017). In France, for more than a decade, the issue of the 'veil' has been a focus for political agitation. Governments of left and right have regarded the foulard, the hijab and the burqa as threats to the republican values of the French state, while secularist intellectuals insisted that Muslims choose between adherence to their religion and participation in public life (Diallo 2018). In Denmark, debates around the policy of separating learners of Danish as a second language from the mainstream school have highlighted the existence of a kind of 'left-wing' chauvinism, which defends the tradition of the 'people's high school', without being willing to admit foreigners to it (Buchardt 2018). In Denmark's early years education, there are similar tensions. A pre-school system seen as 'child-centred' and progressive

(Wall, Litjens and Taguma 2015) is being reshaped by state intervention, so that from the age of one, children from officially categorized 'ghetto areas' will be separated from their parents for at least twenty-five hours a week for mandatory instruction in 'Danish values' (Fekete 2018).

In these dramas, replicated across Europe a version of national identity is being reasserted. Students who have been addressed in human capital terms, with reference to the value of learning to their future position in the labour market, are increasingly interpellated by a discourse of citizenship, in which national values, presented as caught up in a civilizational conflict, are increasingly invoked. Grimaldi and Serpieri write optimistically that national educational cultures help create spaces of 'thought and action … for (re) discovering wider meanings for education and for thinking alternative future societies' (Grimaldi and Serpieri 2014: 177), but their optimism may be misplaced. The 'wider meanings' for education may go beyond those of human capital, but their character may well be more nationalistic than educationalists tend to imagine.

Conclusion

In this chapter we have explored the kinds of flow and pressure, originating outside the field of education, which impact on the education systems of European states.

We have treated neoliberalism in education as a set of processes which prioritize privatization and marketization and which construct subjectivities and policies which favour individuality and competition. We have discussed the devastating social and economic effects on nation states of austerity programmes and we have argued that increasing levels of poverty challenges its earlier claim to reduce unemployment and social inequalities in education. We have argued that this prolonged period of austerity has created other tensions in nation states, associated with the deployment of xenophobic or nationalist themes not only by those in mainstream of neoliberal politics but also by new populist, right-wing parties whose education agenda revolves around protecting a set of values represented as national; which marginalize new and established migrant populations. We have shown the insistence of the EU institutions and the OECD on strengthening further their neoliberal agenda through investing on NPM, their main reform mechanism – and we have also discussed the lack of convergence between such reforms in nation states. In these contexts we have introduced the concept of 'educational formation' to capture the ways in which nation states combine different types of education practice, old and new traditions and ideologies with neoliberal orientations. These reflections and interpretations form a background to the following chapters, which address the educational policies of the European Union as they have moved through boom and crisis, and the patterns of educational contestation within national states.

References

Abramovitz, M. and David, P. A. (1996) Technological change and the rise of intangible investments: The US economy's growth-path in the twentieth century, in D. Foray and B. A. Lundvall (eds), *Employment and Growth in the Knowledge-based Economy*, Paris: Organisation for Economic Cooperation and Development.

Althusser, L. and Balibar, E. (1970) *Reading Capital*, London: New Left Books.

Anderson, P. (2000) Renewals, *New Left Review*, II: 1–30.

Anderson, P. (2001) US elections; Testing formula two, *New Left Review*, II/8: 5–23.

Asatryan, Z., Heinemann, F., Yeter, M., Rubio, E., Rinaldi, D. and Zuleeg, F. (2016) *Budgetary Affairs: How the EU Budget is Used to Encourage It*, Yeter, European Policy Centre (EPC), Brussels (Chapter 7) Directorate General for Internal Policy Department D. European Union.

Barratt-Brown, O. and O'Malley, P. (eds) (1995) *Education Reform in Democratic Spain*, London: Routledge.

Becker, J. (2016) Europe's other periphery, *New Left Review*, II/99, May–June: 39–64.

Blackburn, R. (2011) Crisis 2.0, *New Left Review*, II/72: 33–63.

Blair, T. (1995) The power of the message, *New Statesman*, 29 September: 19–22.

Blair, T. (1996) *New Britain: My Vision of a Young Country*, London: Fourth Estate.

Bruff, I. (2014) The rise of authoritarian neoliberalism, *Rethinking Marxism*, 26 (1): 113–29.

Buchardt, M. (2018) The 'culture' of migrant pupils: A nation-and welfare state historical perspective on the European refugee crisis, *European Education*, 50 (1): 58–73.

Clarke, J. and Newman, J. (2012) The alchemy of austerity, *Critical Social Policy*, 32 (3): 299–319.

Commission of the European Communities (1993) *Growth, Competitiveness, Employment: The Challenges and Ways Forward into the Twenty-First Century*, Brussels: European Commission.

Costa-Kostritsky, V. (2018a) May '18, *London Review of Books*, Blog, 23 May. https://www.lrb.co.uk/blog/2018/05/23/valeria-costa-kostritsky/may-18/

Costa-Kostritsky, V. (2018b) In Persan, *London Review of Books*, Blog, 30 July. https://www.lrb.co.uk/blog/2018/07/30/valeria-costa-kostritsky/in-persan/

Council of Europe, Commissioner for Human Rights (2013) *Safeguarding Human Rights in Times of Economic Crisis*, Strasbourg: Council of Europe.

Dardot, P. and Laval, C. (2013) *The New Way of the World*, London: Verso.

Department for Education and Employment (2001) *Schools Building on Success: Raising Standards, Promoting Diversity, Achieving Results*, London: The Stationery Office.

Department of Education and Science (1976) *School Education in England: Problems and Initiatives. 'The Yellow Book'*, London: Department of Education and Science.

Diallo, R. (2018) A student leader is the latest victim of France's obsession with the hijab, *Guardian*, 28 May.

Embury-Dennis, T. (2018) Italy's deputy PM Salvini called for 'mass cleansing, street by street, quarter by quarter', newly resurfaced footage reveals, *The Independent*, 21 June.

Esping-Andersen, G. (1990) *The Three Worlds of Welfare Capitalism*, Cambridge: Polity.

Euromemorandum (2018) European economists for an alternative economic policy in Europe Euromemorandum 2018. http://www.euromemo.eu/index.html

European Parliament Think Tank (2016) *European Parliament Poverty in the European Union: The Crisis and Its Aftermath*. http://www.europarl.europa.eu/thinktank/en/document.html?reference=EPRS_IDA(2016)579099

European Union (EU-Lex) (2012) Treaty on stability, coordination and governance in the economic and monetary union. https://eur-lex.europa.eu/legal-content/EN/TXT/?uri=legissum:1403_3

Eurydice Report (2015) *Assuring Quality in Education: Policies and Approaches to School Evaluation in Europe*, European Commission.

Fassin, D. (2018) Sure looks a lot like conservatism, *London Review of Books*, 40 (13): 15–17.

Fazi, T. (2016) The EU's banking union a recipe for disaster, *Open Democracy 2016*. https://www.opendemocracy.net/can-europe-make-it/thomas-fazi/eus-banking-union-recipe-for-disaster

Fekete, L. (2016) Flying the flag for neoliberalism, *Race and Class*, 58 (3): 3–22.

Fekete, L. (2018) *Islamophobia in Denmark: From Parallel Societies to the Ghetto List*, London: Institute for Race Relations.

Gamble, A. (2009) *The Spectre at the Feast: Capitalist Crisis and the Politics of Recession*, London: Macmillan.

Gelmini, M.-S. (2008) Quarantanni da smantellare, *Corriere della Sera*, 21/22 August.

Gill, S. (1998) New constitutionalism, democratisation and global political economy, *Pacifica Review*, 10 (1): 23–38.

Grahl, J. and Teague, P. (1989) The cost of neo-liberal Europe, *New Left Review*, 1/174: 33–51.

Grimaldi, E. and Serpieri, S. (2014) Italian education beyond hierarchy: Governance, evaluation and headship, *Educational Management Administration & Leadership*, 42 (4S): 119–38.

Halasz, G. (2015) Education and social transformation in Central and Eastern Europe, *Journal of European Education*, 50 (3): 350–71.

Harvey, D. (2005) *A Brief History of Neoliberalism*, Oxford: Oxford University Press.

Holmwood, J. (2017) *Requiem for the Public University*. Available at: http://publicuniversity.org.uk/2017/05/02/requiem-for-the-public-university/, accessed 20 July 2018.

Holmwood, J. and O'Toole, T. (2017) *Countering Extremism in Schools? The Truth about the Birmingham Trojan Horse Affair*, Bristol: Policy Press.

Hood, C. (1991) A public management for all seasons, *Public Administration*, 69 (1): 3–19.

Hyman, R. (2015) *Austeritarianism in Europe: What Options for Resistance*? Paper for Institute for New Economic Thinking, April 2015. https://www.ineteconomics.org/research/research-papers/austeritarianism-in-europe-what-options-for-resistance

Jones, K. (2009) Patterns of conflict in education: France, Italy, England, in Tony Green (ed.), *Blair's Educational Legacy 13 Years of New Labour*, New York: Palgrave Macmillan US.

Kessler, D. (2007) Éditorial', *Challenge*, 4 October. Available at: http://www.challenges.fr/opinions/1191448800.CHAP1020712/adieu_1945_raccrochons_ notre_pays_au_monde_.html, accessed 20 July 2018.

Keucheyan, R. and Durand, C. (2015) Bureaucratic Caesarism: A Gramscian outlook on the crisis of Europe, *Historical Materialism*, 23 (2): 33–51.

Khan, M. (2017) Macron's £9 billion austerity headache, *Financial Times*, 3 July.

Kouvelakis, S. (2018) Borderland: Greece and the EU's Southern Question, *New Left Review*, II/110: 5–34.

Lemke, T. (2001) The birth of bio-politics': Michel Foucault's lecture at the Collège de France on neo-liberal governmentality, *Economy and Society*, 30 (2): 190–207.

Lopez, A. M. (2017) All precarious? Institutional change and turning points in labour market trajectories in Spain: Insights from narrative biographies, *Employee Relations*, 39 (3): 408–22.

Lundahl, L. (2016) Equality, inclusion and marketization of Nordic education: Introductory notes, *Research in Comparative and International Education*, 11 (1): 3–12.

Mazower, M. (1998) *Dark Continent: Europe's Twentieth Century*, London: Penguin.

McBride, S. and Mitrea, S. (2017) Austerity and constitutionalizing structural reform of labour in the European Union, *Studies in Political Economy*, 98 (1): 1–23.

McNay, I. (1995) From the collegial academy to corporate enterprise: The changing cultures of universities, in T. Schuller (ed.), *The Changing University*, London: Society for Research into Higher Education.

Merkel, A. (2013) Speech at World Economic Forum, Davos, cited by Cecile Barbier Chronology 2013, Key Events in European Policy, ETUI.

Middlehurst, R. and Kennie, T. (1995) Leadership and professionals: Comparative frameworks, *Tertiary Education and Management*, 1 (2): 120–30.

O'Connor, J. (1973) *The Fiscal Crisis of the State*, New York: St. Martin's Press.

OECD (1995) *Governance in Transition: Public Management Reforms in OECD Countries*, Paris: PUMA/OECD.

OECD (2012a) *Reviews of Evaluation and Assessment in Education: Czech Republic*, Paris: OECD.

OECD (2012b) *Economic Policy Reforms: Going for Growth*, Paris: OECD.

Official Journal of the European Commission (2000) Charter of Fundamental Rights of the European Union (2000/C 364/01), 18 December.

Panitch, L. (1987) Capitalist restructuring and labour strategies, *Studies in Political Economy*, 24: 131–49.

Plehwe, D., Neujeffski, M. and Krämer, M. (2018) Saving the dangerous idea: Austerity think tank networks in the European Union, *Policy and Society*, 37 (2): 188–205.

Pollitt, C. (1990) *Managerialism and the Public Services: The Anglo-American Experience*, Oxford: Blackwell.

Pollitt, C. (2003) Public Management reform: reliable knowledge and international experience, *OECD Journal on Budgeting*, 3 (3): 121–36.

Pollitt, C. and Bouckaert, G. (2017) *Public Management Reform A Comparative Analysis – Into the Age of Austerity*, 4th edn, Oxford: Oxford University Press.

Pollitt, C. and Dan, S. (2011) *The Impacts of the New Public Management in Europe: A Metaanalysis*, Coordinating for Cohesion in the Public Sector of the Future (COCOPS) European Commission.

Pollitt, C., van Thiel., S. and Homburg, V. (2007) New Public Management in Europe, *Management Online Review*, October.

Pollitt, C., Thiel, S. V., Homburg, V. and Van Thiel, S. (eds) (2007) *New Public Management in Europe Adaptation and Alternatives*, Basingstoke: Palgrave Macmillan.

Powell, W. W. and Snellman, K. (2004) The knowledge economy, *Annual Review of Sociology*, 30: 199–220.

Power, M. (1997) *The Audit Society: Rituals of Verification*, Oxford: Oxford University Press.

Priestley, M. and Sinnema, C. (2014) Downgraded curriculum? An analysis of knowledge in new curricula in Scotland and New Zealand, *The Curriculum Journal*, 25 (1): 50–75.

Robbins Report (1963) *Report of the Committee Appointed by the Prime Minister Under the Chairmanship of Lord Robbins*, London: HMSO.

Sahlberg, P. (2009) *Finnish Lessons: What can the World Learn from Educational Change in Finland?* New York: Teachers College Press University.

Scharpf, F. (1999) *Governing in Europe: Effective and Democratic?*, Oxford: Oxford University Press.

Seddon, T., Larsen, A., Rasmussen, P., Rönnberg, L. and Tsatsaroni, A. (2015) Policies of 'modernisation' in European education: Enactments and consequences, *European Education Research Journal*, 14 (6): 479–86.

Standing, G. (2011) *The Precariat: The New Dangerous Class?* London: Bloomsbury.

Tiefensee, A. (2018) A big legacy: Wealth in Europe, in H. Meyer (ed.), *Inequality in Europe*. Friedrich-Ebert-Stiftung, Hans Böckler Stiftung, Social Europe. https://www.socialeurope.eu/wp-content/uploads/2018/01/Inequality-in-Europe -final.pdf

Varoufakis, Y. (2018) *Adults in the Room*, 2nd edn, London: Vintage.

Verger, A. and Curran, M. (2014) New public management as a global education policy: Its adoption and recontextualisation in a Southern European setting, *Critical Studies in Education*, 55 (3): 253–71.

Verger, A. and Pages, M. (2018) New public management and its effects in the teaching profession: Recent trends in Spain and Catalonia, in Romuald Normand, Min Liu, Luís Miguel Carvalho, Dalila Andrade Oliveira and Louis LeVasseur (eds), *Education Policies and the Restructuring of the Educational Profession*, Singapore: Springer.

Wacquant, L. (2009) *Punishing the Poor: The Neoliberal Government of Social Insecurity*, Durham and London: Duke University Press.

Wall, S., Litjens, I. and Taguma, M. (2015) *Pedagogy in Early Childhood Education and Care: An International Comparative Study of Approaches and Policies*, London: DfE.

Williamson, H. (2014) Radicalisation to retreat: Responses of the young to austerity Europe, *International Journal of Adolescence and Youth*, 19 (sup 1): 5–18.

2

Educational Policy-Making in Europe 1986–2018: Towards Convergence?

Nafsika Alexiadou and Ken Jones

The Lisbon Declaration of 2000, with its ambition to make the European Union 'the most competitive and dynamic knowledge-based economy in the world', marked a new phase in the development of EU education policy, and encouraged new waves of academic research. Since 2000, the volume, detail and sophistication of academic research have grown considerably and the instruments of EU policy-making, their relationship to the policies of national states and their effectiveness in economic and social terms have all been brought more closely into focus. In the course of this analysis a particular narrative has developed – all the more influential for being unsystematized and unvoiced – which tends to tell a story of a partial but steady process of convergence, in which the policy objectives of member states have become increasingly coordinated and more precise in their requirements. The accent of this account falls on consensus around policy goals, and on the development of the technical means by which they can be realized. It is most evocatively presented by Martin Lawn (2013), who summarizes what he has learned from close investigation of the ways in which knowledge and policy have been connected and elaborated. For Lawn, governance (of education) in Europe is developed through

> public-private partnerships, knowledge-based organizations, agencies, associations and markets. … This activity is often out of sight and excludes politics. It thrives among a new elite of technocrats, professionals and academics, with expert knowledge or skills. … They meet in associations or through projects or networks. They are solving problems, problems in the governing of Europe, through the collection, classification, and analysis of data, the parallel creation of standards or the accumulation of knowledge about problems and development. (20)

In this account, what is notable is the expert character of policy work and the distance of educational process from a wider world of political contestation. The storms of popular controversy over the meaning and the direction of the EU project do not trouble the deeper, long-term activities through which Europe, in its educational dimensions, is being fabricated.

A similar distance between expert and popular strata of activity is noted – in more explicitly critical terms – by Romuald Normand (2010) and Antonio Nóvoa (2001, 2013). For Normand, the work of experts has political effects: it 'gives us the impression that policy makers manage public action with method and rationality' thus 'helping to elaborate a common vision of public issues in education', one of whose consequences is that far-reaching programmes of educational change appear to be common-sense adaptations rather than controversial matters of political choice (Normand 2010: 415). Nóvoa goes further. One of the effects of the prestige assigned to the work of experts is to open a gap between policy-making and democratic politics – a gap which is deliberately maintained by a bureaucratic elite. Nóvoa raises the prospect of 'a permanent orientation in which a suprastate bureaucracy will predominate and put into place a strategy based on criteria of economic rationality that tends to transform politics into a problem of administration and management' (Nóvoa 2001: 254). He thus registers – in a dystopian, rather than a positivist mode – an assumption about the potency of new kinds of policy-making.

This is the context in which this chapter seeks to make an intervention. It sketches a history of EU policy-making in education and training, acknowledging the importance of policy convergence, across Europe, around objectives which are explicitly linked to the economic and social programme of the European Union, and which have been developed within the European Union's institutional framework. Alongside this emphasis, however, it seeks to establish another way of reading policy-making, in which other factors assume a significant position. In this interpretation, inequalities and antagonisms between member states are highlighted, as are the continuously destabilizing effects of social and economic polarization between and within countries. Thus, in parallel with an account of convergence and consensus among policy elites, we try to draw attention to constraints upon and unresolved tensions within European education policy. In order to do this, we aim to move beyond research which directly focuses on educational institutions and networks. Outside the field of research in education, there has been developed a tradition of policy analysis which locates questions of perspectives, strategy and governance in a context where antagonism and conflict are more central, where policy decisions are viewed as both ideologically driven and contestable, and where the rationality and achievability of the goals which the European Union has set for itself are problematized (Streeck 2011; Bickerton 2016; Eley, Paggi and Streeck 2017).

From such a perspective, the orientation of the European Union since the late 1980s has been a complex mix of socially constructive and economically disruptive programmes, with the latter having an increasingly dominant and destabilizing effect. So far as construction is concerned, the historian Geoff Eley (2017) discerns in the 1980s and 1990s, a process of Europeanization which had some purchase on national societies, through the 'objective consequences of cumulative integrative processes, the coalescence of institutional and regulative machinery, and the emergence of a more coherent European project'. As a result, '"Europe" acquired a far stronger … material actuality. The Single European Act and Maastricht solidified a European presence whose penetration downwards into the respective European societies became impressively effective' (2017: 28). In Pochet's narrative, however, this process is in counterpoint to others which are viewed in less positive terms:

> From the outset, the European project has been doubly unbalanced. In the first place, it has been dominated by the logic of economic integration, with the social dimension essentially constituting a by-product of the benefits resulting from this integration. (Pochet 2018)

In this reading, echoed by that of Anderson (1997), Callinicos (2013) and Bickerton (2016), the work of EU institutions as it developed through the 1990s complemented an intensifying process of neoliberalization. Questions of social and economic policy which had been the objects of contestation between political forces at national level were increasingly settled in market-orientated terms, becoming constitutionalized through treaty or judicial ruling, as ground rules for the functioning of the European Union. Thus Scharpf (1999) discusses the rulings of the European Court of Justice, which adjudicated on the limits of government action, and Bickerton (2016: 174) points out that the apparently technical nature of the convergence criteria for Eurozone membership place key aspects of macroeconomic policy out of reach of political challenge.

Other researchers – for example, Streeck (2011, 2017) – add a further emphasis. These policy options, all of which have become more marked in the period since 2008, should be understood in the context of interstate relations: EU institutions may well have developed common norms and reference points, but the Union does not stand above national states; it is rather an arena in which different national interests are played out, in ways which have a decisive influence on policy directions. The European Union is bisected by a tension between dominant and dominated powers, with integrationist tendencies being offset by processes of uneven development and interstate polarization which have been accentuated by neoliberalization. Financial arrangements – such as the Exchange Rate Mechanism (ERM) introduced in 1979 and the full-scale European Monetary Union established in 1999 – are presented as serving not the Union as a whole, but rather the interests of the strongest national capitalisms, in particular, Germany. In this account (e.g. Callinicos 2013) German superiority in technological competition has been reinforced by reductions in the cost of German labour, through fixed exchange rates and by the inability of weaker economies, particularly since the establishment of the Eurozone, to improve their competitiveness through devaluation and inflation. The solution the European Union offers to its failing member states is a European version of structural adjustment, which portrays the sale of public assets, the cutting of welfare and the flexibilization of the workforce as essential means by which problems of productivity and competitiveness can be resolved. In this literature, the existence of policy convergence and coordination, and of tendencies towards economic and social integration, are certainly recognized. These features, however, are set in a context where other questions – including those of power and inequality – have moved to the front of the stage.

Education in the EU integration project

Intertwined with a narrative of coordination and consensus, analysis of EU policy needs thus to appreciate turbulent and disruptive influences. This chapter attempts to depict the relationship over time between a broader field where economic dislocation and inequalities of power are unmistakable characteristics, and a mode of educational policy-making in which normative consensus is a significant tendency. It seeks to recognize external influences that press upon European education policy-making and shape its themes, ambitions and limitations – notably, the effects of fiscal and monetary policy, which vary significantly across member states. At the same time, it tracks the ways in which different national trajectories are brought to converge around a particular set of goals: the systematic expansion of the role of the European Union in the formation of education policy; the increasing importance of a transnational level of policy-making, which operates through the use of soft powers instead of coercive/legal measures; institutional innovations such as the Open Method of Co-ordination which have contributed to the development of a 'European space of education' (Hingel 2001). Through attending to educational policy-making in a wider economic and political context, the chapter aims to contribute to reflection on the effectiveness of the EU project in education.

The years of formation

Within the European integration project, education was a policy area that was comparatively slow to develop. In a period of continuous economic growth, educational reform was not a European-level priority: why make changes at a time when there seemed to be no major problems? The early period of the European Economic Community (EEC 1957–71) was characterized by limited actions confined to the vocational sector, where the Commission was tasked with promoting cooperation in a range of social fields, including 'basic and advanced vocational training' (European Union 1957: art.118). Rhetorically, education was valued as a means of creating a cultural and social community in Europe that reached beyond trade and agricultural matters, but cooperation was slow to materialize because the EEC did not have the policy architecture necessary to move forward.

It was only in the 1970s that institutional forms of cooperation took shape, facilitated by the first enlargement of the Community (to include Denmark, Ireland and the UK) and by an expanded administrative capacity that included education and training under the Directorate General for Research and Science. This was not an easy political accomplishment. According to Hywel Ceri Jones, head of the Commission's first-ever department for education and youth policies, in 1973:

> It took almost 3 years of hard negotiation between the Commission and national governments before the ground rules for educational collaboration were established and a first education action programme set up on a Community-wide basis. (in Pépin 2006: 68)

These developments led to the adoption of the first resolution on education cooperation in 1976. The 'action programme' it introduced was a wide-ranging declaration which endorsed principles of free access and equal opportunity.

It called for closer relations between education systems; it looked to develop cooperation in higher education, and progress in the teaching of foreign languages (OJEC 1976). More concretely, it established an educational database that would allow statistical comparison of different systems. These early stages of cooperation lacked any basis in European treaties, and as a result progress was frequently stalled. Movement only became possible at the end of the 1970s, in the context of growing youth unemployment and gathering recession. At this point perceptions of the potential connection between the social and economic content of the treaty and new forms of educational provision saw education and training brought under a unified Employment, Social Affairs and Education Directorate-General.

The 1980s was a decade of strengthening political cooperation, with education and other areas of cultural and social policy seen as important for further integration. Debates occurred around the teaching of foreign languages, giving a new impetus to the European dimension of education, as well as clearing the ground for cooperation and mobility between universities. This was the decade when initiatives in education and culture began to be developed (Comett, Lingua, 'Youth for Europe'). But the most important development for education in the 1980s had its roots, not in a policy initiative but in a Court of Justice ruling in 1985. In the famous *Gravier judgment* the definition of 'vocational education' (already covered by the Rome Treaty as a Community competence) was expanded to include studies at the level of higher education and gave a wider scope to Article 128 of the Treaty (ECJ 1985). From that point on, there have been many higher education initiatives that included cooperation around student access and the setting of objectives in the areas of multiculturalism, mobility and training for all (Pépin 2006).

In 1987 the ERASMUS mobility programme was launched, which proved to be the most significant instrument of University student mobility and allowed exchange and cooperation between higher education institutions. The original ERASMUS and its later evolutions (Erasmus Mundus, that opened to non-European students, and the Erasmus+ framework that combines several training and youth schemes including the Lifelong Learning programme) have been seen as important cultural achievements for the European Union, in that they contributed to a developing sense of Europeanness. They were also important in a political sense, in that they enabled an intensification of Commission involvement in education and higher education matters so that higher education became more closely aligned with EU social and economic programmes (Corbett 2011).

Education policy at the heart of economic governance – 1990s

The economic and social policies that had united the original six countries of the Common Market during the post-war boom did not survive the neoliberal turn of the 1990s. There occurred what Anderson (1997) called a 'sea-change in official attitudes to public finance and levels of employment, social security and rules for competition' (66). The Single European Act of 1986 (OJEC 1986) and the Treaty of Maastricht's European Community Treaty, effective from 1993, replaced the original constitutive Treaties. They involved the construction of the single market, the establishment of a European Central Bank and a monetary union (the EMU), preparatory to the introduction of a single currency. Politically, they established the importance of the Council of Ministers as central to policy-making: decisions about monetary, fiscal and financial policy would be reached between heads of government, on the basis of 'convergence criteria' – established in the Maastricht Treaty – which sought to organize national economic policies around commitment to the cutting of deficits. In this sense, austerity, understood as a permanent attentiveness to fiscal 'discipline', and a hostility towards demand-led growth, became a lasting feature of the European Union's economic orientation, preceding by nearly two decades the measures taken after 2008 (see Chapter 1 for a fuller account). Committed to price stability, Maastricht required of national governments that they reduced their budget deficits to 3 per cent of national income and kept government debt no higher than 60 per cent of GDP.

Given this kind of regulation, which reflected the orientation of national governments, large-scale Keynesian policies of state investment and public sector expansion were ruled out. In their place was established a repertoire of policies that addressed issues of social cohesion and identified the role of the European Union and of national states in relation to education, training and economic growth. Maastricht established a common European citizenship with the right of free movement, settlement and employment across the European Union. It endorsed a principle of subsidiarity, which encouraged local and regional dimensions of policy-making. It saw the beginnings of regional redistributive policies under the 'cohesion' umbrella, which had an important impact on poorer regions in Southern Europe, and on the post-2004 enlargement countries of Eastern Europe. Significant elements of the European Union's Structural and Cohesion Funds were directed towards the accession countries, which had the effect of making them more attractive as locations for foreign direct investment (Breuss, Egger and Pfaffermayr 2010). Maastricht also involved the formal acceptance of broad social policy goals by the European

Union, with the Treaty of Amsterdam (European Union 1997) inserting a 'Social Chapter' into the acquis – the body of common rights and obligations[1] – of EU member states, with explicit priorities, desired outcomes and frameworks for action. At the same time the European Union continued, in line with the principle of subsidiarity, to 'respect the responsibility' of member states for their education systems', as set out in Articles 149, 126 – EC Treaty (Maastricht consolidated version) and Article 126 (EEC Treaty). These articles, which set the legally defined parameters of EU action, have remained largely unchanged in the subsequent Treaties.[2] In textual terms, the principle of subsidiarity still stands, with no harmonization of regulatory or legal provision allowed for by the Treaty: member states carry the full responsibility for the organization and the content of their education and vocational systems. As we shall see, however, this is a principle which is both qualified by states' involvement in systems of policy coordination, and contradicted, at times of crisis, by the demands made on national educational policies by the Commission and by the European Central Bank.

Both the Single European Act and Maastricht emphasized the development of human resources and education and training, as strategies through which the state could contribute to economic growth, in a context in which its role was limited to working on supply side factors, rather than taking a directive role in economic development (James 2012). Maastricht provided a place for general and vocational education in a dedicated chapter on Education, Vocational Training and Youth: the European Union was committed to the development of 'quality education, encouraging cooperation, supporting and supplementing national action'.

Discursively, and in terms of policy options, the European Union's orientation was dominated by a human capital approach. The 1990s saw the launch of a discourse of 'lifelong learning' that shifted the emphasis from the personal, cultural and social values of education towards its capacity to contribute to employability and pro-market economic growth. A groundbreaking White Paper on *Growth, Competitiveness and Employment* (European Commission 1994), the product of consultation between the Commission and member states, located education and training policy at the heart of the wider economic growth and social policies of the European Union, so that education and training

---

[1] The *acquis communautaire* refers to the cumulative body of European Union legislation since 1958. It consists of primary (treaties and protocols) and secondary legislation (regulations, directives and decisions) and the case law of the European Court of Justice.

[2] Now Articles 165 and 166 in the Treaty on the Functioning of the European Union, Lisbon 2007.

policies became key to the building of a 'knowledge society'. What this meant in practice was identified in a subsequent White Paper, *Teaching and Learning – Towards the Learning Society* (European Commission 1996), the precursor in both the method and content of the mechanisms later used to steer education policies and calls for reform. In the same period the Bologna Declaration of 1999 launched an intergovernmental process in which higher education systems were aligned around common academic structures and objectives, including a credit transfer system, with the aim of establishing a European Higher Education Area that would be internationally competitive. Alignment helped enable student mobility, at the same time as it required a reorganization of national traditions of university education around a single Europe-wide approach. The 'Bologna Process' began outside the Community institutions, as an initiative of education ministers of France, Germany, Italy and the UK, and extended beyond the European Union.[3] Its impact on the European Union, and on member states, was nonetheless considerable (Carlhed 2017; Dakowska and Serrano-Velarde 2018). According to Muller and Ravinet (2008) initial resistance to the EU involvement in the process softened as the advantages of the process became plainer: it enabled countries beyond the European core to 'develop the international embeddedness of their higher education systems, while improving the quality of their own system', not least in terms of the system's capacity to take on 'social issues and equal opportunities'; across Europe it was seen to enable 'the modernisation of education and training systems to make sure these meet the needs of a changing labour market'. This was important, since in the perception of policy-makers there was a rising demand of high skills jobs, innovation and entrepreneurship (Orosz 2013).

The changes of the 1990s established an enduring and definitive connection between core aspects of education and training policy and the overall orientation of the EU economic strategy. At the same time, however – like EU policy in general – the sector was expected to address issues of social policy and social cohesion. The Treaty of Amsterdam called for a widening of access to education and for continuous updating of education systems (Article 2), incorporating education objectives into guidelines (23 and 24) for the economy and employment.[4]

---

[3] In 2018, there are forty-eight participating countries in the Bologna Process and the European Higher Education Area.

[4] 'Member States and the Community shall, in accordance with this Title, work towards developing a coordinated strategy for employment and particularly for promoting a skilled, trained and adaptable workforce and labour markets responsive to economic change with a view to achieving the objectives defined in Article B of the Treaty on European Union and in Article 2 of this Treaty' (Employment Chapter, Article 109n, The Treaty of Amsterdam Union 1997).

Initiatives in the post-Amsterdam period also demonstrated a strong desire at EU level to develop transnational forms of citizenship, a wider project of European integration in which education had an important part (Keating 2009, 2014; Milana 2008; Souto-Otero 2017). Thus, accompanying neoliberal economization there developed a set of policies and initiatives in which access, equity and integration were key terms (Papatsiba 2014; Walkenhorst 2008). Understanding this ensemble, and the shifting relationships between its terms, is key to the interpretation of EU education policy.

Constructing education policy – Lisbon 2000 and after

At Lisbon, in March 2000, the Council of Ministers announced its goal of establishing Europe as the most competitive knowledge economy in the world (European Council 2000) – an objective which throughout the following decade was put to a stringent test. Education was central to the Council's ambitions: the strategy explicitly and directly called for the modernization of education systems and the continuous update of knowledge through life-long learning, as determinants of economic and social future developments (Ertl 2006). In this context, where the goals were set high, but the legal powers of the European Union were limited, education required a steering mechanism which respected national sovereignty but which at the same time was detailed and comprehensive in relation to the programme agreed by the Council of Ministers. Thus the conclusions of the Lisbon Council referred to the Open Method of Co-ordination (OMC), a soft mode of governance, configured through administrative and procedural arrangements rather than through formal constitutional means. The OMC, which was not unique to education, but was particularly effective in the educational field, appealed to those aspects of the European Union's function which have been described as normative – to shared social values, and to overall political directions and goals which have been reached by negotiation and consensus (Pochet 2005; Fink-Hafner, Lajh and Dezelan 2010). It operated as a 'multi-level governance' instrument where informal normative pressures, agenda-setting and mutual policy learning (learning from each other) could be as powerful as legal prescription in the transformation of national policy-making (Lange and Alexiadou 2007).

The OMC operated, in the spirit evoked by Lawn, through a process of consensual alignment, which included the fixing of European guidelines, accompanied by timetables for achieving specific goals; the translation of guidelines into national policies associated with clear targets; the development of benchmarks and indicators in order to compare best practice among member states; and the periodic monitoring, evaluation and peer review of member states' practices organized as mutual learning processes (European Council 2000: para. 37). The 500 or so experts who by 2006 were participating in the work of the OMC around education and training were involved in what Hingel (2001) called the fabrication of a European educational space, a process that seemed to be turning European integration into the kind of technocratic endeavour that Nóvoa deplored, a way of working from which explicit political debates about definitions of quality and efficiency in education were marginalized (Gornitzka 2006). In practice, however, politics – in the shape of the effects on the European Union of economic recession and policy failure – influenced the work of the OMC, and of the European Union's wider education policy, in significant ways.

The 2005 midterm review of the Lisbon strategy highlighted the lack of commitment from (mainly old) member states to the Lisbon strategy, a problem which had led to a fairly weak implementation and ownership of the strategy at national level (Pépin 2011). The review led to the reaffirming of the significance of the strategy and the strengthening of its governance, the OMC. The goals and objectives of the strategy were formally and explicitly incorporated in the launch of the Education and Training 2020 programme (part of the Europe 2020 Strategy) with both the Commission and the Council continuing with the earlier policy of bringing together education, economic growth and labour market needs (Nicaise 2012). The revised Lisbon strategy led to a shift from the 'openness of Lisbon 1 (2000) to the 'bilateralism' of Lisbon 2[5] which put less focus on mutual learning between groups of experts based in national states and more emphasis on a direct relationship between EU institutions, notably the Commission, and individual member states to implement reform' (Tholoniat 2010: 109). As a result, the work of the Commission, in education and in other fields, shifted significantly, with political and ideological themes becoming more explicit, along with a directive rather than a coordinating approach to policy work (Busemeyer and Trampusch 2011).

The Lisbon strategy and its aftermath have also been significant for policy developments in higher education. Even though higher education is governed by similar subsidiarity principles to compulsory education, policy is considerably affected by the use of soft law and coordination mechanisms. In addition, other areas of EU policy as well as legal provisions, on citizenship, free movement and

---

[5] By 'Lisbon 2' the literature refers to the relaunch of the Lisbon process after the publication of the sharply critical Kok report in mid-2000.

competition law have 'spilled over into the HE sector' and have had an impact on policy formation at national level (Gideon 2016: 1045). Working in parallel to the Bologna process, the Lisbon strategy launched in 2000 the European Research Area; these twin policy frameworks have allowed a significant role for the European Commission in higher education policy development, a role which has served to shape fundamental thinking about the objectives of HE. Thus alongside many institutional changes – the design of degrees, the introduction of credit transfer systems and quality assurance systems, the recognition of qualifications – the consistent, Commission-driven emphasis of both the Bologna European Higher Education Area and the Lisbon strategy has been on creating an internationally competitive HE sector in Europe. Higher education discourse employed in both frameworks is organized around topics of economically beneficial activities, modernization reforms and research that contributes to measurable outcomes and is responsive to the needs of industry and the labour market. This focus has raised serious concerns about a redefinition of the role of universities in Europe, and their reorientation towards a more economically oriented mission (Gideon 2016; Keeling 2006; Serrano-Velarde 2015).

Post-2008 and the future of the EU integration project

The architects of the European Monetary Union expected that the launch of the euro would lead to economic convergence within the Eurozone, the group of nineteen states which shared a common currency and whose national banks were coordinated through the Eurosystem. In fact, the combination of monetary union with structural weaknesses in some national economies – weaknesses perpetuated by governments fearful of disturbing clientelistic systems of political support – led in a different direction, towards the exacerbation of old and the rise of new inequalities and hierarchies among member states. What happens, the British economist Wynne Godley had asked presciently,

> if a whole country – a potential 'region' in a fully integrated community – suffers a structural setback? So long as it is a sovereign state, it can devalue its currency. It can then trade successfully at full employment provided its people accept the necessary cut in their real incomes. With an economic and monetary union, this recourse is obviously barred, and its prospect is grave indeed unless federal budgeting arrangements are made which fulfil a redistributive role. ... If a country or region has no power to devalue, and if it is not the beneficiary of a

system of fiscal equalisation, then there is nothing to stop it suffering a process
of cumulative and terminal decline leading, in the end, to emigration as the only
alternative to poverty or starvation. (Godley 1992)

Lacking a system of financial equalization, the Eurozone has endured since
2000 the process of uneven development that Godley anticipated. By entering
the Eurozone at high rates of exchange and giving up the ability to respond
to recession by allowing their currency to devalue, the European Union's
peripheral countries were placed at the kind of disadvantage foreseen by
Godley, a disadvantage from which several have not recovered. The growing
competitiveness of China and other BRICS countries affected all European
economies, but especially those of the EU 'South'. The notion of a globally
dominant European knowledge economy faltered under such pressures. Well
before the recession of 2008, Portugal, Spain, Italy and Greece were experiencing
the effects of competition: construction booms came to an end in Portugal and
Spain; state spending contracted; youth employment rose above 40 per cent
and stayed there: significant protest movements developed among students and
school students (Jones et al. 2008; Jones 2009). Neither national elites nor the
Eurozone had adequate means of counteracting these developments. Member
states were faced with a complex set of problems: how to rescue a banking
system that could not sustain its own losses, while dealing at the same time with
falling tax revenues and increased welfare needs. In the case of states for which
this problem was insoluble at a national level, the Eurozone responded with
bailouts that were conditional on cuts in public expenditure, privatization, and
labour market and pension 'reform' supervised by the Troika of the European
Commission, the ECB and the International Monetary Fund. The European
Union inscribed this approach to economic governance into its constitutional
framework. The Lisbon Treaty (OJEU 2007), which came into force in 2009,
stipulated that member states should avoid 'excessive government deficits' and
that the Commission should monitor the situation of individual member states
'with a view to identifying gross errors'. The Fiscal Compact of 2012 – the 'Treaty
on Stability, Coordination, and Governance in the Economic and Monetary
Union' – was signed by the great majority of member states. Effectively, it
generalized a sharp form of austerity by entrenching the deficit and debt targets
in the Stability and Growth Pact which had been in place since 1997.[6] Signatories

---

[6] https://ec.europa.eu/info/business-economy-euro/economic-and-fiscal-policy-coordination/
    eu-economic-governance-monitoring-prevention-correction/stability-and-growth-pact/history
    -stability-and-growth-pact_en

agreed to amend their constitutions to include the requirement of a balanced budget and to set up a fiscal coordination council supposedly independent of political influence, to monitor compliance. These programmes had the effect of displacing the costs of the crisis onto the populations (employed, unemployed and retired) of member states. The impact on the 'rescued' economies was in several cases devastating (Lapavitsas 2012).

What has been the impact on education of decisions taken at the highest level of policy-making? Approaches which focus too exclusively on the normative elements in EU policy-making, and on the institutional mechanisms which generate them, tend to overlook continuing differences in national interest, and developing tensions between EU institutions, steered by the strongest national powers, and other member states. Yet it is in the context of these significant tensions that we should understand important aspects of EU education policy, and the ways in which the project of promoting education and training as instruments of economic growth run up against the barriers created by long-term recession, and constitutionalized austerity. The financial crisis brought new attention to education and training and their closer coupling with employment strategies, social cohesion and youth training schemes. However, the demand for targeted educational growth was combined with a demand for measures of a countervailing kind – a combination that was especially strong in relation to countries embroiled in debt crises. As a condition of bail out, countries like Portugal and Greece faced demands for simultaneous programmes of educational reform, public spending reduction and labour market flexibilization. In relation to Portugal, for instance, the EU Directorate for Economic and Financial Affairs emphasized that

> the structural reform agenda is comprehensive and frontloaded. … The measures include a reform of the labour market, reinforcement of competition, a review of the judicial system, housing and rental market reform, liberalisation in services sector and network industries, reducing the administrative burden on companies, scaling down the direct involvement of government in the economy, strengthening human capital via further reform of the education system. (European Commission 2011)

Portugal, the Directorate pointed out, is 'still lagging behind in educational achievement'. It stands out as having

> by far the highest share of lower secondary education graduates in the EU, pointing to relatively low aggregate skill levels. Its functional literacy is among the lowest in Europe. … This severely limits the flexibility of employers to adjust

to new demands. The potential pool of skilled workers in tradable sectors is further reduced by a still relatively high share of university graduates entering the government administration, although this trend has recently reversed. At the same time, the allocation of human capital to tradable sectors has been hampered by the relatively high level of wages in non-tradable sectors and in protected professions. (European Commission 2011)

Therefore, alongside strategies to lift levels of skill and rates of upper-secondary qualification, Portugal must embark on a programme of 'redefining the functions carried out by the public sector and reducing and eliminating services that do not represent a cost effective use of public money, as well as streamlining the education system', so that 'the link between curricula and skills needs in the labour market' will also be strengthened.

In this set of prescriptions, which were contested and to some extent modified by the parties of the Portuguese left and centre-left (Finn 2017), what was required of education was not just a paradigm shift relating to its processes and objectives, but a responsiveness to cost pressures, and an acceptance of financial restraint. This combination of demands has proved difficult for Portugal, and for other states, and is an important factor contributing to the tensions and conflicts which attend education reform.

Emerging from crisis?

The case of Portugal illuminates a nexus of structural adjustment and education policy change. The nexus is not only present in crisis situations but also embedded, in a less accentuated form in the workings of the routine policy instruments of the European Union. The European Union's headline statement of strategy, *Europe 2020*, set out targets in five key policy areas – employment and growth, investment, climate change, education and social inclusion (European Council 2009; European Commission 2010). It was not envisaged that the attainment of these targets would be conditional on substantial increases in funding, nor that there would be substantial increases in funding. EU 2020 was based on a commitment to fiscal responsibility and the continued promotion of structural reform, reiterated in its latest assessment of progress as part of the continued focus on the 'virtual triangle': investment, structural reforms and responsible fiscal policies (European Commission 2018a: 1).

Price stability and the 'highly competitive social market' declared by the Lisbon Treaty to be foundational principles of the European Union remained central. Within this parameter, governments have been encouraged to address issues of labour market need, and of social cohesion with education still playing an important role in aligning schooling to labour market needs (European Commission 2018a: 12–13). Providing a measure of inclusion, and a means of improving the employment situation of a large section of the population of member states, became crucial to addressing the legitimation crisis which the European Union, and many national governments, had experienced since the beginning of the century. For these purposes the OMC was seen as too soft a policy instrument, with the European Council emphasizing the need for a 'strong governance framework' and a 'more focused country surveillance' (European Council 2011: 3) that went beyond previous approaches. There were other changes of emphasis too. Before 2008, budgetary policy and planning had been the responsibility of Member States 'with only a limited coordinated overview at EU level of the national efforts' (European Commission 2015); in a new economic era, a different approach was needed, that required *policy learning* of a new type.

'Policy learning', developed between member states, and, at the Commission level, is integral to the European Union. Most of the governance strategies of the education OMC of the last eighteen years relate to the policy learning that forms part of all the reform programmes of the post-Lisbon policy cycles: 'mutual learning' where member states are encouraged to learn from each other's policies, policy exchanges and transfers; self-reflective learning that the Commission and Council engage in through the annual monitoring of progress on the benchmarks and the setting of priorities (Lange and Alexiadou 2010). The early framework for policy learning began with the setting up of eight learning 'clusters' that corresponded to national priorities in various areas of education (European Commission 2006). These evolved towards *Thematic Working Groups* (just 'Working Groups' after 2013) designed to help member states, in collaboration with the Commission, to 'address the key challenges of their education and training systems, as well as common priorities agreed at the European level' (European Commission 2013). The focus and mandates of the *Working Groups* were defined in short cycles (2011–13, 2014–15, 2016–18), and the process involved experts from member states and various peer learning activities.

The Commission itself engages in policy learning through the ET 2020 monitoring of progress of member states against the benchmarks and indicators set, and this represents the most up-to-date information for the process of peer learning among the member states. In addition to the annual monitoring process, a further learning process is the so-called stocktaking exercises, to assess progress made and to set up new priorities. The stocktaking exercise involves the input of member states and stakeholders. A small number of countries have been invited to the exercise. It is interesting to compare the different approaches taken towards the evaluation of ET 2020 (European Commission Strategic Framework – Education and Training 2020) and the focus of different countries on those priorities and emphases respond to their own policy concerns. The Czech Republic urges even more emphasis on the existing priority of early childhood education, and overall supports the current networks of cooperation as well as governance instruments for education policy and modernization of school systems (Czech Republic 2014). Sweden, one of the best performers in many of the education and inclusion indicators (European Commission 2018b; OJEU 2017), shows an overall level of support to the ET 2020, a very strong support to the process of policy learning and implementation through the Working Groups, but cautions against 'common solutions' when it comes to issues of funding (Ministry of Education and Research, Sweden 2014: 6) – a position consistent with the Swedish approach to an active but selective Europeanization (Jacobsson and Sundstöm 2016). These examples accord with Rambla's (2018) finding that the interaction between the Commission and member states is highly complex but also adjusted to suit the different policy priorities of states – albeit that states tend to share many elements of a normative framework (see also Mikulec 2017).

Since the late 2010s, policy learning has taken place with more explicit reference to macroeconomic objectives, and within a more stringent regulatory process. National reform plans have been assessed more precisely, performance targets have become more central, and country-specific recommendations (CSRs) have been published which the Council can use to issue guidance for the kind of reforms seen to be required in member states (Alexiadou 2014; Alexiadou and Lange 2015). The means that the Commission employs to coordinate the macroeconomic policies of member states is the European Semester. Established in 2011, the Semester includes CSRs, monitoring of progress towards the EU 2020 targets and economic forecasts. Its main focus is economic, but recommendations related to education and research nonetheless feature prominently. Though education accommodates a concern with social cohesion, with attention to particular categories of pupils (such as migrant, Roma and asylum-seeker students) and to addressing the widening inequality gaps, it is viewed often from an economic perspective. What the intervention in Portugal dramatized – market economics as the touchstone of education policy – is also present in the Semester's approach, qualifying and limiting the inclusive tendencies of social policy.

Dunlop and Radaelli (2016) emphasize the authoritative character of the Semester process: that no serious contestation of the rules of fiscal discipline and the processes of policy coordination has occurred. A system of 'monitoring, alerts and surveillance' is firmly in place which no member state has wished to challenge (2016: 116). In the processes of the Semester, there is certainly room for high-level bargaining, to increase the room for financial manoeuvre, especially of the more powerful states. However, the overall bias of the Semester is clear: the 'social' is subordinate to the 'economic'; the achievement of social objectives depends on voluntary cooperation; the achievement of economic objectives is mandatory (2016: 116).

In this context, Stevenson et al. (2017) analysed the Semester's effects on education policy-making, looking at the CSRs generated by the Semester process in 2016. They found that objectives related to social inclusion are present in the CSRs. For instance, in many cases there was an emphasis on integrating newly arrived migrants into the school system, and through CSRs the Semester steers funding through priority regions and vulnerable populations (such as the Roma)[7] (Alexiadou 2017; European Commission 2017). However, such goals and funding tended to be framed in terms of their value to the labour market. Slovakia was urged to extend the provision of 'affordable, quality childcare', and this goal was motivated less by arguments for social equality but by reference to the need to 'facilitate the employment of women', who without childcare could not enter the labour market. Likewise, several countries were encouraged to expand higher education but at the same time to strengthen the role of the market in its governance: the Czech Republic was advised to 'accelerate the development and introduction of a new methodology for evaluating research and allocating funding with a view to increasing the share of performance-based funding of research institution'. France was recommended to 'improve the links between the education sector and the labour market, in particular by

---

[7] 'For the 2014-2020 programming period, the EU framework and the European Semester have ensured that there is a strong linkage between policy and funding priorities. The link between implementation of CSRs and the European Structural and Investment Funds ensures that mainstream policy reforms serve inclusion goals. For example, the Commission asked MS that received CSRs calling for enhanced Roma participation in education to select the investment priority "socio-economic integration of marginalized communities such as Roma" and to mainstream Roma inclusion under other relevant priorities (most importantly, "fighting early school leaving and promoting equal access to quality early childhood, primary and secondary education")' European Commission (2017: 5).

reforming apprenticeship and vocational training, with emphasis on the low skilled' (France CSR 2016). Lithuania, similarly, should 'strengthen investment in human capital and address skills shortages, by improving the labour market relevance of education, raising the quality of teaching and pursuing more active labour market policies and adult learning' (Lithuania CSR 2016). As with Portugal in 2011, the horizon of these recommendations was set by economic constraints, so that 'expansionist' recommendations were qualified and undercut by deflationary ones: in 2016, the UK was advised to 'further improve the availability of affordable, high-quality, full-time childcare' (UK CSR 2016) while in the same year, it was urged to 'correct the excessive deficit in a durable manner by 2016-17'.

Conclusion

The insistence of the Semester process on the alignment of national goals to an overall European process of policy development is striking, though not unexpected. In the two decades since the Lisbon Conclusions, the mode of European education policy-making processes has changed from 'soft' to 'harder', with clearer targets and closer monitoring of progress towards them. In terms of its content, policy has wound itself ever more tightly around a policy core in which educational objectives are defined in terms of labour market and productivity needs. While there is clear progress towards the targets set in successive phases of this process, it is difficult to say that policy has successfully addressed the challenges presented by economic stagnation, generational exclusion and high levels of migration. The fundamental reasons for these failings lie outside education, in the economic choices made by the most powerful EU governments. These choices lead education systems towards insoluble difficulties. Education is seen as central to the promotion of social cohesion, generalized knowledge production and public well-being, yet at the same time it is limited by growing problems of funding, and the corrosive effects of social polarization. The technical rationality of EU policy means (extensive discussion of measurable processes and objectives) is thus accompanied by elements of irrationality relating to more general purposes which within the European Union's current orientation are unrealizable. In this sense, education policy-making will continue to be shaped by tensions – sharper now than twenty years ago – which arise from the wider problems of Europe's social and economic order. It is to these wider problems that the next chapters turn.

References

Alexiadou, N. (2014) Policy learning and Europeanisation in education: The governance of a field and the transfer of knowledge, in A. Nordin and D. Sundberg (eds), *Transnational Policy-Flows in European Education Conceptualizing and Governing Knowledge*, 123–40, Oxford Studies in Comparative Education, Oxford: Symposium books.

Alexiadou, N. (2017) Equality and education policy in the European Union: An example from the case of Roma, in S. Parker, N. K. Gulson and T. Gale (eds), *Policy and Inequality in Education*, Volume 1, 111–31, Singapore: Springer.

Alexiadou, N. and Lange, B. (2015) Europeanising the national education space: Adjusting to the Open Method of Coordination (OMC) in the UK, *International Journal of Public Administration*, 38 (3): 157–66.

Anderson, P. (1997) Under the sign of the interim, in P. Gowan and P. Anderson (eds), *The Question of Europe*, 51–76, London: Verso.

Bickerton, C. (2016) *The European Union: A Citizen's Guide*, Harmondsworth: Pelican.

Breuss, F., Egger, P. and Pfaffermayr, M. (2010) Structural funds, EU enlargement, and the redistribution of FDI in Europe, *Review of World Economic*, 146 (3): 469–4.

Busemeyer, R. and Trampusch, C. (2011) Comparative political science and the study of education, *British Journal of Political Science*, 41 (2): 413–43.

Callinicos, A. (2013) Perry Anderson on Europe, *Historical Materialism*, 21 (1): 159–76.

Carlhed, C. (2017) Resistances to scientific knowledge production of comparative measurements of dropout and completion in European higher education, *European Educational Research Journal*, 16 (4): 386–406.

Corbett, A. (2011) Ping Pong: Competing leadership for reform in EU higher education 1998–2006, *European Journal of Education*, 46 (1): 36–53.

Czech Republic (2014) *Education and Training 2020. National Report Questionnaire.* Available at: http://ec.europa.eu/dgs/education_culture/repository/education/policy/strategic-framework/doc/et2020-national-report-cz_en.pdf.

Dakowska, D. and Serrano-Velarde, K. (2018) European higher education policy, in H. Heinelt and S. Münch (eds), *Handbook of European Policies: Interpretive Approaches to the EU*, 260–72, Cheltenham: Edward Elgar.

Directorate for Economic and Financial Affairs, European Union (2011) *The Economic Adjustment Programme for Portugal*, EU Directorate-General for Economic and Financial Affairs. Available at: http://ec.europa.eu/economy_finance/publications/occasional_paper/2011/pdf/ocp79_en.pdf

Dunlop, C. A. and Radaelli, C. (2016) Policy learning in the Eurozone crisis: Modes, power and functionality, *Policy Sciences*, 49 (2): 107–24.

Eley, G., Paggi, L. and Streeck, W. (2017) Interviewed by Carlo Spagnolo. The EU
    Crisis and Europe's divided memories, in *Le memorie divise dell'Europa dal 1945*,
    monographic issue of *Ricerche Storiche*, n. 2: 27–44.

Ertl, H. (2006) European Union policies in education and training: The Lisbon agenda
    as a turning point? *Comparative Education*, 42 (1): 5–27.

European Commission (1994) White Paper, *Growth, Competitiveness, Employment*,
    Brussels: European Commission.

European Commission (1996) White Paper, *Teaching and Learning – Towards the
    Learning Society*, Brussels: European Commission.

European Commission (2006) *OMC Thematic Working Groups in Education and
    Training*. DGVT Meeting in Ireland, 21–2 May 2013, European Commission. http://
    www.eu2013.ie/media/eupresidency/content/documents/dgforvocationaltraining/
    3-OMC-Thematic-Working-Group-in-Education-and-Training.pdf

European Commission (2010) *Europe 2020*, Brussels: European Commission.

European Commission (2011) The economic adjustment programme for Portugal,
    Occasional Papers 79, DG-Economic and Financial Affairs. http://ec.europa.eu/
    economy_finance/publications/occasional_paper/2011/pdf/ocp79_en.pdf

European Commission (2013) *Operational Guide for Clusters and Peer Learning
    Activities in the Context of the Education and Training 2010 Work Programme*,
    Brussels: European Commission.

European Commission (2015) *The EU's Economic Governance Explained. European
    Commission – Fact Sheet*, Brussels, 26 November 2015.

European Commission (2017) Midterm review of the EU framework for national
    Roma integration strategies, *Communication from the Commission to the
    European Parliament and the Council*, Brussels, 30 August 2017. COM(2017)
    458 final.

European Commission (2018a) European semester: Assessment of progress on
    structural reforms, prevention and correction of macroeconomic imbalances, and
    results of in-depth reviews under Regulation (EU) No 1176/2011, *Communication
    from the Commission to the European Parliament, the Council, the European Central
    Bank and the Eurogroup*, Brussels, 7 March 2018. COM(2018) 120 final. Available
    at: https://ec.europa.eu/info/sites/info/files/2018-european-semester-country-report
    -communication_en.pdf

European Commission (2018b) Country Report Sweden 2018, including an in-depth
    review on the prevention and correction of macroeconomic imbalances, *Commission
    Staff Working Document*, Brussels, 7 March 2018. SWD(2018) 225 final. Available at:
    https://ec.europa.eu/info/sites/info/files/2018-european-semester-country-report
    -sweden-en.pdf

European Council (2000) *Presidency Conclusions Lisbon European Council*, Lisbon,
    23–4 March 2000. http://www.consilium.europa.eu/ueDocs/cms_Data/docs/
    pressData/en/ec/00100-r1.en0.htm

European Council (2009) Council Conclusions of 12 May 2009 on a strategic framework for European cooperation in Education and Training (ET 2020). Available at: https://ec.europa.eu/education/policy/strategic-framework_en.

European Council (2011) Council Conclusions on the role of education and training in the implementation of the 'Europe 2020' strategy, *Official Journal of the European Union* (2011/C 70/01).

European Court of Justice (1985) Judgment of the Court of 13 February 1985, *Françoise Gravier v City of Liège*. Reference for a preliminary ruling: Tribunal de première instance de Liège - Belgium. Non-discrimination - Access to vocational training. Case 293/83.

European Union (1957) *Treaty Establishing the European Community (Consolidated Version), Rome Treaty*, 25 March 1957. Available at: https://eur-lex.europa.eu/legal-content/EN/TXT/?uri=legissum:xy0023.

European Union (1997) Council of the European Union, Treaty of Amsterdam amending the Treaty on European Union, the Treaties establishing the European Communities and certain related acts - Final Act, 10 November 1997. Available at: https://eur-lex.europa.eu/legal-content/EN/TXT/?uri=CELEX%3A11997D%2FAFI

Fink-Hafner, D., Lajh, D. and Deželan, T. (2010) The Open Method of Coordination in the global context of policy cooperation, in D. Fink-Hafner (ed.), *The Open Method of Coordination*, 17–34, Ljubljana: Faculty of Social Sciences, University of Ljubljana.

Finn, D. (2017) Luso-anomalies, *New Left Review*, II/106, July–August: 5–33.

Gideon, A. (2016) The position of Higher Education Institutions in a changing European context: An EU law perspective, *Journal of Common Market Studies*, 53 (5): 1045–60.

Godley, W. (1992) Maastricht and all that, *London Review of Books*, 14 (19), 8 October: 3–4.

Gornitzka, A. (2006) The Open Method of Coordination as practice – a watershed in European education policy? *Working Paper 16*. Centre for European Studies, University of Oslo.

Hingel, A. (2001) Education policies and European governance – contribution to the interservice groups on European governance, *European Journal for Education Law and Policy*, 5: 7–16.

Jacobsson, B. and Sundström, G. (2016) The Europeanisation of the Swedish state, in J. Pierre (ed.), *The Oxford Handbook of Swedish Politics*, 515–28, Oxford: Oxford University Press.

James, H. (2012) *Making the European Monetary Union: The Role of the Committee of Central Bank Governors and the Origins of the European Central Bank*, Harvard: Harvard University Press.

Jones, K. (2009) Patterns of conflict in education: England, France, Italy, in A. Green (ed.), *Blair's Educational Legacy: 13 Wasted Years?* 193–217, Basingstoke: Palgrave.

Jones, K., Cunchillos, C., Hatcher, R., Hirtt, N., Innes, R., Johsua, S. and Klausenitzer, J. (2008) *Schooling in Western Europe: The New Order and Its Adversaries*, Houndmills: Palgrave Macmillan.

Keating, A. (2009) Nationalizing the post-national: Reframing European citizenship for the civics curriculum in Ireland, *Journal of Curriculum Studies*, 41 (2): 159–78.

Keating, A. (2014) *Education for Citizenship in Europe: European Policies, National Adaptations and Young People's Attitudes*, Houndmills, Basingstoke: Palgrave Macmillan.

Keeling, R. (2006) The Bologna process and the Lisbon research agenda: The European Commission's expanding role in higher education discourse, *European Journal of Education*, 41 (2): 203–22.

Lange, B. and Alexiadou, N. (2007) New forms of European Union governance in the education sector? A preliminary analysis of the Open Method of Coordination, *European Educational Research Journal*, 6 (4): 321–35.

Lange, B. and Alexiadou, N. (2010) Policy learning and governance of education policy in the EU, *Journal of Education Policy*, 25 (4): 443–63.

Lapavitsas, C. (2012) *Crisis in the Eurozone*, London: Verso.

Lawn, M. (2013) The understories of European education: The contemporary life of experts and professionals, *Sisyphus: Journal of Education*, 1 (1): 18–35.

Mikulec, B. (2017) Impact of the europeanisation of education: Qualifications frameworks in Europe, *European Educational Research Journal*, 16 (4): 455–73.

Milana, M. (2008) Is the European (active) citizenship ideal fostering inclusion within the Union? A critical review, *European Journal of Education*, 43 (2): 207–16.

Ministry of Education and Research, Sweden (2014) *Education and Training 2020 National Report*. http://ec.europa.eu/dgs/education_culture/repository/education/policy/strategic-framework/doc/et2020-national-report-sv_en.pdf.

Muller, P. and Ravinet, P. (2008) Construire l'Europe en résistant à l'UE ? Le cas du processus de Bologne, *Revue Internationale de Politique Comparée*, 15 (4): 653–65.

Nicaise, I. (2012) A smart social inclusion policy for the EU: The role of education and training, *European Journal of Education*, 47 (2): 327–42.

Normand, R. (2010) Expertise, networks and indicators: The construction of the European strategy in education, *European Educational Research Journal*, 9 (3): 407–21.

Nóvoa, A. (2001) The restructuring of the European educational space: Changing relationships among states, citizens, and educational communities, in J. Fink, G. Lewis and J. Clarke (eds), *Rethinking European Welfare*, 249–75, London: The Open University/Sage.

Nóvoa, A. (2013) The blindness of Europe: New fabrications in the European educational space, *Sisyphus: Journal of Education*, 1 (1): 104–23.

OJEC (1976) Resolution of the Council and of the Ministers of Education, meeting within the Council, of 9 February 1976 comprising an action programme in the field of education, *Official Journal of the European Communities*, 19 February 1976. No C 38/1.

OJEC (1986) Single European Act, *Official Journal of the European Communities* (OJ L 169, 29 June 1987).

OJEU (2007) *Treaty of Lisbon Amending the Treaty on European Union and the Treaty Establishing the European Community*, signed at Lisbon, 13 December.

OJEU (2017) Council Recommendation of 11 July 2017 on the 2017 National Reform Programme of Sweden and delivering a Council opinion on the 2017 Convergence Programme of Sweden, *Official Journal of the European Union* (2017/C 261/26).

Orosz, A. (2013) The Bologna process in Slovenia, in T. Kozma, M. Rébay, A. Ohidy and É. Szolár (eds), *The Bologna Process in Central and Eastern Europe*, 285–319, Springer: The Bologna Process and the European Higher Education Area. http://ec.europa.eu/education/policy/higher-education/bologna-process_en

Papatsiba, V. (2014) Policy goals of European integration and competitiveness in academic collaborations: An examination of joint Master's and Erasmus Mundus programmes, *Higher Education Policy*, 27 (1): 43–64.

Pépin, L. (2006) *The History of European Cooperation in Education and Training: Europe in the Making – An Example*, Luxembourg: Office for Official Publications of the European Communities.

Pépin, L. (2011) Education in the Lisbon Strategy: Assessment and prospects, *European Journal of Education*, 46 (1): 25–35.

Pochet, P. (2005) The OMC and the construction of social Europe, in J. Zeitlin and P. Pochet (eds), *The Open Method of Co-ordination in Action: The European Employment and Social Inclusion Strategies*, 37–82, Brussels: Peter Lang.

Pochet, P. (2018) The European pillar of social rights in historical perspective, *European Politics and Policy,* London School of Economics. Available at: http://blogs.lse.ac.uk/europpblog/2017/11/14/the-european-pillar-of-social-rights-in-historical-perspective/

Rambla, X. (2018) The politics of early school leaving: How do the EU and the Spanish educational authorities 'frame' the policy and formulate a 'theory of change', *Journal of European Integration*, 40 (1): 83–97.

Scharpf, F. (1999) *Governing in Europe: Effective and Democratic?*, Oxford: Oxford University Press.

Serrano-Velarde, K. (2015) Words into deeds: The use of framing strategy in EU higher education policy, *Critical Policy Studies*, 9 (1): 41–57.

Souto-Otero, M. (2017) Neo-liberalism, discursive change and European education policy trajectories, in P. Kennett and N. Lendvai-Bainton (eds), *Handbook of European Social Policy*, 284–301, Cheltenham: Edward Elgar Publishing.

Stevenson, H., Hagger-Vaughan, L., Milner, A. and Winchip, E. (2017) *Education and Training Policy in the European Semester: Public Investment, Public Policy, Social Dialogue and Privatisation Patterns across Europe*, Brussels: European Trade Union Committee for Education.

Streeck, W. (2011) The crises of democratic capitalism, *New Left Review*, II/71, September–October: 5–30.

Streeck, W. (2017) The return of the repressed, *New Left Review*, II/104, March–April: 5–19.

Tholoniat, L. (2010) The career of the Open Method of Coordination: Lessons from a 'soft' European instrument, *West European Politics*, 33 (1): 93–117.

Walkenhorst, H. (2008) Explaining change in EU education policy, *Journal of European Public Policy*, 15 (4): 567–87.

3

England: The Limits of Conservatism

Ken Jones

England is home to education policies which set the country apart both from its smaller UK neighbours – which possess devolved powers over their school systems – and from most other countries in Europe. Whereas Wales and Scotland have invited OECD policy reviewers to evaluate and advise on their educational achievements and programmes, England has followed a different route, not seeking a conversation with European policy-makers, and basing itself on what an influential Secretary of State for Education called the 'common sense of the British people' (Gove 2009). The country's adherence to a market model of education, in school and universities, is especially strong; it has also developed an approach to school curriculum, assessment and governance which is detached from OECD orthodoxy and makes only occasional, and idiosyncratic, reference to education in other countries (Schleicher 2017). England's distinctive educational character can in part be explained by considering the perspectives and commitments of the Conservative Party, which has been in government for twenty-seven of the last forty years, and the achievements and limitations of modern Conservatism will be an important focus of this chapter.

However, the peculiarities of English education are explicable, also, by broader and longer-term factors that go beyond the politics of a single party. England's education system – like that of the UK as a whole – has been decisively shaped by the UK's position in the world economy, and by the ways in which politics, society and culture have been influenced by it. This dialectic of global relations and domestic formation has been much explored by historians (e.g. Hobsbawm 1968; Anderson 1987; Rubinstein 1993), who offer an interpretation of Britain's trajectory in which the country's initial socio-economic advantages are claimed to have contributed to its later failings. In the eighteenth and nineteenth centuries, Britain developed a vast empire, a globally significant financial system, and an industrial base that rested on mineral extraction and first-wave manufacturing activities. Yet the state which presided over these achievements was, in terms of its capacity for economic planning, weaker than its French, German or American competitors (Green 1991). Successful in enabling imperial expansion, and in creating the conditions for a global flow of large-scale financial transactions, the state was much less effective in supporting the modernization of long-established industries which were incapable of modernizing themselves and – governed by a political elite in which agrarian and finance capital were much more strongly represented than manufacturing – Britain became 'locked into an industrial structure that was slow to adapt and change as the domestic and world economies developed' (Kitson and Michie 2014). Neither of the world wars which Britain fought resolved these difficulties, and from the 1970s it began a sharp and as-yet-unended phase of deindustrialization – which state policies accelerated rather than counteracted. In the long period of Conservative rule between 1979 and 1997, manufacturing 'shrank to 17 per cent of UK gross value added by 1997, compared to 26 per cent in Germany' (Blackburn 2018: 5). Educational investment did not counteract this tendency. Research and development was much lower as a proportion of GDP than in other countries: 1.7 per cent in the UK in 2015 compared with 2.8 per cent in the United States and 3 per cent in Germany (OECD 2018a). Spending on Further Education – which included most technical courses – was no higher in 2017 than in 1990 (Bellfield and Sibieta 2017).

Britain's relative decline was an effect of policy failure and the path dependencies resulting from its economic structure. Especially so far as England was concerned, it also included a specific intellectual dimension. In Wales and in Scotland, policy-making was strongly shaped by intellectual traditions which saw education as an element within a common national culture. Even in conditions of economic decline, appeals to policy principles of equal opportunity and inclusion retained their force. Policy discourse in England was much more likely to be shaped by other cultural influences, in which the concerns and preferences of elites were presented as models to which the multitude should aspire.

Much of Britain's social and cultural capital – its universities, private school system and cultural institutions – was accumulated in the imperial period. But rather than serving as a resource for modernization, the late nineteenth-century intelligentsia which drew on this capital tended to position itself against industrialism, and to share the cast of ideas of the aristocracy, 'repudiating bourgeois origins and miming a synthetic gentility and ruralism' – so that the bias of culture secreted what Anderson (1987) calls a 'deeply conformist and conservative cult of countryside and [London] club'. This intellectual tradition, with a base in journalism and the humanities, and strong links to political elites, regarded education not from the point of view of economic need, but from that of cultural reproduction, the culture in question being understood in traditionalist terms, with a strong high cultural inflection. Fears of cultural decline, aversion to cultural diversity, fascination with English identity and distaste for cultural democratization were deeply embedded in this tradition, which extended far into the twentieth century, and continued to shape English education policy – and the wider politics of national identity – well into the twenty-first (Jones 2015). 'We have the character of an island nation', David Cameron told European leaders in 2013, and 'we can no more change this sensibility than we can drain the English channel' (Cameron 2013).

Thus while England is neoliberal in its political economy, this neoliberalism is embedded in a social formation in which an economic policy based on financialization, services and an open market is linked with a political and social orientation that emphasizes sovereignty and national tradition. This chapter seeks to explore the effects of this policy combination on the development of the English educational formation, across the four decades since 1979. In the process, it suggests a three-phase periodization of neoliberalism in education: a 'destructive' phase in the 1970s and 1980s, when established institutions and practices were discredited and undermined; a phase of construction that lasted from the 1988 Education Reform Act, through the Labour governments of 1997–2010 to the election of 2010; and finally a phase in which the policy innovations of early periods were accelerated and intensified – in a continuing context of austerity – to the point where their sustainability was called into question.

The productivity of neoliberalism

A programme for education was a late arrival in Conservative policy-making, elaborated only after Thatcher's third election victory in 1987. It had been preceded by more than a decade's campaigning by the think-tanks, networks and pamphleteers of the right. The Black Papers of the 1960s and 1970s were important because they embedded in the education politics of Conservatism a destructive, critical element that was essential to the side-lining of previously dominant policy approaches, and to the defeat of those social agents who had elaborated them. They constructed a discourse which was not in itself neoliberal but which provided material which could be reworked in neoliberal terms, launching a polemic against education which held it responsible for the undermining of a unified national culture, and for betraying the principle of allegiance to established political and social authority. Reform, the editors of the Black Papers argued, was taking a course that led away from 'standards' and the disciplined educational order that was their precondition; it was therefore letting down those who most needed the support of the school: working-class children (Cox 1992).

Seven years after the publication of the last of the Black Papers, the Adam Smith Institute's 'Omega File' of 1984 took their argument a stage further: the indifference of the educational establishment to what was claimed to be popular aspiration for good-quality education was not an accident, but followed inexorably from the nature of a system which had been removed from the pressures of the market place, to be 'put under political direction and control'. Operating on an assured state-provided income, schools were 'complacent about existing practices'. They 'failed to innovate' in any constructive sense, while at the same time they were 'all too susceptible to the political whims of teachers', some of whom found it 'easier to spout their political prejudices to their charges than to make the intellectual effort to master a real subject'. The school could not regenerate itself, since, with the best will in the world, teachers could not escape the pressures of a monopoly situation.

The Omega File was one of many documents and articles that claimed to identify the causes of educational crisis (Jones 1989) and helped create the context for the legislative programme of late 1980s Conservatism. The Teachers' Pay and Conditions Act of 1987 abolished national negotiating rights, and enabled school managements to exert more effective control over teachers' work. The local authority most associated with progressive and equality-orientated reform, the Inner London Education Authority, was abolished. In ways like these, the ground was cleared for a new, constructive period of neoliberalism, with institutions and dynamics significantly different from those of earlier decades.

The policy turn was formalized in the major achievement of educational Conservatism, the Education Reform Act of 1988. The legislation clinched the destruction of the educational culture which had developed between 1944 and 1979, and began the work of creating a different one, in which old social actors were marginalized and new ones rendered powerful. What it created was in a political sense successful: it established enduring ground rules for schooling that have endured for more than thirty years. (The Labour Party, following three election defeats, retreated from its historic commitment to equality-orientated reform, and from its acceptance of teacher professionalism as an agency of change.)

In several respects, the ERA reflected a rising international policy orthodoxy, in which public services were exposed to external audit, tighter management and competition; it had its analogues in other European countries, from Sweden (see Alexiadou and Rönnberg in this volume) to France (see Dreux, this volume). Likewise, in some respects Conservative neoliberalism acted as a modernizing force, linking education to other policy objectives, and bringing order and greater fairness to a haphazard system; by 1987, the separate two-tier exam system at 16+ had been brought to an end, and a common examination, the GCSE, had been introduced. Adding to this, the ERA established the national curriculum, a universalistic form of provision which ensured among other things that the curriculum provided for girls no longer denied them access to scientific and technological education. Thus, Conservative-led changes significantly increased curricular and institutional access, in ways that seemed to conform to the classic pattern of post-war schooling, and even to speed up the processes by which it expanded provision and certification to new age cohorts and social groups.

However, the provisions of the Act embodied not only these global principles but also the tangled themes of a distinctively national movement, English Thatcherism. If the national curriculum was a modernizing measure, it was of a Janus-like kind. It combined measures of inclusiveness with curricular preferences which looked back to old hierarchies and divisions. The curriculum was designed on a subject basis, and in its essentials replicated the grammar school curriculum of the earlier part of the century (Simon 1988). Its content at several important points reflected the traditionalist, ethnocentric preferences of ministers and pressure groups. The emphasis was on British history, European art and music and English literature, informed by an unwillingness to acknowledge cultural diversity. In the 1990s, under a new prime minister, John Major, these influences were for a time to grow stronger, contributing to a complex pattern of reform – a universalism with archaic elements, expressed in the form of root-and-branch hostility to pedagogy and curricula as they had developed in the post-war period. It is this combination which is key to the understanding of neoliberalism in its English variant, and possibly in other countries too: the 'education formation' of Conservative neoliberalism has always included an element of tradition, not simply as decoration but as a substantive element, shaping curriculum policy.

A (regressive) modernization programme driven by an activist state was combined with extensive, market-orientated change. The establishment of a market, or quasi-market, constituted by schools which operated as financially autonomous units under the leadership of managements deploying techniques intended to improve a school's market position, was meant to supply the local dynamism that would complement centrally directed reform – an English enactment of the New Public Management principles which were becoming a global orthodoxy. Arrangements informed by principles of competitiveness were interwoven with state regulation of a stronger and more intrusive kind than had existed before 1979. The devolved school system was steered and regulated by new agencies created by the ERA and by subsequent legislation in 1992–4. Ofsted, the Office for Standards in Education, carried out detailed inspections of schools; the Teacher Training Agency produced specifications for what was in effect a national curriculum for teacher education; and the School Curriculum and Assessment Authority stipulated the school curriculum and provided for national testing. This system of regulation and competition, centralization and autonomy constituted the set of forces that would drive change.

The effects of Conservatism's intense programme of institutional innovation were felt by teachers, students and parents. Teachers experienced a weakening of their unions, an increase in their workload, the monitoring of their work by line managers, heads and inspectors and the loss of much of their classroom autonomy. The authoritative status of the national curriculum tended to foreclose arguments about educational purpose: especially as the testing system developed, questions of purpose and process became less a centre of debate initiative and controversy than a set of matters that had been pre-decided, outside the school.

The ERA's emphasis on performance, the establishment of a common 16+ examination in 1985–7, the expansion of higher education and an occupational shift away from industrial work strengthened trends towards certification and participation. In the process, a new student culture, in which successful examination performance had a central part, came into being: the new structures, rhythms and expectations of education exerted an influence on students that was both more extensive (involving greater numbers) and more intensive (encouraging a greater subjective investment in schooling). The ERA also had implications for parents. Conservatism sought to reshape institutions and to demolish professional networks of interest that were deemed bureaucratic.

Rhetorically, 'parent power' played a major part in this project: governing bodies had been opened up to parents, increasing amounts of information about school performance had been made available and ministers appealed for support over the heads of professionals to parents as consumers. It was as individuals, rather than as a group of voters, that parents were intended to exert their most powerful influence: by exercising their right of choice, they would apply a market pressure upon schools. Parents were encouraged to become 'skilled choosers' (Gewirtz, Ball and Bowe 1995; Vincent and Ball 2006), attentive players in the differentiated system.

So far, this account has focused on education in schools. In Higher Education, the picture differed. The Conservatives came to office in 1979 without a programme for universities, except to cut their funding. In the 1980s, as with schools, a programme took shape – but it was not of the same kind as that which reshaped schooling. Appeals to tradition were not a significant part of the Conservative repertoire, and Conservatives tended to view academic culture and traditions as obstacles to change (Watson and Bowden 1999). Margaret Thatcher saw 'state-funded intellectuals' as an interest group whose practices required scrutiny and curtailment. She attacked the 'cloister and common room' for disparaging the creators of wealth in Britain, and in particular for criticizing the programme of her government (Harrison 1994). When, after a brief period in which they contemplated reducing levels of participation in higher education, Conservative Secretaries of State developed more elaborate views, they became eager advocates of increased student access (Watson and Bowden 1999). Expansion of the university sector was accompanied by new kinds of management and governance. The Research Assessment Exercise (RAE) of 1986 began a process whereby the research conducted in university departments was laid open to external scrutiny and evaluation, whose outcomes would determine a significant part of universities' funding. Government had found a means of linking funding to quantifiable, competitive performance, and in doing so introduced a new logic of action to universities: the force of academic autonomy as a principle underlying academic work and status was called into question (Dorey 2014). When the ERA deprived academics of the right to tenure – a status that protected them from redundancy and dismissal – the power of university leaders to manage staff in the name of efficiency and quality of performance was further increased (Dennison 1989). These large-scale changes in the way that academic work was funded, organized and motivated occurred against a background in which the economic function of higher education was constantly stressed: higher education's links with the corporate world should be strengthened; its value should be calculated on the basis of its contribution to economic growth. Above all, it had to offer 'value for money': the level of funding per student should fall – as indeed it did, by 25 per cent between 1987 and 1994 (Watson and Bowden 1999).

A continuing phase of construction: New Labour

The long period of Conservative rule ended in 1997, but policies developed under Conservatism, for schools as well as universities, were retained and elaborated by subsequent governments, in new inflections of neoliberalism.

At a Conservative Party dinner, in 2002, Margaret Thatcher was asked what was her greatest achievement. She replied, 'Tony Blair and New Labour. We forced our opponents to change their minds' (Burns 2008). So far as education was concerned, Mrs Thatcher was right. Elected in 1997, Labour – 'New Labour' in Blair's parlance – accepted a pattern of accountability and governance based on the ERA, and on the regulatory system centred on Ofsted that had been developed in the early 1990s. Labour's first major legislation – the 1998 School Standards and Frameworks Act – took as its starting point the inviolability of much Conservative law-making. It retained testing, league tables, the national curriculum and local management of schools. Alongside these legacies, there were new initiatives. To build on the post-1988 system, New Labour increasingly turned to the private sector; its belief in competition as the driving force of progress inclined it to regard the sector as, in the words of its chief policy adviser, a force 'uniquely capable of managing change and innovation' (Barber 1998). It followed that business, equipped with such qualities, should have a strong role in the future development of the public sector, including schooling and higher education. By the end of the New Labour period, private sector interests were securely established in the everyday processes by which the English school and college system was steered and governed (Ball 2007): Labour had introduced 'academies', outside local authority control, to raise standards; outsourcing of services such as inspection and school improvement had become commonplace.

Narratively, Labour endorsed Conservative accounts of English educational history. Previous governments had accepted Britain's economic and occupational structure as unchangeable. Its bedrock was a largely 'unskilled' working population which had possessed 'jobs for life' in local industries (Department for Education and Employment 2001: 4). An undynamic economy produced a school system in its own image. In the supposedly static society of 1944–76, there was no strong demand for certification and there was a 'general acceptance that only a minority would reach the age of 16 with formal skills and qualifications' (2001: 4). Comprehensive reform had not done enough to challenge this acceptance, and by setting 'social' as opposed to 'economic' goals – emphasizing egalitarianism at the expense of standards – it had contributed to stasis. Overreacting to the failings of the 11+ exam and dominated by the 'ideology of unstreamed teaching' (Blair 1996: 175), it had failed to differentiate among students and to 'link different provision to individual attitudes and abilities' (DfEE 2001: 5). One of the results was mass illiteracy; another, relatively slow rates of economic growth.

In this story, despite a huge investment in their recruitment and training, teachers were depicted not as a source of change but a barrier to it – 'forces of conservatism', in Blair's words (R. Smithers 1999). The post-war state had created teachers in their hundreds of thousands, managed them only lightly, allowed them to develop cultures both radical and inertial and set them to work in a system of low-level mass schooling. Government had kept its distance from the workings of the system, sponsoring but not directing educational expansion and reform, and relying on teachers and local authorities, not central intervention, to secure school-level change. This was an error Labour pledged not to repeat. Developments in IT enabled Labour governments to set up an apparatus of accountability that could set targets and monitor in detail schools progress towards them. Within schools, it encouraged moves towards performance-related pay. At the political level, it ensured that teacher influence on educational policy was minimal.

In these ways, Labour embedded essential characteristics of neoliberalism within the English school system. However, the education formation that developed under New Labour differed in significant ways from its Conservative predecessor. The emphases on investment, and social inclusion, were stronger. Between 2000 and 2010, public spending on education grew by more than 5 per cent a year – the fastest growth since the 1970s (Chowdry and Sibieta 2011). Labour intended to maintain public education as a system to which the great majority of the population would want access. The governments of Blair and Brown were also more open to curriculum change than Conservative governments had been. Blair's own preferences blocked reforms to the examination system that would have done something to integrate academic and vocational tracks, but in other ways, Labour cautiously endorsed reform: it funded programmes of cultural and creative education (Jones and Thomson 2008), and promoted inclusive practices around issues of ethnicity and race. These initiatives did not mark a decisive break with educational conservatism but they did inflect educational practice in different ways.

Like governments in other OECD countries, New Labour's policies for higher education were framed by its understandings of globalization and the knowledge economy. Government's role was to 'educate and retrain for the next technologies, to prepare the country for new global competition, and to make [it] a competitive base from which to produce the goods and services people want to buy' (Blair 1995). In the belief that the knowledge economy required higher skills on the part of a broader section of the population, New Labour set ambitious targets. In 2003, it expected 50 per cent of the relevant age-group to be involved in higher education by 2014, and introduced funding schemes and access programmes intended to meet this target (which in England was never attained). Such schemes were socially positive, in terms of encouraging and supporting overall access to higher education, but they did not alter a pattern in which entrance to elite universities was dominated by students from independent schools (Harrison 2011; Sutton Trust 2011). Like the Conservatives, New Labour accepted that the state could not bear the entire costs of the expanded system. In 1998, Labour had established individually paid, means-tested tuition fees as an element of university funding – institutions were allowed to charge up to £1,000. In 2004, this maximum was increased to £3,000. These measures ended the principle of free, public higher education. Students were instead supported through a complex mix of maintenance grants for the poorest, loans and part-time paid work.

In these ways, New Labour developed a system of higher education which did not so much break from Conservatism as draw the main lines of Conservative policy more boldly. The system was massified, diverse and unequal; it was focused on the employability of graduates and the adequacy of university-produced knowledge to business needs. Likewise, as in the 1990s, it was both fiercely competitive, in terms of inter-institutional competition for student numbers and research funding, and strongly regulated, in terms of the accountability of universities to the bodies that funded them. These were conditions that had powerful effects on the internal life of universities: the routines of academic management were shaped by an economic logic.

Both insecurity of employment and intensification of work increased: by 2009, 34 per cent of British academics worked on some kind of temporary contract, while numerous studies reported higher work-loads, longer hours and more intrusive styles of management (Archer 2008; Higher Education Statistics Agency 2010; Ogbonna and Harris 2004). By 2010, when the Labour government left office, neoliberal principles were arguably reflected more strongly in higher education than in schools: universities operated without the cultural baggage that impeded schooling from adjustment to marketization.

Austerity

Like Thatcher in 1979, the Conservative-led coalition which came to office in 2010 exploited an emergency in order to launch a radical programme of cuts and restructuring, which was continued under the 'Conservative-only' governments elected in 2015 and narrowly returned to office in 2017. Under David Cameron, the long Conservative revolution, begun by Thatcherism, resumed, in both economic and ideological form – this time with goals that were even more ambitious. As Chapter 1 suggested, the rationale for this programme was an interpretation of the crash of 2008 as the consequence of government overspending. From this point of view, Britain's economy could only be rebuilt through severe constraints on the public sector, linked to a flexibilization of the workforce that would reduce pay costs and lead to economic expansion. The intention of Cameron, like that of Thatcher, was to construct a programme which could 'accomplish a long-needed restructuring of economy and society, and create at the same time a spirit of national unity' (Newman and Clarke 2012: 305). Restructuring involved a prolonged period of cutback – the Institute for Fiscal Studies estimated that government policies for a total real-terms cut to per-pupil spending of around 7 per cent over the six years between 2015–16 and 2021–2 (IFS 2017).

In the context of Britain as a whole, the English educational formation was unique. In Scotland – as well as Northern Ireland and Wales – financial austerity was accompanied by efforts to hold on to and develop an educational agenda which avoided strong measures of privatization, sought some kind of partnership with professional interests and redesigned curricula along more inclusive lines. None of this was true of England. In their higher education policy, the governments of 2010–17 took the combination of marketization and central control to a new level. In their policy for schools, they accelerated privatization, toughened the system of data management and inspection that held schools to account and introduced changes to curriculum and assessment that reinforced the borders between academic and vocational education – developing a curriculum for the former of these, but not the latter. They thus replayed the historic themes of the English educational formation, in which the links between education and 'industry' were weak, and one of the main purposes attributed to education was the fight against cultural decline.

William Davies (2018) draws attention to the importance of the personal formation and disposition of the group of Conservatives which shaped social and economic policy after 2010: they brought to Conservatism a taste for political symbolism accompanied by a lack of policy expertise. Educational politics since the 1970s could be discussed in similar terms. It has been a breeding ground for Conservatism activists of a particular sort – strongly committed ideologically, deeply opposed to dialogue with educational interests, traditionalist in their conception of teaching and learning, market-focused in their policy innovations (see also Exley and Ball 2010; Jones 1989). Cameron's first education secretary, Michael Gove, belonged to this lineage, and made a strong contribution to its renewal. It was in his period in office that the policy trends of previous decades were accelerated, and that both elements of the combination established in the Thatcher period – market-orientated neoliberalism and a cultural-traditionalist approach to curriculum and assessment – were accentuated. Liberated by the Coalition's presentation of itself as an emergency regime that would use forceful measures to exit from a once-in-a-century crisis, Gove seized the opportunity to pursue a strategy of restructuring that was simultaneously destructive and creative, compressing the patterns of the eighteen years of Conservative policy under Thatcher and Major into one four-year ministerial span. Destructively, he concluded that, more than twenty-five years after the Education Reform Act, which was supposed to have settled such matters, there was still much to be done to break the influence of progressive educational ideas and the organizations that harboured them. Creatively, he aimed to extend the achievements of the Thatcher period, so that schooling was reinvigorated by competitive mechanisms, private sector influence, tight control from the centre and what he saw as academic rigour.

This double policy was evident in the programme for the expansion of academies, and the introduction of free schools. Labour had seen academies as path-breaking institutions, limited in number, that mobilized the management capacity of the private sector, to replace established urban schools that were deemed to be failing (Machin and Vernoit 2010). The coalition government significantly increased the pace and scale of this programme and it became the government's 'chosen vehicle for school reform' (Machin and Vernoit 2010). In 2010, just 6 per cent of secondary schools were academies. By 2014, the percentage had increased to 55 per cent, with 13 per cent of primary schools also transferring to academy status (Department for Education 2014). Alongside this rapid shift, the Academies Act 2010 enabled the setting up of 'Free Schools', autonomous, state-funded schools run by many different providers, including parents, teachers and religious groups. By 2015, 255 such institutions had opened.

This fragmentation of the school system, which entailed the transfer of public assets to private trusts, entailed a sharp decline in the influence of elected local councils. It was accompanied also by an assertion of central control, more rigorous than any previous system, over the work of teachers. Regarding national pay scales as a collectivist relic, Gove proposed that school managements should be able to set each teacher's pay level on an individual, performance-related basis (Stevenson and Wood 2013). This would tend to shrink further whatever element of individual professional autonomy teachers still possessed, at the same time as it made them into more flexible instruments for the transmission of official educational agenda. Performance-related pay was one element in a larger system of regulation that was driven above all by the constant measurement of pupil progress and attainment. Ofsted held schools accountable for exam and test results, and head teachers who failed to deliver on these indicators were likely to be dismissed. This external pressure was passed on to teachers, who were expected to demonstrate that each of their pupils was making continuous progress against specified criteria. The outcome of this data-driven system was not only an increase in workload that teachers found difficult to bear but also a sense on their part that a new form of education was being created, in which test-based performance was valued above all other kinds of goal. 'Since Christmas [six months ago], I have only taught literacy and numeracy', wrote one primary school teacher, who had prepared her class for Key Stage 2 tests. 'When asked their favourite subject, "wrote another," [my pupils] say English or Maths because they don't know anything else.' At secondary level, the same complaints about a narrow curriculum, focused on preparation for high-stakes tests and prioritizing skills of rote learning, were commonplace (Sherrington 2017). It was not only teachers who voiced such criticisms. The OECD, in the form of the head of its Education Division, Andreas Schleicher, began to present the English approach to curriculum and assessment as an outlier among member states, unusual in its emphasis on rote learning and memorization, and overly narrow in its approach to curriculum design (Schleicher 2017).

The marketization of higher education

In its final months, Labour had established a review panel, chaired by the former Chief Executive of British Petroleum Lord Browne and charged with drawing up a new system of financing higher education – a system that would lessen the need for government support, while allowing an expansion of student numbers. Browne's solutions, which were published under the Coalition government, were more than technical. Their essence was that investment in higher education would be funded through student debt. State funding for the teaching of arts, humanities and social sciences degrees should be withdrawn; all students would have access to interest-bearing loans to pay for tuition, which they would pay back when they earned more than £21,000 (McGettigan 2013). The government accepted the proposal to replace state funding, with loan-backed student funding, capping the new level of tuition fees at £9,000.

Thus the 'burden of financing higher education teaching [shifted] towards students and away from central government' (Crawford, Crawford and Wenchao 2013). The resultant restructuring was equally fundamental: it established the basis on which higher education could be marketized, not, as in the past, through competition between different institutions which were all largely state-funded, but rather through the entry into the system of private, for-profit companies. These, just as much as 'public' universities, would be enabled to recruit students with access to the loans system. The teaching grant which the state had previously paid to public institutions had given them what ministers called a 'significant advantage' that no private provider could match. 'Our funding reforms', claimed the Higher Education Minister, David Willetts, in 2011, 'will remove this barrier because all HEIs will – in future – receive most of their income from students via fees. This reform, of itself, opens up the system' (quoted in McGettigan 2013: 3).

The Higher Education Act (2017) consolidated these changes, putting the 'regulatory architecture of a market-based education firmly in place' (Holmwood 2017). It made it easier for profit-seeking institutions to enter the market for undergraduate degrees and as it lifted from existing universities some of the responsibilities associated with public bodies, it increased their capacity for financial maneuverability. It set in place arrangements for institutions which scored well against government criteria for student satisfaction and future student earnings to raise the level of fees they charged. At the same time, the strengthening of an 'impact agenda' for funded research required of researchers that they aligned their work with the interests of its potential users. Higher Education thus became more clearly a field characterized by financial turbulence, in which success was determined by effectiveness in meeting the employability needs of students, and the research and development needs of businesses and the public sector. The mechanisms by which these correspondences were to be assured were those of market competition, and target-setting by the state.

Limits

It is forty years since Thatcher came to power, more than thirty years since the Education Reform Act. Looking back across boom and recession, these events still seem important markers of changes that continue to reverberate in education. The governments of David Cameron (2010–16) in many ways resumed the course set by Thatcher, but in doing so raised the intensity of educational change to a new level. Yet for all this, it is difficult to see English neoliberalism as having reached a triumphant stage. Compared with the period of its emergence in the 1980s, and its first constructive steps in the following decade, neoliberalism in English education is a fuller, more developed programme. There are few hiding places from its systems of surveillance and performance management systems, and few organized points of resistance. Nevertheless, at central points of its project, its unsustainability is apparent, its incoherence is evident and its future is not guaranteed.

Most evidently, the commitment to austerity made by Cameron's governments and renewed by Theresa May, prime minister from 2016, resulted in a school system damaged by cuts, a child population affected by rising levels of poverty, and a cohort of sixteen- to thirty-year-olds disenchanted with the ways in which a decade without income growth has limited their options. Even in the heyday of neoliberalism, the polarization of the labour market and the economic exclusion of youth were emergent problems. By 2017, the year of an ill-timed election which greatly reduced the authority of the Conservative government, the problems had become clearer.

Students are educated as never before. The number of years they spend in formal education has increased. They gain ever greater numbers of qualifications. Yet the connection between educational success and secure, well-paid employment is a tenuous one. Policy has found no answer to this problem. In the job market, as it exists rather than as it is imagined by policy-makers, young people are both overqualified, relative to the jobs on offer, and underemployed in relation to the hours per week they are called on to work. Employment, for school and university leavers, is in most areas available, but it is not a guarantee of adequate pay levels or long-term security (Allen and Ainley 2012; OECD 2018b). High status jobs are increasing in number, but compared to other developed countries, the UK has a relatively large number of people working in low-paid, low-skilled jobs.

The second problem relates to social class. In many ways, education in Britain now is more equitable than it was seventy years ago. Special education, though grossly underfunded, is constructed around a principle of inclusion (Galton and MacBeath 2015). Gender inequalities have been vastly reduced though gender pay gap remains high. Overt forms of institutional racism have diminished. Gay, lesbian and transgender issues, 'promotion' of which the law sought to prohibit in the 1980s, have now become a touchstone of 'British values', as one of what a Conservative Education Secretary called the 'many facets of British culture' (*Pink News* 2015). Class inequality has been harder to address. This is not for want of discussion. The need for schools to address class-related patterns of differences in attainment and outcome has been an urgent theme in the speeches of Conservative ministers. Yet, as could be expected in a society experiencing higher levels of inequality, the social class gap remained strong. In the words of the government's Commission on Social Mobility (2017), England was 'in the grip of a self-reinforcing spiral of ever-growing division'. The pattern of previous decades was accentuated: access to education steadily increased, across all classes, but the most prestigious courses and institutions were dominated by wealthier social groups. When this pattern is placed next to that of the stratified labour market, the conclusion is plain: the inequalities that reformers in earlier generations aimed to eliminate continue to exist. Education is caught up in, and continues to reproduce, these inequalities.

A further problem relates to the culture and management of educational institutions. Successive governments have placed the burdens of achieving educational success on the shoulders of teachers and students. In the present situation, where the individual benefits of education are uncertain, students are nevertheless required to work more intensely than ever, and from an earlier age: without success in competition, they are lost. At the same time, teachers and lecturers, in most cases long since deprived of their autonomy, and facing inspection, performance management and other elements in the battery of management control, are also under great pressure (Warner 2015): work is a place of stress, and the school, so often acclaimed as a site of self-development, becomes in the view of many who labour there a place where broader visions of educational possibility have been cancelled. It is difficult to see how the disparity between the work demanded and the rewards that accrue from it, individual and social, cannot lead to a physical or mental disengagement from the system on the part of large numbers of students and teachers. Problems of recruitment and retention among teachers (National Union of Teachers 2018), and the rising level of protest by academics against increasing insecurity and lower pay and pensions are some of the symptoms of a deepening educational discontent (Yaqoob 2018).

Finally, there is the emerging problem of the legitimacy of Conservative reform in the eyes of those who should be among its close supporters. British politics since 2016 has been dominated by the Brexit referendum and its aftermath. Here the themes of sovereignty, allegiance and national identity which were Conservatism's distinctive contributions to policy for schooling have been replayed on a larger, national stage, eclipsing, in the rhetoric of the referendum, arguments that related to economic activity or to regional inequalities. To an extraordinary degree, pro-Brexit Conservatives have rejected the position of employers' groups: 'fuck business', said the Foreign Secretary, when told of some criticism that had been made of Brexit. In a politer register, the same rejection is occurring in policy for schooling. One of the most striking features of the education policy landscape in the period 2015–19 has been the gulf that has opened between the educational programme of government and the expectations and preferences not just of educationalists, but of employers. Andreas Schleicher's OECD critique of English schooling was echoed in 2018 by Paul Drechsler, president of the Confederation of British Industry (Drechsler 2018). Calling for a new approach to policy-making, Drechsler asked whether the 'ideological commitments' of politicians held too firm a grip. 'Perhaps old habits die hard', he commented. The old habits in question arise, of course, from the historical depths of English Conservatism, habits which pre-existed neoliberalism and have combined with it to damaging effect. In its policies for curriculum, examinations and assessment, Conservatives find themselves enumerating old themes – the uncrossable divide between academic and vocational education, the necessity of a subject-based curriculum, the intellectual worthlessness of an educational philosophy based around creativity, the value of a selective education system. These were the maxims of Conservative thinkers in the immediate post-war decades, and the ideas which enjoyed a second wind when the Black Papers became successful. They still furnish the minds of Conservative policy-makers, but their rationality as a response to England's deep social and economic problems is seriously in question.

References

Allen, M. and Ainley, P. (2012) *The Great Reversal*, London: RadicalEd.

Althusser, L. (1969) Contradiction and overdetermination, in *For Marx*, Harmondsworth: Penguin.

Anderson, P. (1987) The figures of descent, *New Left Review*, 1 (161): 20–76.

Archer, L. (2008) The new neoliberal subjects? Young/er academics' constructions of professional identity, *Journal of Education Policy*, 23 (3): 265–85.

Ball, S. J. (2007) *Education Plc: Understanding Private Sector Participation in Public Sector Education*, London: Routledge.

Barber, M. (1998) *Creating a World-Class Education Service*. Speech Delivered to North of England Education Conference, Bradford, January.

Bellfielid, C. and Sibieta, L. (2017) *Long-Run Comparisons of Spending per Pupil across Different Stages of Education*, London: Institute for Fiscal Studies. https://www.ifs.org.uk/uploads/Presentations/IFS%20Education%20Presentation%20270217.pdf

Blackburn, R. (2018) The Corbyn project, *New Left Review*, II/111, May–June: 5–36.

Blair, T. (1995) The power of the message, *New Statesman*, 29 September: 19–22.

Blair, T. (1996) *New Britain: My Vision of a Young Country*, London: Fourth Estate.

Burns, C. (2008) Margaret Thatcher's Greatest Achievement: New Labour, *Conservative Home*, 11 April. http://conservativehome.blogs.com/centreright/2008/04/making-history.html

Cameron, D. (2013) EU speech at Bloomberg, 23 January. https://www.gov.uk/government/speeches/eu-speech-at-bloomberg.

Chowdry, H. and Sibieta, L. (2011) *Trends in Education and School Spending*, London: Institute for Fiscal Studies.

Clarke, J. and Newman, J. (2012) The alchemy of austerity, *Critical Social Policy*, 32 (2): 299–320.

Commission on Social Mobility (2017) *Social Mobility in Great Britain: Fifth State of the Nation Report*, London: Social Mobility Commission.

Cox, B. (1992) *The Great Betrayal: Memoirs of a Life in Education*, London: Chapman.

Crawford, C., Crawford, R. and Wenchao, J. (2013) *The Outlook for Higher Education Spending by the Department for Business, Innovation and Skills*, London: Institute for Fiscal Studies.

Davies, W. (2018) What are they after? *London Review of Books*, 40 (5), 8 March: 3–5.

Dennison, J. (1989) Higher education policy in the United Kingdom – reformation or dissolution? *The Canadian Journal of Higher Education*, XIX (1): 87–96.

Department for Education (2014) *Schools, Pupils and their Characteristics*, London: Department for Education.

Department for Education and Employment (2001) *Schools Building on Success: Raising Standards, Promoting Diversity, Achieving Results*, London: The Stationery Office.

Dorey, P. (2014) The legacy of Thatcherism for education policies: Markets, managerialism and malice (towards teachers), in C. Hay and S. Farrell (eds), *The Legacy of Thatcherism,* Oxford: Oxford University Press/British Academy.

Drechsler, P. (2018) *Education is More than Knowledge Alone, Speech to Association of School and College Leader.* London: Confederation of British Industry Press Release, 9 March. http://www.cbi.org.uk/news/education-is-more-than-knowledge-alone/

Exley, S. and Ball, S. J. (2011) *Something Old, Something New ... Understanding Conservative Education Policy*, in H. Bochel (ed.), *The Conservative Party and Social Policy*, Bristol: Policy Press.

Galton, M. and MacBeath, J. (2015) *Inclusion: Statements of Intent*, London: National Union of Teachers.

Gewirtz, S., Ball, S. J. and Bowe, R. (1995) *Markets, Choice and Equity in Education.* Buckingham: Open University Press.

Gove, M. (2009) What is education for? *Speech to Royal Society for Arts*, 30 June.

Green, A. (1991) *Education and State Formation: The Rise of Education Systems in England, France and the USA*, Basingstoke: Macmillan.

Harrison, B. (1994) Mrs Thatcher and the intellectuals, *Twentieth Century British History*, 5 (2): 206–45.

Harrison, N. (2011) Have the changes introduced by the 2004 Higher Education Act made higher education admissions in England wider and fairer? *Journal of Education Policy*, 26 (3): 449–68.

Higher Education Statistics Agency (2010) *Free Online Statistics – Staff*. https://www.hesa.ac.uk/stats-staff

Hobsbawm, E. (1968) *Industry and Empire: From 1750 to the Present Day*, Harmondsworth: Penguin.

Holmwood, J. (2017) *Requiem for the Public University*, Campaign for the Public University. https://publicuniversity.org.uk/2017/05/02/requiem-for-the-public-university/

Institute for Fiscal Studies (2017) *A Comparison of Manifesto Proposals on School Spending in England*, 26 May. https://www.ifs.org.uk/publications/9252

Jones, K. (1989) *Right Turn: The Conservative Revolution in Education Policy*, London: Radius.

Jones, K. (2015) *Education in Britain 1944 to the Present*, Cambridge: Polity.

Jones, K. and Thomson, P. (2008) Policy rhetoric and the renovation of English schooling: The case of creative partnerships, *Journal of Education Policy*, 23 (6): 715–27.

Kitson, M. and Michie, J. (2014) *The Deindustrial Revolution: The Rise and Fall of UK Manufacturing 1870-2010*, Centre for Business Research, University of Cambridge Working Paper No. 459.

Machin, S. and Vernoit, J. (2010) *Academy Schools: Who Benefits? CentrePiece*, Centre for Economic Performance: LSE. http://cep.lse.ac.uk/pubs/download/cp325.pdf

McGettigan, A. (2013) *The Great University Gamble: Money, Markets and the Future of Higher Education*, London: Pluto Press.

OECD (2018a) Research & development statistics. http://www.oecd.org/innovation/inno/researchanddevelopmentstatisticsrds.htm

OECD (2018b) *Education at a Glance*, Paris: OECD.

Ogbonna, E. and Harris, L. C. (2004) Work intensification and emotional labour among UK university lecturers: An exploratory study, *Organization Studies*, 25 (7): 1185–203.

Pink News (2015) Nicky Morgan Backs Ofsted over Decision to Ask Christian Schools about Gay People, 29 January.

Rubinstein, W. D. (1993) *Capitalism, Culture and Decline in Britain 1750-1990*, London: Routledge.

Schleicher, A. (2017) What can English education learn from other countries, Lecture to the Education Policy Institute, London, 8 November. Available at: https://epi.org.uk/wp-content/uploads/2017/11/EPI-2017-Annual-Lecture-Andreas-Schleicher.pdf

Sherrington, T. (2017) We need to ditch Progress 8, *Schools Week*, 15 July.

Simon, B. (1988) *Bending the Rules: The Baker 'Reform' of Education*, London: Lawrence & Wishart.

Smithers, R. (1999) Unions angered by Blair attack on teachers, *Guardian*, 22 October.

Stevenson, H. and Wood, P. (2013) Markets, managerialism and teachers' work: The invisible hand of high stakes testing in England, *International Education Journal: Comparative Perspectives*, 12 (2): 42–61.

Sutton Trust (2011) *Degrees of Success: University Chances by Individual School*, London: Sutton Trust.

Vincent, C. and Ball, S. J. (2006) *Children, Choice and Class Practices: Middle-Class Parents and their Children*, London: Routledge.

Warner, M. (2015) Learning my lesson, *London Review of Books*, 37 (6): 8–14.

Watson, D. and Bowden, R. (1999) Why did they do it? The Conservatives and mass higher education, 1979–99, *Journal of Education Policy*, 14 (3): 243–56.

Yaqoob, W. (2018) Why we strike, *London Review of Books*, Blog, 16 February. https://www.lrb.co.uk/blog/2018/02/16/w-yaqoobgmail-com/why-we-strike/

4

Great and Small Expectations: The French Education System

Guy Dreux

Translated into English by Elise Brault-Dreux

For thirty years or so, French education has been designed to serve the economy. Responsible for the production of 'human capital', it is expected to respond to the evolution of the labour market. Compelled to contribute to gains in productivity, the educational system – from nursery school to university – is submitted to ever more detailed plans of action which seek to carry out the European strategy defined in Lisbon in 2000 – that is, to make Europe 'the most competitive and dynamic knowledge-based economy in the world' (European Council 2000). The 2008 crisis did not alter these goals, though public funding became more constrained. The situation in the last few years has further confirmed the trend: successive governments have one after the other tried to seek practical means to fulfil EU ambitions. Europe 2020 ordains, for instance, that the proportion of fifteen-year-old pupils with poor skills in reading, mathematics and sciences must fall below 15 per cent, and at least 40 per cent of people aged between thirty and thirty-four must have a university degree (European Union 2010).

France must attend to this European framework at the same time as it tries to address policy issues of reducing educational inequalities that are specifically French. This chapter focuses on these combined economic and equality-related concerns, and the ways in which they are addressed by the Macron presidency's 2018 education reforms.

The *baccalauréat*: The rise and fall of a symbol

It was with a well-practised strategy of policy staging – when an official commission delivers its report in a 'sort of public drama, the drama of the reflection over public issues' (Bourdieu 2012: 48) – that the government of Emmanuel Macron, whose election was mainly based on the discourse of 'revolution', announced its reform plans for the bac: 'one revolution that we really need is the transformation of our schools' (Macron 2017). Following the British nineteenth- and twentieth-century model of a 'Royal Commission', the 'Mathiot Report' delivered on 24 January 2018 to the education minister, Jean-Michel Blanquer, was the outcome of consultations with experts, key figures or wise people who were enlisted in the 'performance' of 'a new legitimate definition of a public issue' (Mathiot 2018; Bourdieu 2012: 51–2).

The 'novelty' of the scene resides in the identity of the protagonists who perform the play. So far as both form and content are concerned, the propositions of the Mathiot report – which mainly seeks to reduce the number of tests for the final assessment in favour of a continuous assessment – exactly meet the wishes expressed by Jean-Michel Blanquer a few years back (Blanquer 2014) and are a good match for the programme of neoliberal reform advocated by some politicians, such as Luc Chatel[1] and replicated in reports of the European Union. The purpose of the current report then is to give a new legitimacy and political weight to propositions that were formulated some time ago.

The Report insisted on the current unfitness-for-purpose of the *baccalauréat*. It was quickly followed by the announcement of the reform of high school (14 February) and of the reform of access to university – the ORE law was approved on 15 February. Taken as a whole, these measures amounted to a new logical continuum, stretching from three years before the *bac* to three years after ('Bac–3/Bac+3'). This new organization of upper-secondary and tertiary education in France, prefigured by Blanquer (2014) rests on two main phases: In Blanquer's words,

> the first [phase], which starts after the *maternelle* (nursery school) and ends at the end of *collège* (secondary school) corresponds to the provision of a common base of knowledge and skills. Moving from simple to complex knowledge and skills, it is meant to provide all French children with the basic elements a person, a citizen, must know in our century. The second period starts right after the first year of the lycée and ends when the individual starts his / her professional career, therefore encompassing higher-education and / or professional training. Like the first period, but more intensely, it must also prepare young people for continuous professional development throughout their life, a life where

---

[1]   In 2012, Luc Chatel, then minister for education during the Sarkozy presidency, expressed his wish to 'put new value on' the *baccalauréat*; he suggested 'a greater amount of continuous assessment', http://www.cafepedagogique.net/lexpresso/Pages/2012/03/13032012_Chatelattaquelebac.aspx

one never stops learning since, by definition, 'living is learning' ('la vie est un apprentissage'). (Blanquer 2014: 91)

The three quasi-concomitant reforms that aim to reshape Blanquer's 'second period' ascribe a decisive, strategic function to 'orientation', to guidance – which is presented as the means to link study to employment, individual choice to occupational outcome. The engagement letter Blanquer addressed to Mathiot stated the priorities of reform: 'The ambition is at once to simplify its [the *baccalauréat*] organization, to maintain its function of giving access to higher education, in the context of the fundamental question of guidance, [and] to re-establish its credibility in making it a determining rite of passage in our pupils' future achievement.' The report in response proposes 'a *baccalauréat* that has been modified in order to improve guidance for higher education' (Mathiot 2018: 4, 9). The reform of the *lycée* curriculum is likewise intended to facilitate student guidance, substituting for the three general tracks – S (sciences), ES (economics and social sciences) and L (literature) – a diversity of teachings chosen by the pupils at the end of their first year of high school, which are supposed to facilitate and foreshadow a specific higher-education degree course. The reform also allocates a more significant amount of time to the elaboration of the pupils' vocational projects – this as early as the first year of high school. As for higher education, detailed reforms are yet to emerge, but all indications are that universities, too, will need to address questions of guidance, given the 'rapid evolution of knowledge, technologies and jobs'.[2]

Histories of the *bac*

The full significance of the reforms cannot be understood outside the history which is their ambition to change. Created in 1808, the *baccalauréat* eventually imposed itself as the *satisfecit* required to have access to higher education and above all to the best careers. A social 'barrier' separating those who have access to higher education from the others and, at the same time, a 'level', or a certification of the holder's general knowledge, the *baccalauréat* was for a long time seen as a sign distinguishing class membership of the French bourgeoisie (Goblot 1925/2010). For in France, till the 1970s, there were two different parallel school systems which were socially segregated: the 'primary' system for working-class

---

[2] 'From now on, the role of school is decisive and educational public policies must seriously take into account the issue of guidance. Each pupil must acquire the skills necessary to make the right choices throughout their life and of course, first and foremost, when leaving high-school' (Daniel Filatre 2017: 3).

children from the age of six to the *certificat d'études* (taken aged fourteen); and the 'secondary' system delivered by *lycées* for children from the bourgeoisie, from the age of six till the *baccalauréat*. Till the 1970s, only a small part of a student generation – most of whom were from privileged backgrounds – took the *baccalauréat*.[3]

Behind this educational sign lay a deep sociological transformation: the bourgeoisie's acceptance that in order to reproduce itself and to reproduce its economic capital and domination, it had to provide a new form of legitimacy, and prove its merit with a qualification that recognized its possession of cultural capital. It was this very transformation which was recognized in Edmond Goblot's book in 1925: economic, political and social evolutions, as well as the exigencies of war, impelled the bourgeoisie to set out evidence of its superiority through the official recognition of its intellectual worth. This was the *baccalauréat's* role and symbolic meaning.

Yet, since the second wave of high-school democratization in the 1980s, which increased access to upper-secondary education[4] – mainly justified by reference to the modernization of the economic system and the necessary improvement of skills among the workforce – the *baccalauréat* has become a mere *accessit* that entitles the holder to enter higher education, but no longer ensures access to the best positions on the market. Analysing the effects of credential inflation, experts point out the permanent increase in labour market demands for diplomas and qualifications and, at the same time the relative devaluation of the *baccalauréat* (Duru-Bellat 2006). Even more worrying, because of the alarming first year failure rate at university,[5] what has been seriously and increasingly questioned is the essential academic value of the *baccalauréat*, that is, its capacity to certify a level required to study at university.

The fact that the *baccalauréat* is no longer a 'level' (which provided expectations for academic success), nor a 'barrier' (since 79 per cent of the student generation

---

[3] For a discussion of the evolution of the *bac* into different tracks, and the relation of tracking to social inequality see Chapoulie 2017.

[4] 170,000 *bac*-holders in 1968 (that is, 20 per cent of a generation), then 250,000 in 1985 (that is, 30 per cent of a generation), 400,000 in 1991 and 500,000 in 1995 (that is, 63 per cent of a generation). The success rates at the exam also significantly increased: from 60 per cent up to 87 per cent between 1960 and 2017. See Duru-Bellat (2013).

[5] What is commonly pointed out and commented upon is that 60 per cent of the students do not pass their *licence* (three-year degree) after four years spent studying at the university. Among the 2012 *bac*-holders, who started university in September 2012, 28.4 per cent passed their *licence* within three years, 41 per cent within four years. So the commonly mentioned '60 per cent' (which encompasses all types of *baccalauréat* – that is, the general track and the professional, technical ones) is therefore often contested. See Stromboni (2017).

passed it in 2017[6]) is now utilized to justify the reform of both the high-school system and the first three years of university. This is the immediate context of Mathiot's reforms. The argument of the current government is that the main consequence of university democratization (in the 1980s and 1990s) was a massification of the total number of pupils and students, which led to a decreasing value of diplomas, especially in the case of the *baccalauréat*. The explicit purpose of Macron's government is to give value again to the system, not by improving the conditions of study of the 'new students' (i.e. lower-class students who would not have gone to university before the 1990s), but by improved methods of school and professional guidance – guidance in the sense of orientation to future careers, and the educational pathways which might lead to them.[7]

The 2018 reform seeks a reduction in the number of disciplines, more significant, and more individualized, specialization of courses, and a larger amount of time devoted to guidance.[8] Reform at the level of higher education gives universities the capacity to check high-school pupils' results before admitting them, and to require an improvement in certain skills.[9] This is a change of historical significance: since it was first created, the *baccalauréat* had been in effect the first stage in higher education; it allowed each bac-holder entry to the system, to pick any kind of degree offered by universities. What is jeopardized today is this freedom of choice; the scale of student demonstrations in various universities in the spring of 2018 demonstrated a widespread desire to regain this freedom (Costa-Kostritsky 2018; Stangler 2018).

The specific challenge to the French education system: The question of equality

Is there a 'crisis of performance' in the French school system? The pattern of PISA test results, across a long period, suggests that there is. There are various studies to show that between 1999 and 2013 the performance of CE2 pupils (eight-year-old primary school children) in French and mathematics declined

---

[6] 643,800 *bacheliers* in 2017.
[7] Guidance ('orientation') is a strongly established feature of secondary and tertiary education in France. For instance a 2009 law set up a 'public lifelong guidance service' 'to guarantee all people access to free, full and objective information on occupations, training, certifications, job opportunities and remuneration levels as well as access to quality, networked guidance, advisory and assistance services'. See https://www.euroguidance.eu/guidance-system-in-france
[8] The Mathiot report about the *baccalauréat* reform overtly announces a high-school reform.
[9] This reform, called 'Loi Vidal' or 'Loi Orientation et Réussite de Etudiants' (law for the guidance and success of students), was passed on 25 February 2018.

by fourteen points on the PISA scale, and to reveal that spelling skills have significantly weakened over thirty years (CNESCO 2018). Likewise, in the most recent round of PISA tests, France had alarming results. The peculiarity of France is that both the proportion of students with good results and the proportion of students with difficulties are higher than in the other OECD countries, thus complicating the analysis that night be derived from a study of mean scores. In mathematics, for instance, the mean performance of French students deteriorated significantly between 2003 and 2012 – and in addition the gap between the results of privileged and underprivileged students became particularly wide.[10]

More seriously, it is in France, of all the countries participating in the 2015 PISA survey, that the influence of 'socio-economic background is strongest. PISA's calculations suggest that in France, socio-economic background accounts for more than 20% of the results obtained by 15-year-old students, as compared to an average of only 13% for other OECD countries' (OCDE, PISA 2015). Among all student populations with an underprivileged background, it is the French who most frequently said to 'have difficulties' (40 per cent against 34 per cent globally). Conversely, among students from a privileged background, it is the French who most frequently 'achieve excellent results' (18 per cent against a global average of 16 per cent).

In the French system, then, education inequalities are clearly correlated to the parents' social status. 'On average across the OECD countries, a one-unit increase on the PISA index of economic, social and cultural status is associated with an increase of 38 score points in the mathematics assessment; in France, this rises to 57 points an increase which corresponds to more than a "school year"' (OCDE, PISA 2015: 8). PISA also reveals wide performance gaps and social inequalities relating to course type, with predictable correlations between social class and programme of study – general education, technical education or professional training. Again, what is a particular cause of concern is the enduring and increasing nature of these inequalities. If we take into account that a school year corresponds to thirty-eight score points on the PISA index, the performance gap between the most privileged and the least privileged pupils was equivalent to 2.7 school years in 2000 and 3.5 in 2012 (Felouzis 2014: 57).

---

[10] The number of pupils with difficulties in mathematics keeps increasing: 17 per cent in 2003, 22 per cent in 2012 and 24 per cent in 2015. But, pupils from lower backgrounds are overrepresented in vocational education, a field which is clearly less 'performant' than general courses (by forty-three points for PISA 2015).

A school system that increases inequalities

These results are all the more disappointing and worrying since the struggle against inequality at school has been one of the enduring political battles fought since the end of the 1970s. Out of these battles a worrying paradox has emerged: it is not just that social inequalities in schooling have not been successfully addressed by action plans which initially sought to fight them; it is also that inequalities may actually turn out to have been strengthened by these plans. In the 1960s and 1970s within the 'collège unique',[11] there developed a pedagogy supposedly adapted to the working classes, who were assumed to inhabit a culture remote from that of the school, and characterized by poor linguistic and cultural skills (Terrail 2016). This ambition to adapt the school to the educational difficulties of working-class students – whether they were real or teacher-constructed we will leave to one side for now – may in fact have endlessly postponed the moment of learning, as 'phases of exploration' were multiplied, along with the creation of 'motivating situations'. Favouring 'fun' activities, 'familiar representations and material evocations' to better match a 'hypothetically poor inclination for school knowledge and limited cognitive and cultural skills' seems from a current perspective to have been absolutely unproductive. As it seemed to lower its expectations and intellectual ambitions for the pupils who were thought to be weak, the school system might in the end have actually produced the very difficulties which it initially intended to fight with its 'differentiated instruction'.

Likewise, since the creation of educational priority zones (ZEPs) in 1981, additional resources have been allocated to schools in disadvantaged areas. But these plans of action, compared with those carried out in several other countries after the 'PISA shock', were both less ambitious and more embedded. In the long run they therefore have noxious effects, especially in the form of a 'labelling effect': the best students or the socially most favoured seek to leave schools in the ZEP; teachers do not want to teach in them and so on. These negative effects clearly counterbalance the positive effects expected when class sizes are reduced and financial resources are lifted slightly above the average (Mons 2013).

---

[11] The 1959 Berthoin reform, to meet the country's needs for more skilled engineers, created the 'collèges d'enseignement general' (general education secondary schools) and hence raised the age of compulsory education from fourteen to sixteen. The subsequent Haby Reform (11 July 1975), which launched the 'collège unique', put an end to the parallel system of primary education for the masses and secondary education [high-school] for the bourgeoisie – two systems that were clearly socially distinct. The 'collège unique' is quite often described as the outcome of a long process of secondary school democratization, but what it has produced goes along a new problematic situation in terms of a pedagogy that derived from unprecedented social heterogeneity.

As a consequence of policy change, social evolutions and school-level practice, there have emerged what some sociologists (Felouzis, Liot and Perroton 2005) have called 'school ghettos' in which has accumulated a mass of economic and social difficulties – an accumulation which has led to deteriorated conditions of learning that themselves have grown worse as more privileged layers have elaborated strategies to avoid these schools (Felouzis et al. 2016; Felouzis, Liot and Perroton 2005). Family strategies to evade the 'carte scolaire'[12] and to search out better conditions of learning for their children were seen to be justified by studies which measured the 'crucial role' of 'peer effects' on school performances (Brodaty 2010).

A market that relies on panic and fear

The three reforms (*baccalauréat*, high school and university) created a continuum between 'Bac–3 and Bac+3'. They thus spoke to a wide swathe of the population: the *baccalauréat* and higher education have become the horizon of expectations for the bulk of families[13] and the debates around the 'value' of the *baccalauréat* concentrate all the uncertainties around the 'value' of the French school system as a whole. They address a situation in which complex and apparently contradictory patterns have taken shape. As more and more students pass their diplomas and degrees, educational inequalities increase – there is a widening gap between high-performing students and those in difficulties (Felouzis 2014). The relationship between the expansion of education and the 'mediocre' achievements of students becomes a political issue.[14] It is as though the school system which produces – even reinforces – social inequalities were carrying out its democratizing ambition by distributing *counterfeit money*, titles and diplomas whose value is low, not only on the labour market but also in relation to the skills and knowledge necessary for higher education. France thus seems to be affected by a defiance, even a form of panic, regarding its own school system, which may well account for the success of the phrase 'inflation scolaire' (Duru-Bellat 2006). Out of this situation arises Macron's project: *baccalauréat* reform is quite symptomatically designed to give back some 'value' to the

---

[12] The *carte scolaire*, introduced in 1963, defines in geographical terms the catchment area of each educational institution, and thus serves as a basis for allocating student numbers and teaching posts. Unless exempted for some allowable reason, every pupil should attend the school whose location corresponds to their home address.

[13] In 2016, 62.2 per cent of *bac*-holders entered university.

[14] It has certainly been an issue for Emmanuel Macron. 'Now, however, the performance of our schools has become mediocre' (Macron 2017: 97).

diploma, a value which dropped due to bac-holders' massive failure in the first years of university.

This mistrust of the school's capacity to provide good-quality teaching and to maintain high standards is also evident in other socially significant choices: the privileged classes' interest in forms of alternative schooling,[15] the commercial success of all the products labelled 'Montessori', the success of private initiatives that offer certifications of skills and standards, and the increasing market for remedial courses (Lehoux 2018). If these new markets are revelatory agents of a form of panic, they also work to strengthen current trends in which the economic capital at the disposal of families is an increasingly important factor in students' achievement – it is no longer so dependent on translation into cultural capital to become a force for educational success (Bourdieu 1986). Since the end of the 1980s, the 'social selectivity' of diplomas (measured by the closeness of the relationship between students' social background and the status of their degree) has increased in the '*grandes écoles*'[16] and is no longer decreasing for postgraduate degrees (Albouy and Venecq 2003; Albouy and Tavan 2007).[17] These developments put an end to important aspects of the movement towards a democratization of education – admittedly a slow movement, but one that attracted many supporters, in all corners of the world of education, and whose existence was noticeable throughout the twentieth century. It is quite tempting to draw a parallel with the most conspicuous tendencies observed by Thomas Piketty about economic and wealth inequalities – inequalities which declined throughout the twentieth century but which have been increasing since the beginning of the twenty-first century (Piketty 2001, 2013).

Post-2008 France: A business-orientated education system

Since 2008 education has been increasingly seen as an essential factor of economic growth and a weapon in the fight against unemployment.[18] (This is the context in which appropriate 'orientation' is regarded as essential.) In France, as elsewhere,

---

[15] 'Les Ecoles alternatives séduisent l'élite', *Les Echos*, 25 March 2016.

[16] The 'grandes ecoles' are higher education establishments that lie outside the main framework of the public university system. They are highly selective and prestigious institutions; their graduates tend to dominate the private and public sectors of French society.

[17] Albouy and Vanecq (2003). Even if for the working-class children the chances to obtain a higher education degree were multiplied by three between the 1948–51 and 1975–7 generations, they still remain three times lower than the chances of the upper-middle-class children (77 per cent for 25 per cent).Albouy and Tavan (2007).

[18] In the first months of 2018, the unemployment rate in France reached 9.2–21.4 per cent for fifteen- to twenty-four-year-olds. Le Point (2018).

governments have seen economic performance as dependent on human capital formation, on innovation encouraged by the autonomy of, and competition between, universities, on the business-orientated reprofessionalization of education, and on the increased status of research and on its transferability to socio-economic sectors (Aghion and Cohen 2004). The quality of education is now measured, therefore, by its contribution to economic performance and in consequence, in periods of crisis, the efficiency and effectiveness of the education system is called into question. For Blanquer, as Minister of Education, the tasks for education are clear; its legitimacy directly depends on its ability to contribute to an economic recovery:

> Unemployment among the youth is unacceptable … . All the projects we undertake seek to reduce it considerably. On that condition only can a necessary confidence be restored between school and society so that, in the end, pupils can be confident about themselves and their future. (Blanquer 2017: 5)

Blanquer's strictures arise from the wider ambitions of the Macron presidency. Low competitiveness – source of trade deficit – and labour market rigidity – source of unemployment – are for Macron, as for Francois Hollande, his predecessor, the two main challenges faced by the French economy, and they have faced the challenges in similar ways. On 8 August 2016, Hollande's government, in spite of massive protests, announced a labour law reform whose purpose was to make things easier for companies to hire and fire employees. A few days later, on 17 August, Macron, then Minister of Economy, Industry and Digital Affairs, completed a preface to a book (Kramarz and Tibi 2016) that set the doctrines of economic science (presented in the singular, as an unequivocal set of teachings) against the irrationalism of trade union resistance, an uninformed 'blocage syndicale'. The argument of the book was clear: to be successful, the economy (understood as a continuous 'creative-destructive mechanism') directly depends on the way in which social, political and economic institutions carry out the transfer/transformation of resources between old and new labour activities. Orientating resources, capital and employment towards developing new activities was becoming crucial to the destructive-creative process, and in this context finding effective measures of labour reallocation was key. This was an argument to which Macron lent his weight. 'We firmly believe', he wrote, in defence of the 'flexibility' of labour, 'that France can be reformed so as to offer a better future to its citizens. And we are sure that these reforms must be carried out in the light of the science of economics' (Kramarz and Tibi, 2016: 28). Once president, Macron signed, in September 2017, five orders which were supposed to extend Hollande's 2016 reform and make it easier for companies to put an end to permanent employment contracts, following the common neoliberal reasoning that in order to boost employment, lay-offs have to be made easier.

To this perspective was added another, with particular resonance for education. In order to deal with France's problem of competitiveness, Kramarz and Tibi proposed a new ambition. Governments should steer investment towards partnerships between universities and private R&D activity. The country should become 'the centre of venture capital in Europe' by mobilizing and yoking together its new companies and its best 'academic institutions', so that globally competitive academic clusters, comparable to Stanford, Berkeley and MIT, could be developed (Kramarz and Tibi 2016: 171–3). Naturally, this would tend to favour selectivity, in the form of the '*pôles d'excellence*' (centres of excellence) launched in 2010, following the passing of the law on university autonomy in 2009. Partnerships and new funding would contribute to reducing the gap between France's high position in league tables for the production of scientific knowledge – it ranks seventh in the world (HCÉRES 2018) – and its much more lowly position in league tables for the application of scientific knowledge in the form of innovation. As in other European countries, the concern has been to create a closer link between scientific achievement and its economic uses.

An education system for an entrepreneurial mindset

The future of French society is in this way depicted by advocates for neoliberal change in the form of an economy led by innovation and contract flexibility, where information becomes essential to promote one's skills and seize opportunities on the labour market. The entrepreneurial mindset is being put forward as a means of determining behaviours and decisions in a society that offers opportunities to adaptable individuals. At school level, this has become a paradigm which has been increasingly taken up. In 2014, when he was still the president of a leading business school, rather than a senior government minister Blanquer was already observing with satisfaction a better relationship between education and business, the result of countless initiatives and partnerships between teachers and company directors. The 'school – company week', for instance, was organized by the Ministry of Education to 'bring together education and business' and offer opportunities to pupils, to 'develop their taste for entrepreneurship', to 'boost their desire to learn' and to be better informed and guided. Blanquer (in the same spirit as the Italian Buona Scuola programme discussed in Chapter 8) wanted to take this further "by spreading among our pupils the entrepreneurial mindset our country of which our country is in so much need." This could be concretized, he suggested, in the form of workshops, role plays, creation of junior companies in schools (Blanquer 2014, 116).

Blanquer's words perfectly echo what François Hollande (then president) declared in 2013, during the annual conference on entrepreneurship: 'The stimulation of the entrepreneurial mindset in our country, is first and foremost the role of school. … A set of courses on entrepreneurship will be developed and taught from the first year of secondary school to the end of high-school' (Soulé 2013). School-company 'partnerships' would allow companies to take part in various education activities. They would promote *learning by doing*, on the basis of which principle pupils are often encouraged to carry out market research, to imagine small companies or start-ups, to have a positive approach to business in general, to see it as an innovating and self-realizing force where individual qualities prevail over academic knowledge. In all of this, there is a certain ignorance of reality, for the companies imagined by the pupils are invariably very idealized: workers are absent, only leading positions are considered, and conflicts are non-existent.

From a sociological or historical point of view, all these initiatives participate in a reversal or a diversion of values, well summarized by the French researcher, Lucie Tanguy: 'The watchword "*apprendre pour entreprendre*",[19] launched in the early 1980s by Jean-Pierre Chevènement, then Education Minister, had been subverted to become "*entreprendre pour apprendre*"'[20] (Tanguy 2016: 13). Much was at stake, therefore, in the attempt to create new elements in the culture of schooling.

Access to university and econometrics of higher education

Spreading the entrepreneurial mindset also means encouraging individuals to see themselves as entrepreneurs of their own life (Dardot and Laval 2017), and to commit themselves and, especially, to invest in higher education. In France, university tuition fees for national diplomas are low and are set by a ministerial

---

[19] *Apprendre pour entreprendre* is the title of the book written by Jean-Pierre Chevènement and published in 1985.
[20] '*Entreprendre pour apprendre*' is the name of one of the main organizations, approved by ministers, which offer training courses 'to develop the entrepreneurial mindset among young people ranging from 8 to 25 years old … , to increase their employability' or 'guide' them. For the year 2016–17, 1,400 entrepreneurs, 2,800 teachers and 27,000 pupils were involved in the activities of this organization. http://www.entreprendre-pour-apprendre.fr/

order.[21] Because of the university funding crisis, an increase of tuition fees has been under serious consideration. This solution remains taboo and politically tricky, but a growing number of voices argue that the idea of free higher education should be relinquished. The arguments they deploy are based on neoliberal premises. According to human capita theory, there is supposed to be a contradiction between, on the one hand, universities funded by public means and, on the other, the private benefits that accrue for degree holders. This theory, which rejects public good arguments for free or low-cost education, argues in favour of an increase in tuition fees, using as justification sociological research which has revealed an overrepresentation of the well-off and an underrepresentation of the underprivileged in universities.[22] It is argued that a 'fairer' system, closer to a 'social optimum', would be to define a lower rate of subsidy for higher education, so that the rich were not subsidized through general taxation. This, according to some economists, would be a move based on principles of social justice (Gary-Bobo 2006).

From the principle of guidance to the introduction of Parcoursup

According to Robert Gary-Bobo, a neoliberal economist who took part in Emmanuel Macron's electoral campaign, the massive failure rate of university students who hold a professional and technical *baccalauréat* ('different in form and content from "general" *baccalauréat*, and prepared in specific professional technical schools') draws attention to a very specific institutional problem: that of the guidance of these students towards courses where their academic chances of success are extremely low. This leads Gary-Bobo towards the idea of a system which would combine guidance with selection, and orientation would be based on an estimation of the likely level of a student's success. The selection-guidance system would enable students to enrol in courses adapted to their skills rather than lose themselves in over-general degree courses which, most of the time, are mere stopgap solutions. 'We must keep in mind that specific efforts and a better use of public funds can improve youth employment' (Gary-Bobo 2017: 47). These propositions have been carried out in Blanquer's recent reform of the admission system for university: under the name of 'Parcoursup'. The reform

---

[21] For 2016–17, the fees were 184 euros for a licence (three-year degree), 256 euros for a master and 391 for a doctorate. But a university can set its tuition fees when it offers a diploma specific to its own institution.

[22] In 2015, 10.8 per cent of the university students were working-class and 30 per cent were middle-class (children of executives). Workers amount to 20.8 per cent of the population aged fifteen and over, and executives, 18 per cent.

embodies the 'selection-guidance' principle floated by Gary-Bobo: a process enabling universities to select their future students, while appearing also to be attentive to the talents and interests of individual students.

Concretely, 'Parcoursup' is a government portal which all secondary school pupils must use to apply to higher education courses in various universities. A university cannot deny access to a student. But it can demand of them that they attend refresher courses in various disciplines considered essential for the courses chosen. The portal enables students to nominate specific university courses. Students are then informed of the outcome of their applications – whether they have been accepted on the course or whether they are required to attend refresher courses. For some students, entry to well-subscribed or prestigious courses will be straightforward. For others it will be more problematic.

Gary-Bobo sees this encounter between selectors and applicants as a market relationship in which both categories are provided with econometric information that can enable rational choices. In this view, students need to be better informed about the content of degree courses offered by universities as well as about their own likely employability when they graduate. Information on salaries and the quantitative study of the labour market integration of university graduates, according to the university they attended and the courses they followed, should become 'fundamental principles', and this would result in an 'extraordinary update' of continuous, reality-based data (Gary-Bobo 2017: 49). There would be a dual benefit. On the one hand each student would be able to make their own well-informed choices; on the other, the publication of these data would further encourage competition between universities, which would be incited to improve the quality of their work, and to propose solutions that 'increasingly fit the social demand' (Gary-Bobo 2017: 49). It follows from these emphases that universities – just like business schools[23] – should then be ranked, no longer according to academic criteria (related to cultural values and to research), but on the basis of standards set by companies and thus directly deriving from business. The salary levels of former students now become the main indicator of the value of each university and of its courses (cf. Chapter 3 in this volume on England).

This new econometrics of higher education could of course facilitate a system of student loans. It would enable students to calculate their expected gains, to optimize their choice of courses having regard to their application's chances of

---

[23] It is actually quite revealing that on the welcome page of ESSEC (*Ecole Supérieure de sciences économiques et commerciales*, a prestigious business school), we are given the average 'first salary' of the former ESSEC students. Also, tellingly, Jean-Michel Blanquer had been at the head of this school since 2013 when he became education minister.

success, and it would enable the banks to better consider the risks of each loan application. But for the moment, the reform focuses on providing information to students and teachers and on encouraging competition between universities for the students they need.

The management of expectations

Let us summarize the argument and narrative of the chapter so far. Beyond the official discourse, what is at stake is the increase of success rates in higher education – to meet France's European commitment – while observing the principle of freedom of choice for each pupil.[24] The work around guidance, the principle which is supposed to improve students' chances of success in the pathway they are guided towards, is from the government's perspective a necessary action to create a correspondence between student choice, school and university reform, and economic success. Much of its social and political significance, however, may lie elsewhere, in the relationship between schooling, inequalities and legitimation (Laval et al. 2011).

While official texts mention a mere effort to 'follow-up' and 'inform' students in the development of their professional projects, the real ambition is beyond doubt to reduce the failure rate (at school and university) which is increasingly seen as the direct consequence of poor guidance. In other words, when it comes to guidance, 'informing' must actually be understood as a taking into account of reality, that is, of the chances of success. The teachers' mission then is not so much to indicate or point out the existence of various possible degree courses nor the existence of professional careers enabled by possession of such or such a degree. Instead the teacher's focus should be on the need to make their pupils lucid, realistic and rational in relation to the situation with which they are presented by contemporary labour markets. In Bourdieu's words (1970), the pupils must subjectively interiorize their objective chances of success. To achieve a future that can be deemed successful, they must apply to specific degree courses in accordance with the current statistics of the real situations. This presupposes the teachers' taking on the 'cooling out function' about which Clark, adapting Goffman, was talking in 1960: in contexts of mass higher education, teachers must act on their pupils' representations and expectations so as to make them 'realistic' (Clark 1960).

---

[24] 'Each bac-holder must have the opportunity to have access to higher-education and, at the same time, their chances of success and of obtaining a diploma must be maximized' (ibid.: 12).

These processes can also be digitalized, with new products that are advertised as being helpful for choices of courses and applications. *Inspire-orientation.org*, a website recently launched on the market, has been officially approved by the Ministry of National Education. With a few questions on the type of *baccalauréat* (S, L, ES or professional and technical), about the overall profile of a school's results, the student's academic and non-academic interests and so on, the website claims that it can propose the types of degree courses or programme best adapted to the 'pupil's profile': 'With Inspire, [the founder] wants to offer all high-school pupils, whatever their background, all the keys to map out their higher-education. He believes in the true power of algorithms to offer the best advice and guidance to high-school pupils.'[25] The official purpose is to 'be able to broaden the scope of possibilities for high-school pupils'. But beyond this prospect – at first glance quite laudable – what is now of fundamental interest is how the algorithms used by this platform actually work. Besides weighting the pupils' grades/results with the national ranking of their *lycée*, 'the algorithm checks the coherence between the internet users' replies to the website questions and the national statistics about the students' profile and results in each degree course or programme'.[26] In other words, guidance is in fact reduced to a mere checking process that makes sure that applications are in accordance with the sociological reality and the academic results already observed in higher education. The future students' chances of success on such or such a degree courses or programme are assessed on the basis of the profile of the students who are already studying in these courses or programmes.

Parents are also formally enrolled in the tasks of guidance. Several plans designed to 'inform' families at the end of secondary school have already been tested and assessed in terms of their effects on the types of applications the families subsequently made. The plan was primarily based on two meetings between the heads of the secondary schools and parents of pupils with difficulties. This quite simple and inexpensive initiative is 'enough to slightly improve the families' ability to anticipate and to broaden the range of courses considered possible', in order to reduce the number of school dropouts and, meanwhile, to make the pupils' application more realistic, in accordance with the reality of the pupil's level and of the socio-economic context. Such a process of 'adjustment of anticipations

---

[25] https://www.inspire-orientation.org/qui-sommes-nous
[26] 'Un algorithme pour trouver son orientation', *Le Monde*, 13 March 2018.

and aspirations' may also even claim to fight against tendencies towards school dropout' (Goux, Gurgand and Maurin 2014).[27]

In these new situations, a sociology of 'educational aspirations' is starting to take shape in France. It points out the new importance given to the issue of guidance and it also reveals new tendencies in the organization and practices of certain schools. For instance, Sophie Orange points out that out of a group of 900 students studying in BTS (a two-year vocational training certificate starting after the *bac*) between 2008 and 2011, 53 per cent, when they started, had planned to pursue their studies at the end of their two-year degree (and it was the sole ambition of 40 per cent of them). Two years later, only 28 per cent had actually done this. For Orange, this is a sign that there must have been an underlying action, an effect of the educational institution on the students' representation of their own future, on their expectations (Orange 2013). In this insight, she took the measure of an emerging educational reality. Educational aspiration is becoming increasingly calculable. Reduced to its most classic mathematical form, it becomes an expectation, a reasonable aspiration weighted by the probabilities of success. And it is on this expectation that all the actors of education (pupils, teachers and parents) base their aspiration, ambition and, especially, their calculations.

Conclusion: A conservative revolution

The policy of Emmanuel Macron and Jean-Michel Blanquer is grounded on an undeniably coherent theory. But this strong political ambition is based on the belief that pedagogical methods, augmented by efficient digital environments, may be strong enough to annihilate social determinisms. This is an unlikely scenario. Indeed the current policy seems to confirm an opposite tendency, towards determinism: all national and international assessments keep revealing the undisputable existence of social determinisms – in France more than anywhere else, but in France like everywhere else. Policy is not so much aiming to change this situation, as to reshape the pathways along which it operates. The fact that universities can now select students on the basis of their grades and take into account the 'level' – that is, the 'rank' – of the high school they come from draws a more immediate and more open correspondence than in the past

---

[27] 'Two years after this simple and inexpensive initiative, the dropout rate which used to reach 20% in the test group, fell to 15%', Goux, Gurgand and Maurin 2014: 4.

between the ranking of institutions in higher education and the ranking of high schools. This threatens to freeze the current hierarchies in higher education and to reinforce, at an even earlier stage, the logics of social reproduction. In that sense, the 'revolution' that was announced may well turn out to be a conservative revolution, which may give way to still further disillusionment.

References

Aghion, P. and Cohen, E. (2004) *Éducation et Croissance*, Paris: La documentation française.

Albouy, V. and Tavan, C. (2007) Accès à l'enseignement supérieur en France, *Economie et Statistiques*, no. 410.

Albouy, V. and Vanecq, T. (2003) Les Inégalités sociales d'accès aux grandes écoles, *Economie et Statistique*, no. 361: 27–52.

Blanquer, J.-M. (2014) *L'école de la vie*, Paris: Odile Jacob.

Blanquer, J.-M. (2017) 'Préface' à *L'Etat de l'école 2017*, Paris: Ministère de l'Education Nationale, Novembre 2017.

Bourdieu, P. (1970) *La reproduction*, Paris: Minuit.

Bourdieu, P. (2002) The forms of capital, in J. Richardson (ed.), *Handbook of Theory and Research for the Sociology of Education*, 241–58, Westport, CT: Greenwood.

Bourdieu, P. (2012) *Sur l'Etat*, Paris: Raisons d'agir/ Seuil.

Brodaty, T. (2010) Les effets de pairs dans l'éducation: une revue de littérature, *Revue d'économie politique*, 120 (5): 739–57.

Chapoulie, J.-M. (2017) Schooling in France: From organizational to informal inequality, *Annals of the American Academy of Political and Social Science*, 673 (1): 235–50.

Clark, B. R. (1960) The cooling out function, *The American Journal of Sociology*, 65 (6): 569–76.

CNESCO, Conseil National de l'Evaluation du Système Scolaire (2018) *Ecrire et rédiger: Enjeux et état des lieux acquis des élèves et évolution de l'enseignement*, Paris, March.

Costa-Kostritsky, V. (2018) May '18, *London Review of Books*, Blog, 23 May. https://www.lrb.co.uk/blog/2018/05/23/valeria-costa-kostritsky/may-18/

Duru-Bellat, M. (2006) *L'inflation scolaire*, Paris: Seuil.

European Union (2010) Strategic framework – Education & Training 2020. http://ec.europa.eu/education/policy/strategic-framework_en

Felouzis, G., (2014) *Les inégalités scolaires*, Collection 'Que sais-je?', Paris: PUF.

Felouzis, G., Fouquet-Chauprade, B., Charmillot, S. and Imperiale-Arefaïne, L. (2016) *Comment l'école amplifie les inégalités sociales et migratoires?* CNESCO, Paris: mars.

Felouzis, G., Liot, F. and Perroton, J. (2005) *L'apartheid scolaire*, Paris: Seuil.

Filatre, D. (2017) *Réformer le premier cycle de l'enseignement supérieur et améliorer la réussite des étudiants*, Rapport général de la Consultation sur la réforme du premier cycle de l'enseignement supérieur, 19 October 2017.

Gary-Bobo, R. (2006) Education, efficacité économique et justice sociale: une approche rawlsienne, *Revue d'Economie Politique*, Paris: Dalloz, no. 116: 2.

Gary-Bobo, R. (2017) *Performance sociale, financement et réformes de l'enseignement supérieur*, Paris: Presses de la Fondation nationale des sciences politiques.

Goblot, E. (2010) *La barrière et le niveau. Etude sociologique sur la bourgeoisie française moderne* [The Barrier and the Level. A sociological study of the modern French Bourgeoisie], Paris: Alcan (3rd ed. Paris: Presses Universitaires de France, 1925).

Goux, D., Gurgand, M. and Maurin, E. (2014) *Implication des parents et prévention du décrochage scolaire, Rapport final d'évaluation*, Ecole d'Economie de Paris, Fonds d'expérimentation pour la jeunesse, Ministère de la ville, de la jeunesse et des sports, June 2014.

HCÉRES (2018) *Rapport sur la position scientifique de la France dans le monde, 2000-2015*, Paris: HCÉRES.

Kramarz, F. and Tibi, P. (2016) *Plus de marché pour plus d'Etat!*, Paris: Eyrolles.

Laval, C. and Dardot, P. (2017) *The New Way of the World. On Neoliberal Society*, New York: Verso.

Laval, C., Vergne, F., Clément, P. and Dreux, G. (2011) *La nouvelle école capitaliste*, Paris: La Découverte.

Lehoux, E. (2018) *Payer pour réussir*, Paris: Syllepse.

Le Point (2018) Le chômage est remonté début 2018, 23 May. https://www.lepoint.fr/economie/le-chomage-est-remonte-debut-2018--23-05-2018-2220807_28.php

Lisbon European Council (2000) Presidency conclusion. Available at: http://www.europarl.europa.eu/summits/lis1_en.htm#a

Macron, E. (2017) *Revolution*, London: Scribe.

Mathiot, P. (2018) *Baccalauréat 2021*, Rapport remis à Jean-Michel Blanquer, Ministre de l'éducation nationale, 24 January 2018.

Mons, N. (2013) Évaluation standardisée des élèves et inégalités scolaires d'origine sociale : discours théoriques et réalité empirique, in C. Maroy (ed.), *L'école à l'épreuve de la performance: les politiques de régulation par les résultats*, 33–50, Louvain: De Boeck Supérieure.

OCDE (2015) *Note par pays Programme International pour le Suivi des Acquis des Elèves (PISA) Résultats de PISA 2015*, France.

Orange, S. (2013) *L'autre enseignement supérieur. Les BTS et la gestion des aspirations scolaires*, Paris: PUF.

Piketty, T. (2001) *Les hauts revenus en France au XXe siècle*, Paris: Grasset.

Piketty, T. (2013) *Le capital au XXIe siècle*, Paris: Seuil.

Soulé, V. (2013) Ecole: Hollande impose les patrons sur le programme. *Libération*, 1 May. Available at: https://www.liberation.fr/societe/2013/05/01/ecole-hollande-impose-les-patrons-au-programme_900301

Stangler, C. (2018) Signs of a French Spring, *Jacobin,* 4 March. https://www.jacobinmag. com/2018/04/france-student-worker-strikes-macron

Stromboni, C. (2017) Les 60% d'échec à la fac masquent une réalité plus complexe, *Le Monde*, 30 August.

Tanguy, L. (2016) *Enseigner l'esprit d'entreprise à l'école. Le tournant politique des années 1980-2000 en France*, Paris: La Dispute.

Terrail, J.-P. (2016) *Pour une école de l'exigence intellectuelle*, Paris: La Dispute.

Vacchino, O. (ed.) (2013) *Vers l'e-gouvernance Pour une nouvelle administration numérique*, Paris: CNDP.

5

Global Ideas and Their National Embeddedness: The Case of Swedish Education Policy

Nafsika Alexiadou and Linda Rönnberg

Sweden has been a social democracy with a strong emphasis on constructing education for equality and for prioritizing the social and citizenship functions of schooling. This was the product of a welfare regime that followed active redistributive politics in welfare and education in the period between 1930 and the mid-1970s, further underpinned by a generous and universal welfare state. But this began changing with the economic recession of the subsequent period that, in education policy, was accompanied by the rolling back of state expenditure and functions. Extensive decentralization reforms, the introduction of new public management techniques for the regulation of the competing public and private schools and the introduction of a publicly subsidized private system of education resulted in one of the most marketized and privatized schooling systems in Europe (Blomqvist 2004). Over the last fifteen years, the private school market has become increasingly strong, especially in the upper-secondary levels, and is dominated by 'edu-business', large groups of companies that offer schooling in a 'chain' model. At the same time Sweden retains the 'school for all' ideal, at least at the level of rhetoric, as an underlying feature of national education identity whereby all children have the same opportunity to achieve. This continues to be an important dimension to the policy narrative of education reforms, despite increasing evidence that socio-economic and ethnicity dimensions have a growing impact on children's education performance (OECD 2015; Grönqvist and Niknami 2017).

In terms of welfare politics in general, the famous so-called Swedish welfare model has increasingly been called into question. Sweden was not affected as much as other European countries by the financial crisis of the late 2000s.

Lessons from the financial crisis in the early 1990s led to reforms of policy instruments and governing, and have been put forward as reasons for the comparatively moderate impact on the Swedish financial situation in the late 2000s (cf. SCB 2009). Even if not explicitly connected to austerity measures in this later period, the Swedish redistributive model of providing comprehensive public welfare has been seriously challenged, and even argued to be 'nothing more than a comfortable set of references ... that more describes a longing for the past than it does of contemporary Swedish politics' (Miles 2011: 267). Within this context, national education policy and its connections to international ideas and practices have been shaped in particular directions, reflecting both domestic redefinitions of the welfare state and a national approach to wider international developments.

In this chapter we discuss Swedish education policies as particular national configurations of global and European trends, by focusing on the remaking of social democratic education purposes and ways of organizing education, and in the national response to questions of integration and inclusion. We draw on a similar position as Lundahl (2005), Wahlström (2016) and Waldow (2009) who highlight the influence of unacknowledged international policy borrowing of ideas in Swedish education policy-making. These refer both to the spread of discourses around the benefits of decentralization and marketization and of the wider reform agendas as these emanate from OECD and the European Union (Waldow 2009). Our analysis is presented in three parts.

First, we discuss the evolution of education policy in Sweden over three time periods, and its selective adaptation and adjustment to discourses of neoliberalism. In this part we describe the transformations of the welfare state and the ways in which national-local-institutional relations have changed, with a mix of state and non-state actors involved in the delivery of schooling. We also explore the parallel developments of systematic privatization of schools on the one hand and their coexistence with the older and still present discourses of equality for all on the other.

We then move to discuss two aspects of policy that show the complex relations between contexts, actors and institutions involved in these changes: drawing on two different research studies, we (a) present and analyse the fairly new phenomenon of Swedish school chains that provide schooling internationally, and in doing so illustrate the international spread of privatized school models, and the global dissemination of ideas around the role of schooling as a commodity; and (b) discuss the policies and unintended consequences that emerge from the Swedish response to the European Union call for the production of a National Strategy for Roma Integration. We frame this part with a brief summary of the relations of Sweden to the European Union, highlighting the sometimes ambiguous tensions between a pro-EU stance and a coexisting narrative of national independence and autonomy.

Taken together, these case examples point to features of national discourses of equality against the reality of school privatization and decentralization, and the definitions of equality policies that have not been universally accepted in how they address, for instance, questions of minority representation in the official narratives. Our analysis draws from research that conceptualizes the shifts in education policy processes as framed by neoliberal ideologies that have a global reach. We also connect to debates around the embeddedness of such travelling ideas in national and local settings, as well as the consequences of this localization for schooling outcomes, and the often unintended transformation of policy agendas from their original intention (Jones et al. 2008; Sundberg and Wahlström 2012). We take up the call that we need to explore the ways in which the global flows of education ideas, purposes and governance mechanisms become embedded in national contexts in very different ways, and reflect varying national and local histories and tensions around education policy, economic imperatives, and myths of integration and national identity.

The state and education policy: Transformations and developments

Early changes to the Swedish welfare model

In the period 1945–70, Sweden constructed universal welfare policies that combined social insurance and high levels of economic transfers between groups in the population, hence its classification as a social democratic welfare regime. A system of 'well-functioning negotiated corporatism' brought economic/corporate, trades union and political actors together over extensive modernization projects, such as the further development of the comprehensive school – already in place since the nineteenth century (Sejersted 2011: 225). In the early years of the post-war period, education was seen as a core dimension of social and economic progress, a view similarly held in other parts of Europe. But, in Sweden, in contrast to liberal or conservative European welfare states, this view of progress gave education an active role in equalizing opportunities and life experiences and balancing social differences. Non-selective and non-differentiated nine-year comprehensive schooling was introduced in 1962 and 'good elementary education and equal access to secondary and higher education were regarded both as a matter of social justice, and as an important precondition for economic growth and prosperity' (Lundahl 2005: 149).

This policy approach to education, combined with a high proportion of GDP investment, meant that in the early 1970s Sweden enjoyed a very high participation of young people in the upper-secondary school (post-compulsory, students aged sixteen to nineteen) that hosted both academic and vocational courses. The regulation of teaching and schools was performed through a national curriculum, and the central state had control over resources, organization, employment issues and the daily work of schools. 'Equivalence' was a very central value of the education system, denoting an emphasis on equality and equal standards of schooling for all children regardless of geography or socio-economic status (Telhaug et al. 2004).

This settlement began to change with the economic crisis of the early 1970s, when Swedish industries were severely hit and the country faced a major recession. Politically, the Social Democrats were under attack, both from the left and the right.[1] The left argued that the promise of equality and reduction of social injustice did not materialize and blamed the stifling top-down central state policies, while the right criticized the inefficiencies of a cumbersome, costly and bureaucratic welfare state (Blomqvist 2004). The political right employed these discourses effectively and together with industry managed to set the policy agenda and reinstall faith in private enterprise and the market (Lundahl 2002). The concepts of individual responsibility, choice, competition and entrepreneurship became increasingly visible in the 1980s, although they gained policy momentum later. Interestingly, it was the Social Democrats who throughout the 1980s advocated decentralization, an opening to private schools that encouraged pedagogic innovations, the introduction of NPM and alternative financing and management of the public sector as ways to modernize public services (Alexiadou and Lundahl 2016). As Wiborg (2013: 4213) argued, the

---

[1] The Social Democrats held office for large parts of the twentieth century and the early 2000s: the years 1932–76, 1982–91, 1994–2006 and 2014–still. From the 1980s onwards, the Social Democrats have formed minority governments, except for the most recent period when the Social Democrats and the Green Party have formed a minority coalition (Jarl and Rönnberg 2015).

Social Democrats 'were put in a situation that made it difficult for them to reject neo-liberal policies as a way of giving citizens more choice'. Education became one of the main policy spheres where these new ideas were tried. This context prepared the way and framed the far-reaching reforms of the next decade which changed fundamentally the role of the state in how education services were provided, funded and regulated.

The rise of the local state and the reforms of the 1990s

From an international perspective, the Swedish reforms of the 1990s are interesting not only in terms of the internal national conversations about the size and function of the welfare state but also because of the similarities of the debates to those held in other countries. Thus, (i) marketization of public services was discussed as an efficient and effective way for the allocation of public resources that, combined with decentralization, would lead to democratic renewal; (ii) parents and children would have increased voice over their schooling and more choice of schools by allowing the private sector to enter public education; and (iii) schools would increase the quality of education they offer, they would be more publicly accountable and responsive to their clientele, and more efficient since they would compete for resources.

These political rationales framed the introduction of radical decentralization reforms in the education sector, whereby some of the functions performed earlier by the central state were now delegated to the local level, that is, to municipalities and schools. Municipalities became responsible for the employment of all teacher categories and head teachers, a new funding system was introduced, and schools were given considerable autonomy to decide on instruction content and methods, teaching hours and class sizes. At the same time, NPM inspired reforms were also introduced, with objectives-driven governance structures whereby school quality and performance were to be made publicly visible and used to hold schools and municipalities to account. School heads had considerable scope for enacting the national curriculum framework within the economic parameters given to them by municipalities (Hanberger et al. 2016).

During a right-wing coalition government in 1991–4, these reforms were accompanied by legislation that allowed private actors to establish private, independent schools (so-called free schools), as well as the introduction of vouchers that enabled parents and children to choose between education providers and so transfer resources through school choice. This early school market applied to both public and private compulsory and upper-secondary schools (Lundahl 2002). Initially, private schools received 85 per cent of the average pupil cost in state schools, which for a short period allowed private schools to introduce low-level user fees. Arguing on social justice grounds, the Social Democratic Party abolished this possibility when back in power in 1994, and instead decided that private schools should be fully tax-funded on an equal basis to public ones. Taken together, several political decisions such as (a) allowing parents to choose any school they wished for their child, public or private, free of charge, (b) introducing a national voucher system, (c) instigating liberal regulations about who could operate a free school and (d) operating generous regulations for issuing licences for free schools, all came together in forming the particularities of the Swedish free school model (Jarl and Rönnberg 2015).

The state monopoly of schooling was thereby broken (Lundahl 2002) and the Social Democrats, who earlier had opposed public funding of private schools, were by the late 1990s, fully endorsing the principle of parental choice between publicly funded private and public schools (Wiborg 2013). There is no straightforward answer as to why the Social Democratic Party revised their agenda. The importance of particular actors pushing for reform, such as Göran Persson when appointed as Minister of Education, along with more structural transformations, such as the increasing importance of the middle class as electoral basis for the party, has been proposed as parts of possible explanations (Jarl and Rönnberg 2015; Lidström 1999).

After these reforms, schools were responsible for devising their work plans, and teachers had to design individual plans for students, with the evaluation of quality delegated to the level of the municipality. Still, the central state retained the broader responsibility of controlling the national tests, conducting national evaluations, enforcing the law, granting permissions to operate free schools, the national curriculum and assessment, as well as to set the aims and goals of education in the Education Act (Rönnberg 2012). The initially weak control of the quality of education was the responsibility of the Swedish National Agency for Education (SNAE, Skolverket), that was later reinforced by the establishment of the Swedish Schools Inspectorate (Skolinspektionen).

Accelerating privatization: 2000–today

Educational privatization policies have put significant marks on Swedish education and contributed to a fundamental transformation of the Swedish education system (Lundahl 2016). Initially the expansion of free schools was rather slow, but the last fifteen years have shown two trends. First, there has been a dramatic growth of registration in privately operated schools. In 2015–16, about 15 per cent of all compulsory school pupils and 25 per cent of pupils at upper-secondary level attended free schools (SNAE 2017). The proportion of pupils attending these schools varies across the country, and the largest shares are found in the three largest cities, that is, Stockholm, Gothenburg and Malmö. In these urban areas, free schools are attended by about one-fourth of the students at compulsory level, and every second student (50 per cent) at upper-secondary level (SNAE 2017). These figures indicate that free schools are far from marginal traits in the Swedish school system but rather an integrated, and in some urban areas even dominating, part of it.

Second, the nature of the private school providers has changed. A distinctiveness of the Swedish free schools is that they can be run as limited liability companies, they are allowed to distribute surplus to their owners and shareholders and they are not legally obliged to reinvest any profits in the school (Erixon Arreman and Holm 2011). As a result, for-profit education companies are now dominating the private school market. At the outset, this was not the case and in the 1990s, foundations, cooperatives and other non-profit organizations were the most common free school owners. The share of students attending free schools run by for-profit corporations has now spiked to about two-thirds of all free school students at the compulsory level and 85 per cent at the upper-secondary level (SNAE 2014). In addition, we observe a concentration of ownership, with the eight largest school companies now educating 40 per cent of all free school students (SNAE 2014). The school market and its actors are rapidly changing through acquisitions, buyouts and even bankruptcies (Holm 2017).

These privatization reforms were accompanied by a tighter set of regulations promoted by the SNAE and by an intensified school inspection scheme, performed by the Schools Inspectorate (SI), which has extensive policy powers and possibilities for imposing sanctions (Carlbaum 2016). Testing of student performance has also been intensified and subjected to stricter central control. Now, national testing is more widely used and introduced in earlier stages of compulsory school and cover a range of school subjects. Grading, and at what age it should be introduced, have been long-standing issues of political debate. Today, formal grading begins when pupils are in grade 6 (age twelve), but written assessments are issued from the first grade in all subjects, even if not in the form of grades (Jarl and Rönnberg 2015). A heated issue concerns how a statistically observed difference between national test results and grades should be interpreted. This has spurred a debate on so-called grade inflation and joy grades (Novak and Carlbaum 2017), implying that teachers give their students a higher grade than reflected in their performances on national tests. It should be added though that grading is not supposed to be exclusively based on national test results. Still, given the far-reaching competition between schools to attract students, in the wake of the privatization school choice reforms, doubts have been raised over the perceived 'fairness' in these test and grading systems. As a result, the National SI has been assigned to reassesses teacher's grading on national tests. Novak and Carlbaum (2017: 685) argue that this has affected teachers and the public perception of teachers, by adding to national 'mistrust in the teaching profession' by facilitating 'a game of naming and shaming'. The Inspectorate and the SNAE are also responsible for administering easily accessible information systems on school test results and grading. School reports from the Inspectorate are also publicly available. These are just a few examples of current efforts to provide accessible quantitative and qualitative information to parents and students – and to the wider public. Research has found that the use of data and indicators that are promoted through such information, transparency and accountability systems tend to steer the focus of both school management, teachers and students, running the risk that the broader goals of schooling, such as citizenship, social inclusion and justice, can be devalued in practice (Hanberger et al. 2016).

The justifications for the privatization reforms at the time of their introduction concerned the anticipation of positive outcomes for the consumers of education, arguing for more choice for all students and parents, and not only for the selected few or the elite; better academic performance, and, a more responsive, accountable and efficient education system. Introducing and facilitating competition between education providers assumed higher efficiency in school governance, and an improved and more professional teaching and managerial education cadre. Now, twenty-five years since the early privatization reforms, it is certainly the case that parents and students have more school choice available, and more information is produced in order to compare the performance of different municipal and private schools (Lundström and Rönnberg 2015).

But the ambition to raise academic standards has not been realized, and there is a rapid increase in the performance differences *between* schools as well as a higher homogenization of school populations (Gustafsson et al. 2016; Grönqvist and Niknami 2017). Several studies have identified segregation trends in Swedish schools, whereby school composition seems to reflect a degree of white flight but also self-selection as a result of school choice, and where both socio-economic background and ethnicity become important (Bunar and Ambrose 2016; Östh et al. 2013; cf. OECD 2015). These patterns are accentuated at the upper-secondary school level where the 'school for all' is differentiated into academic and vocational tracks, and where social and institutional identities of students contribute to further selective and segregating outcomes with particularly negative consequences for the more socially disadvantaged students (Erixon Arreman 2014). These issues are turned into contemporary education policy priorities, and framed as a need to reinforce the overall education policy ambition of retaining and reconciling equality and 'a school for all' in a situation of far-reaching educational marketization.

Current policy debates: Bringing discourses of equality (even more) back in?

In the 2010s, concerns had grown about the drawbacks following in the wake of these reforms and several government commissions have been instigated to propose reforms and revised legislation in this area. Partial restorations, such as a stricter licensing and inspection system, have been implemented, but, as it was stated in a parliamentary commission report from 2013, 'Free schools are here to stay' (SOU 2013: 56). Even so, privatization remains the core of recent policy debates. After a steep decline in performance in PISA 2012, Sweden commissioned a report to the OECD to 'diagnose' and suggest 'treatments' for the Swedish school system. The resulting report ended up criticizing the Swedish school choice system on grounds of equity and for lacking adequate accountability systems (OECD 2015). These issues were then taken up by a national commission which ended up proposing 'active school choice' (SOU 2017: 35) as a possible solution to some of the identified weaknesses, for instance its segregating effects with implications for increased injustice. In parallel to these suggestions, restrictions on school owners extracting profits and stricter ownership regulations are also on the national political agenda. A commission advised the government to impose 'profit restrictions' (SOU 2016: 78), that is, not to abolish profit-making in the free school sector. This was however met by intense lobbyism and campaigning from free school owners, their organizations and the political centre-right (Lundahl and Rönnberg 2016). There is no political majority to support such profit restrictions and the proposal was turned down by the Parliament in June 2018 (Riksdag minutes 2017/18: 127). At the moment, only the Left Party has an explicit agenda to completely abolish profit-making in education.

At the same time, there are continuing and intensified political pressures for ensuring educational equivalence and equity. For instance, 'an equal school' is outlined as one out of three main priority areas under the current government, addressing issues such as segregation, increasing divides between groups of pupils and between schools as well as education of newly arrived immigrants and refugee pupils (Government 2017). In fact, the school choice and privatization reforms would probably not have been possible, had they not been linked to the right for *all* parents, and not just the privileged, to choose the school they preferred. However, as it started to become evident that the Swedish free school model had failed to realize all the high expectations and hopes, pressures for 'equality' measures are gaining prominence (Gustafsson et al. 2016). In this context however, where there is no discussion of an overhaul of privatization or marketization reforms, even though *equality in education* is prominent in legislation, it becomes closer to the notion of *equal access to choice of education*. Importantly enough, these developments are embedded in a system that (still) displays strong equality features, such as avoiding streaming and tracking, nurturing democratic teacher-student relationships, differing specialization to later stages of education and offering second chances for transitions within schooling and for accessing university, free of charge. Older but still-cherished ideas of a 'school for all' are combined with 'privatization the Swedish way' (Lundahl et al. 2013), resulting in a policy amalgamation with tensions that are hoped to be merged to coexist. Judging from recent proposals put forward on active school choice (SOU 2017: 35), the problems of segregation and declining student performance are to be addressed through targeted measures, but the fundamental principles of school choice, competition and privatization are not seriously challenged politically.

In the next parts, we look at two aspects of education policy, selectively drawing on our empirical research, in order to illustrate various features of the relationships between state and non-state actors, their manifestations on issues of the mobility and national embeddedness of policy ideas and their intersection with issues of inclusion and equality.

Education as a Swedish export and trade

The extent and scope by which some of the Swedish for-profit education companies have expanded have led to quite a new situation in Sweden. These companies have been perceived as attractive investment opportunities, displaying more promising profit margins (from a tax-funded voucher) compared to more established parts on the economy (cf. SOU 2016: 78). This has aroused financial interest in free school companies, and many of them are now public limited liability companies registered on the Swedish stock market exchange. During the last decade, these Swedish for-profit free school companies have also moved abroad to search and explore new 'markets' to sell their services. Next, we introduce some of the actors that are moving Swedish education as policy export from the national to the international domain. We focus on Sweden's three largest school companies and how the cultural constructions of the national narratives of for instance 'equality' are (re)framed as education is moved across national and cultural borders by these businesses.

Three Swedish school companies going global

Kunskapsskolan, the third-largest free school operator in Sweden at the compulsory level, was the first Swedish free school company to move abroad. Kunskapsskolan entered the English market in 2008, initially as a sponsor of two Academy schools, in order to 'boost its chances of expanding into other countries' (TES 2008). A rapid international expansion then followed, and the company now operates in Sweden, the UK, the Netherlands, India, the United States and the Middle East. Today more than 80 schools are operated by Kunskapsskolan or using their KED-programme, attended by 20,000 students and employing 2,000 teachers (Kunskapsskolan Education 2017).

Kunskapsskolan's expansion to England was headed by one of the main Swedish edu-preneurs, Anders Hultin. Hultin worked at the Ministry of Education 1991–4 as adviser for the Moderate Party and helped design the free school system (Svensson 2014). Hultin was part of the team that founded Kunskapsskolan in 1999, and in 2007 he moved to England. He marketed the Swedish model of free schools, which was put forward as a model for reform by the Conservatives in the 2010 election campaign. He then went on to work for GEMS Education and Pearson before returning to Sweden as CEO of the John Bauer school chain (JB) during its bankruptcy. Hultin now owns his own school chain and recent endeavours include the 'Nordic international school' based in Sweden but connected to an international network of schools, and the company NordicEd, specializing to provide consultancy and operate schools in emerging economies (Rönnberg 2017).

Kunskapsskolan's KED-programme forms the basis of the business model. This programme is signified by personalized learning and the student is mentored and aided by teachers and supported by resources such as a particular IT-portal, premises, time and learning materials. The conception of individualized learning has strong support and history in Sweden, framed by efforts of previously described policy narratives of equivalence and equality; to enable every child to reach her/his full potential, regardless of background and geographical origin. In Kunskapsskolan's Indian schools, this is framed as 'all people are different – they learn in different ways and at different rates. It is our task to meet this challenge. Regardless of his or her ability, each student has the right to a personal challenge every day' (Kunskapsskolan India 2018). Another characteristic promoted to the Indian market is the idea of the teacher as 'a partner and coach committed to ensuring student success' (Kunskapsskolan India 2017), which echoes another feature often associated with the Swedish education system; its comparably egalitarian and democratic orientation and relationships between teachers and students (cf. OECD 2015). Kunskapsskolan's Indian schools, despite charging fees, are framed as intended to be schools for the masses and not exclusively for the elite. In this way, the company connects to and tries to amplify the 'social democratic' ethos associated with the Swedish stereotypical international image.

But there is a clear intention of amalgamation with the local contexts in which they operate. Kunskapsskolan has employed curriculum writers working to adapt the KED-programme to suit quite different 'markets' and localities, in Europe and beyond. Schools, the company states, 'follow the relevant curriculum in each location, as well as the national, state and other local standards in each market' (Kunskapsskolan Education 2017). Thus, we see how Kunskapsskolan seeks to combine its educational philosophy, as manifested in the KED-approach, with the particularities in different local settings, geographies and different cultural histories. The CEO of Kedtech, a joint venture between Saab and Kunskapsskolan Education, expresses their intentions and rationale in the following way:

> You cannot run a school in India in the same way you run a school in Sweden, or the UK, or the USA. ... Our conclusion is to make 'glocal' schools. International in the sense they are connected in a network ... but extremely local in their content

and adaptation to local cultures and habits. … Kedtech's Arab International Learning Portal [is] currently being developed by teams in Jeddah, Dubai, Delhi, the UK and Sweden … the portal will fuse the CIE curriculum with Islamic studies, Arabic language, history, culture, and other social sciences to provide … a 'glocal' educational programme. (*Education Journal Middle East* 2015)

The next chain, Internationella Engelska Skolan (IES) was an early actor in the Swedish school market, founded in the early 1990s by a former science teacher from the United States. Today IES operates more than twenty compulsory schools in Sweden, hosts more than 15,000 pupils and claims long waiting lists for entry to their schools. Swedish free schools have to be open for all and cannot be selective, but the time in waiting list is a valid admission criteria. IES also has a clear intention of 'blending' and aims to provide a 'mix of the best of Sweden and the English-speaking world' and 'an inclusive international English school environment for students of all backgrounds and origins' (IES 2017). IES also operates a school in England, and the founder of IES stated the ambition in England was 'to show the children that they did not have to follow in their parent's footsteps, and that they could become and achieve whatever they want in life' (CEO, quoted in *Veckans Affärer* 2017). In other words, ideas of equality and education as a means of promoting social mobility traditionally anchored in the Swedish education policy setting are used as a way of arguing for, and legitimizing international operations, in this case from Sweden to England. In 2016, IES also entered the Spanish market, by purchasing a family business operating private schools with education in English, with the intention of further expansion into Spain (IES 2018).

Finally, AcadeMedia, the largest Swedish free school chain, describes itself as the leading provider of independent education in northern Europe and as the second largest education provider in Sweden, as only the City of Stockholm is larger (AcadeMedia 2015). The company has 550 preschools and schools, 14,000 employees and almost 140,000 pre-school children and students across Sweden. Recently the company has embarked on an international expansion, initially by acquiring Norway's largest pre-school operator in 2014 and later by entering the pre-school market in Germany in 2016. AcadeMedia depicts this as an important market with future possibilities:

The market for independent for-profit providers is currently in its infancy and consists of several small providers. These players constitute attractive add-on acquisitions for AcadeMedia in its efforts to be a leading independent preschool provider in the market. (AcadeMedia 2018)

In the press releases following the take-over, AcadeMedia emphasized the Scandinavian pre-school model and how this acclaimed world leading approach is attracting international interest (AcadeMedia 2016). The German version of the press release talks about an award-winning Scandinavian pre-school approach, with its focus on nature, movement and democracy (Joki 2016).

Education companies and their transnational moves

Companies such as Kunskapsskolan, IES and AcadeMedia were made possible by national policies of educational privatization. As these businesses move from the national into the global arena, certain 'Swedish' features (and not others) become highlighted and advertised. These features are connected to certain perceptions of for instance equality, democracy and social mobility. But the perceived 'Swedishness' is also remoulded and re-embedded within the 'global' as the educational services are adapted and marketed to the foreign markets: images of the 'Swedish', 'Scandinavian' and 'Nordic' are translated and amalgamated in relation to the non-Swedish settings. In these processes, transcending national boundaries and cultures, we see how nationally embedded narratives of equality, individualization and social mobility are transformed and repackaged into 'saleable' products or arguments as they are moved and 'sold' to different national contexts.

Challenges and remouldings of national narratives of equality and the role of non-state actors in these processes are at focus also in relation to the Swedish approach to policy on Roma inclusion. Before looking at this case in more detail, the next section provides a brief orientation to the relationships between Sweden and the European Union more generally, as a way of framing the subsequent example of the Swedish national response to EU inclusion policies.

Sweden and the European Union

During the late 1980s there were intense arguments in Sweden with regard to its involvement in European integration. According to Johansson (2017: 3), these arguments related to sovereignty, autonomy, the welfare state and the social model, that 'remained obstacles to legitimizing membership'. The discourse that dominated the debate, leading to Sweden joining the European Union in 1995, was that many contemporary economic, environmental, political and social problems were no longer possible to address by individual nations in isolation. Still, Sweden was seen as a 'reluctant European' (Gstöhl 2002: ix) and opted for what researchers called the *calculus of sovereignty*: the voluntary loss of formal sovereignty through EU membership, promoted as an increase in real sovereignty through gains in efficiency of governance (Johansson 2017). This argument was particularly strong among the Social Democratic elites, drawing on the experience of the French economic crisis in the 1980s, and the Swedish one in the early 1990s (Johansson 2017).

A second point of public debate in the early 2000s was the issue of Sweden's possible participation in the euro. Following a national referendum advising against, subsequent Swedish governments have adopted a dual political approach of being out of the Eurozone, but very much participating in 'quiet networking' and the political processes in both the Commission and the Council, combined with a low degree of Europeanization of national politics (Lindahl and Naurin 2010; Miles 2011). During the last ten years, Sweden seems overall more comfortable with full membership of the European Union, but not with further integration especially in relation to the monetary union. In addition, selected issues such as the regulation of the labour market continue to be internally divisive for the Social Democrats (Miles 2011). Still, the official position of successive governments has been one of pro-EU politics, pursued in relatively low visibility and detaching EU issues from overt domestic politics (Jacobsson and Sundström 2016; Lindahl and Naurin 2005).

In the field of education, Sweden followed a similar political approach as its more general involvement in European integration, that is, active but quiet networking in the OMC education processes, what Nordin (2014: 153) called 'silent' Europeanization. It has been argued that EU recommendations have had an impact on national education policy. Successive governments used these as a legitimating argument for particular policies, making Sweden a 'policy borrower', and rarely questioning or challenging the entrepreneurial discourses used as arguments for education and higher education reform (Quintans 2015: 49). The more implicit and quiet approach towards the European Union in education and higher education began to change after about 2013, when Sweden seeks policy guidance from the European Union and the OECD on selected education policy areas, such as early school leaving (Nordin 2017).

In the following section, the national-European interactions in the form of setting up and implementing a national strategy on minority issues are discussed.

The National Strategy for Roma Inclusion and the myth of equality

In 2012, the Swedish government launched a National Strategy for Roma Inclusion 2012–32 (Government Communication 2012, henceforth 'the Strategy') within the context of the European Union request to member states to develop National Roma Integration Strategies around four areas of policy: education, employment, health and housing.[2]

The Roma Swedish minority[3] is small (estimated at about 50,000) but disadvantaged in all these four areas of public policy as well as discriminated in public life (Government White Book 2014). The process of producing a Strategy started back in 2006 (before the request by the European Commission) with the appointment of a Delegation for Roma Issues. The Delegation produced an overview and analysis on the situation of the minority (SOU 2010: 55, often referred to as Roma Rights Report), and identified an 'almost unbreakable pattern of social, economic and political exclusion and marginalization' (SOU 2010, 35). The Report drew attention to issues of Roma representation in Swedish politics, but also raised fundamental issues around economic injustice, cultural and identity politics. In that respect, it corresponds to the EU policies of inclusion that target economic development (through an emphasis on wider economic growth and individual employability), anti-discrimination measures, and also measures that aim at combatting educational segregation and the recognition of minority issues (European Commission 2016). The Report went through a consultation period and resulted in the government communication to the Swedish parliament: *A Coordinated Long-Term Strategy for Roma Inclusion 2012-2032* (Government Communication 2012). This is the document that Sweden submitted to the European Commission, as its National Roma Integration Strategy (NRIS).

For the purposes of this chapter we draw on a recent study that explored the evolution and rationale of the Strategy, an example of a policy initiative that emerged as a response to the EU inclusion policies (Alexiadou and Norberg

---

[2] 'A coordinated long-term strategy for Roma inclusion 2012–32' (Government Communication 2011/12:56); 'Roma Rights—A Strategy for Roma in Sweden' SOU 2010: 55; 'Education and Training 2020 National Report'.

[3] The discussion here only refers to the Roma Swedish citizens, the population that the Strategy applies to. Children of EU Roma migrants to Sweden are a different category and a very problematic case since Sweden applies a narrow (and weak) interpretation of international conventions in relation to entitlement to schooling for non-resident migrants, leaving Roma migrant children mostly without access to education, and in 'a legal laguna' (Harris et al. 2017: 253).

2017). There are two interesting dimensions around the Strategy in Sweden that we wish to highlight as relevant here: The first relates to the explicit targeting of the minority for social policy solutions, an approach that raises questions on the governance of equality policies but also the unintended consequences they produced. The second issue refers to the implementation of the strategy. Consistent with other decentralized policies, the government has put the onus of implementation on municipalities, something that has implications for the effectiveness of the policy.

The Strategy for Roma inclusion draws quite explicitly on a human rights framework, and raises issues of economic marginalization, and cultural recognition for the Roma as a distinct group. The achievement of inclusion and integration is to be pursued through closing the welfare gap between Roma and non-Roma, reversing the disempowerment of the Roma people, and restoring trust between the minority and majority population. But the issue of equality produced a number of strong responses when the Report opened up to consultation, both from Roma and non-Roma organizations. The specific targeting of the minority was seen as against Swedish law that applies a rights-based approach to all citizens equally, with no special dispensation for particular groups (Chancellor of Justice, in Alexiadou and Norberg 2017). When it comes to singling out a minority for special resources or treatment, this is seen as politically difficult as a municipality project officer suggests, '*It is very un-Swedish to design a Strategy based on an ethnic group … why should some people be entitled to special protection?*' But the strongest reaction against the targeting of the minority came from several of the Roma NGOs. They argued that the Roma Rights Report casts them as a disempowered 'object for change' and as powerless victims by a mainstream society that was unfairly portrayed as perpetrating racism. For these Roma NGOs the Report, despite its good intentions, was strengthening stereotypes and embedding further discriminatory assumptions about the Roma. Instead, the Roma organizations who responded to the Report endorsed the human rights discourse and departed from structural explanations for the poverty and marginalization of the majority of the Roma population. They articulated a position of agency and active citizenship that draws on fairly neoliberal assumptions underpinning educational success, and labour market participation: '*We do not understand all cases when a company or employer don't want to employ a Roma as ethnic discrimination, but rather due to lack of education*' (The Delegation and Forum with Roma and Sinti 2010, in Alexiadou and Norberg 2017). Such responses demonstrate the tensions between state policies that attempt to bring identity issues at the centre stage of policy-making, and the positions of minorities that perceive racial politicization of inclusion as producing *more* rather than *less* discrimination (Helakorpi et al. 2018; Marushiakova and Popov 2015). Still, the whole process since the mid-2000s has resulted in more dialogue and a clearly improved relationship between the Roma and the authorities (Harris et al. 2017).

The second dimension to this policy development that we wish to highlight concerns the relationships between transnational, national and local levels. The EU Framework for National Roma Integration Strategies up to 2020 has adopted the approach of *explicit* but *not exclusive* targeting of the Roma minority both in the way it distributes structural funds and in relation to the Member States reporting on progress. As with similar EU initiatives, it is up to member states to decide on resource allocation and specific policy to address integration. The Swedish report originally adopted an exclusive targeting of the Roma, but following the consultation process, the final Strategy included fewer targeted measures of tangible effect, albeit still exclusively focusing on the Roma minority. In the final Strategy the authorities are urged to mainstream the work around Roma inclusion into the routine workings of the administration. In relation to education, the Strategy aims to combine institutional inclusion of Roma pupils in the common school, with added elements of cultural and linguistic support for the maintenance of the Roma identity. These take the form of training around fifteen to twenty 'bridge builders' a year in education and other social services, and the raising of cultural awareness in the school system in general (where there is still a poor record in relation to the Roma). This mainstreaming of policy has the following consequences:

a. The integrated nature of the policy means that there are no specific education goals for Roma children, and there is a very small budget[4] for the implementation of the Strategy. As Erik Ullenhag, the minister responsible for integration (2010–14) argued, Sweden emphasized in its Strategy a 'sustainable' and 'mainstreamed inclusive policy', without the need for special funds (in Alexiadou and Norberg 2017).

b. Sweden adopted in its Strategy the Europe 2020 targets on education,[5] and argued that high quality general education applies on the same terms to

---

[4] Forty-six million SEK was allocated for the period 2012–15.
[5] By 2020, the share of early leavers from education and training should be less than 10 per cent; and, the share of 30- to 34-year-olds with tertiary educational attainment (4) should be at least 40 per cent (Council of the European Union, 2009). Council conclusions of 12 May 2009 on a strategic framework for European cooperation in education and training ('ET 2020'). *Official Journal of the European Union* (2009/C 119/02).

Roma and non-Roma students. In a rather ambivalent set of statements, however, the Strategy identifies the need for 'more systematic knowledge-gathering process ... to obtain a better picture of the situation and needs of Roma children in order to identify the measures that need to be taken' (Government Communication 2012: 28), something that proves to be very difficult in a country that does not register the population by ethnicity. As a result, the municipalities are made responsible for this knowledge-gathering, as well as for the implementation of the Strategy without additional budgets, nor the capacity to survey the extent of the problem by gathering statistical information.

So, by focusing primarily on cultural recognition issues but without the full involvement of Roma representatives in its formation, the Strategy alienated its intended Roma minority target who seem to have adopted a liberal approach of ethnic invisibility in their preferred politics of inclusion. And, without any serious economic support for educational, health, employment or social inclusion projects, the municipalities are left to implement a Strategy that relies on the positive long-term goal of 'equality for all' but with few further incentives to change the existing practices. When questions of ethnicity, identity and marginalization become entangled with education achievement (or underachievement) tensions are likely to emerge that the Strategy has not really prepared for. In this respect, it reflects the European Union approach to the governance of Roma inclusion. They both recognize the complexity of the problem and the intersectional nature of Roma student underachievement, but advocate fairly liberal approaches to their policy solutions (Alexiadou 2017; Brüggemann and D'Arcy 2017).

Conclusion

In this chapter, we sought to analyse and situate Swedish education policy and point to some of its current challenges and debates by initially looking at the historical division and reform of state-local responsibilities in education. We also provided two case illustrations pertaining to issues and dilemmas in policy-making and policy implementation in the light of challenging national/global/local relationships. Our exploration of Swedish education policy illustrate that policies and enactments, on the one hand, need to be seen and understood in close connection to global and international agendas, but that they, on the other hand, become situated in a quite particular social democratic historical setting. As an example, strivings for (certain perceptions of) equality coexists alongside aggressive privatization, and, as the case of the Swedish education company export illustrates, may even be used as a 'selling point' when moved from the national to the international domain. The Roma Integration Strategy example displays the recurrent interactions with and embeddedness of European initiatives in national policy contexts and highlights how these are formed and shaped by the particularities of the Swedish national setting, but also the crucial role played by different state and non-state actors in these policy processes. This exploration of the Swedish case can offer empirical input for further elaboration about issues relating to (i) the complexities of global/national/local relationships in education policy and practice, (ii) the (still) localized and situated character of education policy and (iii) how particular national circumstances, policy histories and narratives become decisive for the enactment of global and general policy ideas and reforms.

References

AcadeMedia (2015) Kvalitetsrapport 2015 [Quality report 2015]. Available online: https://utbildning.academedia.se/wp-content/uploads/2014/03/Kvalitetsrapport-2015.pdf, accessed 16 November 2017.

AcadeMedia (2016) Academedia etablerar sig i Tyskland [AcadeMedia establishes in Germany]. Available online: https://utbildning.academedia.se/2016/01/12/academedia-etablerar-sig-i-tyskland/, accessed 16 November 2017.

AcadeMedia (2018) Our market. Available online: https://corporate.academedia.se/en/about-academedia/our-market/, accessed 29 August 2018.

Alexiadou, N. (2017) Equality and education policy in the European Union: An example from the case of Roma, in S. Parker, K. N. Gulson and T. Gale (eds), *Policy and Inequality in Education*, 111–13, Singapore: Springer.

Alexiadou, N. and Lundahl, L. (2016) Reforming Swedish education by introduction of quasi-markets and competition, in H. Gunter, E. Grimaldi, D. Hall and R. Serpieri (eds), *New Public Management and the Reform of Education: European Lessons for Policy and Practice*, 66–80, London and New York: Routledge, Taylor & Francis.

Alexiadou, N. and Norberg, A. (2017) Sweden's double decade for Roma inclusion: An examination of education policy in context, *European Education*, 49 (1): 36–55.

Blomqvist, P. (2004) The choice revolution: Privatization of Swedish welfare services in the 1990s, *Social Policy and Administration*, 38 (2): 139–55.

Brüggemann, C. and D'Arcy, K. (2017) Contexts that discriminate: International perspectives on the education of Roma students, *Race Ethnicity and Education*, 20 (5): 575–8.

Bunar, N. and Ambrose, A. (2016) Schools, choice and reputation: Local school markets and the distribution of symbolic capital in segregated cities, *Research in Comparative and International Education*, 11 (1): 34–51.

Carlbaum, S. (2016) Equivalence and performance gaps in Swedish school inspection: Context and the politics of blame, *Discourse: Studies in the Cultural Politics of Education*, 37 (1): 133–48.

Education Journal Middle East (2015) Cover interview: A fine blend, 16 September. Available online: http://www.educationjournalme.com/features/cover-interview%3A-a-fine-blend_170, accessed 17 November 2017.

Erixon Arreman, I. (2014) Student perceptions of new differentiation policies in Swedish post-16 education, *European Educational Research Journal*, 13 (6): 616–39.

Erixon Arreman, I. and Holm, A.-S. (2011) Privatization of public education? The emergence of independent upper secondary schools in Sweden, *Journal of Education Policy*, 26 (2): 225–43.

European Commission (2016) *Assessing the Implementation of the EU Framework for National Roma Integration Strategies and the Council Recommendation on Effective Roma Integration Measures in the Member States — 2016.* COM (2016), 424.

Government (2017) *Mer kunskap och jämlikhet i skolan* [More knowledge and equality in education]. Available online: http://www.regeringen.se/regeringens-politik/regeringens-prioriteringar/mer-kunskap-och-okad-jamlikhet-i-skolan/, accessed 16 November 2017.

Government Communication (2012) *En samordnad och långsiktig strategi för romsk inkludering 2012–2032* [A coordinated long-term strategy for Roma inclusion 2012-2032], Skr. 2011/12:56, Stockholm: Kulturdepartementet.

Government White Book (2014) *Den mörka och okända historien - Vitbok om övergrepp och kränkningar av romer under 1900-talet* [The dark and unknown story – assault and degrading treatment of Roma during the 20th Century], Ds 2014:8, Stockholm: Kulturdepartementet.

Grönqvist, H. and Niknami, S. (2017) *Ankomst och härkomst. En ESO-rapport om skolresultat och bakgrund* [Arrival and origin. An ESO-report on student performance], rapport till Expertgruppen för studier i offentlig ekonomi 2017:3, Stockholm: Wolters Kluwers.

Gstöhl, S. (2002) *Reluctant Europeans: Norway, Sweden, and Switzerland in the Process of Integration*, London: Lynne Rienner Publishers.

Gustafsson, J.-E., Sörlin, S. and Vlachos, J. (2016) *Policyidéer för svensk skola* [Policy ideas for Swedish schools], Stockholm: SNS.

Hanberger, A., Carlbaum, S., Hult, A., Lindgren, L. and Lundström, U. (2016) School evaluation in Sweden in a local perspective: A synthesis, *Education Inquiry*, 7 (3): 349–71.

Harris, N. Ryffé, D., Scullion, L. and Stendahl, S. (2017) Ensuring the right to education for Roma children: An Anglo-Swedish perspective, *International Journal of Law, Policy and the Family*, 31 (2): 230–67.

Helakorpi, J., Lappalainen, S. and Mietola R. (2018) Equality in the making? Roma and Traveller minority policies and basic education in three Nordic countries, *Scandinavian Journal of Educational Research*. DOI: 10.1080/00313831.2018.1485735

Holm, A.-S. (2017) En skolkoncerns uppgång och fall [A free school company's rise and fall], *Utbildning & Demokrati*, 17 (1): 87–101.

IES (2017) Welcome from the CEO. Available online: https://engelska.se/about-ies/welcome-ceo, accessed 5 June 2017.

IES (2018) History. Available online: http://corporate.engelska.se/about-ies/history, accessed 29 August 2018.

Jacobsson, B. and Sundström, G. (2016) The Europeanisation of the Swedish state, in J. Pierre (ed.), *The Oxford Handbook of Swedish Politics*, 515–28, Oxford: Oxford University Press.

Jarl, M. and Rönnberg, L. (2015) *Skolpolitik. Från Riksdagshus till klassrum* [Education Politics: From the Parliament to the Classroom], Stockholm: Liber.

Johansson, K. M. (2017) Sweden and the European Union, *Oxford Research Encyclopedia of Politics*, 1–18, EPublication.

Joki (2016) Münchener Kita-Kette Joki wird vom skandinavischen Marktführer AcadeMedia übernommen. Available online: http://www.joki-kinderbetreuung.de/archiv/assets/Pdfs/Presse-fuer-Website-160111.pdf, accessed 16 November 2017.

Jones, K., Cunchillos, C., Hatcher, R., Hirtt, N., Innes, R., Johsua, S. and Klausenitzer, J. (2008) *Schooling in Western Europe: The New Order and Its Adversaries*, Houndmills: Palgrave Macmillan.

Kunskapsskolan Education (2017) About us. Available online: http://www.kunskapsskolan.com/aboutus.4.1d96c045153756b0c14d5714.html, accessed 16 November 2017.

Kunskapsskolan India (2017) Best school in India. Available online: http://ked.edu.in/, accessed 5 June 2017.

Kunskapsskolan India (2018) Vision. Available online: http://ked.edu.in/introduction/vision-and-values/, accessed 29 August 2018.

Lidström, A. (1999) Local school choice policies in Sweden, *Scandinavian Political Studies*, 22 (2): 137–56.

Lindahl, R. and Naurin, D. (2005) Sweden: The twin faces of a euro-outsider, *Journal of European Integration*, 27 (1): 65–87.

Lindahl, R. and Naurin, D. (2010) Out in the cold? Flexible integration and the political status of euro-outsiders, *European Union Politics*, 11 (4): 485–510.

Lundahl, L. (2002) Sweden: Decentralization, deregulation, quasi-markets – and then what? *Journal of Education Policy*, 17 (6): 687–97.

Lundahl, L. (2005) Swedish, European, global, in D. Coulby and E. Zambeta (eds), *Globalization and Nationalism in Education. World Yearbook of Education 2005*, 147–64, London: Routledge Falmer.

Lundahl, L. (2016) Equality, inclusion and marketization of Nordic education: Introductory notes, *Research in Comparative and International Education*, 11 (1): 3–12.

Lundahl, L., Erixon Arreman, I., Holm, A. and Lundström, U. (2013) Educational marketization the Swedish way, *Education Inquiry*, 4 (3): 497–517.

Lundahl, L. and Rönnberg, L. (2016) And what happened next? Managing the Swedish school choice revolution, *Paper Presented at the European Conference of Educational Research*, Dublin, Ireland, 23–6 August 2016.

Lundström, U. and Rönnberg, L. (2015) Att styra skolan med marknaden som förebild [Governing education by using the market as a model], in S. Lindblad and L. Lundahl (eds), *Utbildning – makt och politik* [Education – power and politics], 141–63, Lund: Studentlitteratur.

Marushiakova, E. and Popov, V. (2015) European policies for social inclusion of Roma: Catch 22? *Social Inclusion*, 3 (5): 19–31.

Miles, L. (2011) Looking back on Sweden's 'twin faces': Reflections on Sweden and European integration, in C. Alvstam, B. Jännebring and D. Naurin (eds), *I Europamissionens Tjänst* [At the service of the European Commission], 265–73, Gothenburg: Centre for European Research, Gothenburg University.

Nordin, A. (2014) Europeanisation in national education reforms: Horizontal and vertical translations, in A. Nordin and D. Sundberg (eds), *Transnational Policy Flows in European Education: The Making and Governing of Knowledge in the Education Policy Field*, 141–57, Oxford: Symposium Books.

Nordin, A. (2017) Towards a European policy discourse on compulsory education: The case of Sweden, *European Educational Research Journal*, 16 (4): 474–86.

Novak, J. and Carlbaum, S. (2017) Juridification of examination systems: Extending state level authority over teacher assessments through regarding of national tests, *Journal of Education Policy*, 32 (5): 673–93.

OECD (2015) *Improving Schools in Sweden. An OECD Perspective*, Paris: OECD.

Östh, J., Andersson, E. and Malmberg, B. (2013) School choice and increasing performance difference: A counterfactual approach, *Urban Studies*, 50 (2): 407–25.

Quintans, J. (2015) *A Matter of Democracy: EU Soft Law in the Education Area*, Master Thesis in European Studies, Gothenburg: University of Gothenburg.

Riksdag minutes (2017/18:127) *Riksdagens protokoll torsdagen den 7 juni*. [*Riksdag minutes, Thursday June 7*], Stockholm: Riksdagen.

Rönnberg, L. (2012) Reinstating national school inspections in Sweden: The return of the state, *Nordic Studies in Education*, 32 (2): 69–83.

Rönnberg, L. (2017) From national policy-making to global edu-business: Swedish edu-preneurs on the move, *Journal of Education Policy*, 32 (2): 234–49.

Sejersted, F. (2011) *The Age of Social Democracy. Norway and Sweden in the Twentieth Century*, Woodstock: Princeton University Press.

SCB (2009) *Sveriges ekonomi. Statistiskt perspektiv* [Sweden's Economy: a statistical perspective], Stockholm: SCB.

SNAE (2014) Privata aktörer inom förskola och skola. En kartläggning av enskilda huvudmän och ägare [Private actors in preschools and schools. A survey of private providers and owners], *Rapport 410*, Stockholm: Skolverket.

SNAE (2017) Beskrivande data 2016. Förskola, skola och vuxenutbildning [Descriptive statictics 2016. Childcare, education and adult education], *Rapport 452*, Stockholm: Skolverket.

SOU (2010:55) *Romers rätt - en strategi för romer i Sverige* [Rights of the Roma – a strategy for Swedish Roma], Stockholm: Kulturdepartementet.

SOU (2013:56). *Friskolorna i samhället* [Free schools in society], Stockholm: Fritzes.

SOU (2016:78) *Ordning och reda i välfärden* [Welfare in order], Betänkande av Välfärdsutredningen, Stockholm: Finansdepartementet.

SOU (2017:35) *Samling för skolan. Nationell strategi för kunskap och likvärdighet.* [Rallying for school. National strategies to raise knowledge and increase equity], Stockholm: WoltersKluwers.

Sundberg, D. and Wahlström, N. (2012) Standards-based curricula in a denationalised conception of education: The case of Sweden, *European Educational Research Journal*, 11 (3): 342–56.

Svensson, S. (2014) Oligarkerna. Vinnarna i slaget om välfärden [Oligarchs. Winners in the battle of welfare], *Rapport 4*, Stockholm: Tiden.

Telhaug, A. O., Mediås, O. A. and Aasen, P. (2004) From collectivism to individualism? Education as nation building in a Scandinavian perspective, *Scandinavian Journal of Educational Research*, 48 (2): 141–58.

TES (2008) Swedes bring personal touch to academies, *Times Educational Supplement*, 4 April.

Veckans Affärer (2017) För 20 år sedan trodde få på lärarens nystartade bolag – i dag driver hon ett miljardimperium [20 years ago few believed in the teacher's new business – today she runs a billion SEK empire], 6 March.

Wahlström, N. (2016) A third wave of European education policy: Transnational and national conceptions of knowledge in Swedish curricula, *European Educational Research Journal*, 5 (3): 298–313.

Waldow, F. (2009) Undeclared imports: Silent borrowing in educational policy-making and research in Sweden, *Comparative Education*, 45 (4): 477–94.

Wiborg, S. (2013) Neo-liberalism and universal state education: The cases of Denmark, Norway and Sweden 1980–2011, *Comparative Education*, 49 (4): 407–23.

6

From Public Education to National Public Upbringing: The Neoconservative Turn of Hungarian Education after 2010[1]

Eszter Neumann and György Mészáros

Alongside other public policy areas, states mediate and translate global economic restructurings and steer local societies by their education policies. The following analysis is inspired by the world-systems approach, in particular studies on the operation of the state in semi-peripheral countries. Education policy-making in Eastern European countries cannot be comprehensively understood without considering the implications of global positionality and the ways in which it shapes the broader context of domestic ideological and political struggles. The struggles that divide local Eastern European elites characteristically revolve around their country's integration into global hierarchies and are embedded in the country-specific constellations in which these societies have reintegrated into global capitalism after the fall of the Soviet Union. Our analysis concentrates on how these ideological struggles, which deeply determine domestic and international elite alliances and the political projects of the local elites, have shaped Hungarian education policy-making in the last decades (Gagyi 2016).

In this chapter, we are interested in how, in the context of the changing economic and social conditions of the global financial crisis, these ideological frameworks mediate transnational educational policies and shape education policy-making in Hungary. The bulk of our analysis concentrates on the remaking of Hungarian education in the wake of the financial crisis by a nationalist–populist elite bloc. However, to highlight and contextualize these landslide changes, we first need to

[1] We owe special thanks for the helpful remarks and critical comments to the editors, to Ágnes Gagyi, Tamás Gerőcs, Eszter Kovács, Ágnes Patakfalvi-Czirják, and Ildikó Zakariás and to the members of the Working Group for Public Sociology 'Helyzet'.

briefly summarize the nature of the symbolic political struggles of the decades following the regime change in 1989.

The symbolic political struggles of post-socialist elites and the 'catching-up' project

Following the regime change in 1989, Hungary has fully reintegrated into the capitalist world economy. This economic reintegration has taken place under the unfavourable conditions of high public debt, a lost Comecon market and a higher demand for external capital than is available. With the privatization of state socialist industry, the means of production were transferred to national and transnational capitalists (the biggest investors were German, US and French companies), and the enormous state and industrial debts accumulated during the late decades of state socialism were inherited by the post-socialist state.

After the collapse of the Soviet bloc, the 'competing modernities' discourse of the cold war era was once again replaced by the 'West-centred' modernization discourse of the nineteenth century. Accepting the asymmetric global hierarchy in which Eastern European societies were positioned subordinately to 'developed' Western societies, the post-socialist political project of 'catching up' renders the development of core Western societies as a universal model and 'lagging behind' as an inherent characteristic of semi-peripheral societies. The identity politics and economic strategies enacted by Eastern European political elites are strongly intertwined with the project of 'catching up' with Europe and the ambition to improve the country's position in the ladder of symbolic recognition. Since the regime change, two dominant economic–political blocs with divergent political ideologies of developmentalist illusion have solidified in Hungary. For two decades, a 'Westernist' market-liberalizing position stood against an 'Eastern-nationalist' and economically protectionist position.

The earlier bloc, represented by the coalition of late socialist technocrats tied to the Hungarian Socialist Party (MSZP) and of liberal intellectuals connected to the liberal Alliance of Free Democrats (SZDSZ), propagated modernization through Western integration and positioned itself as the representative and local mediator of Western values. The political rhetoric of this *antipopulist–Westernist elite bloc* rejected the popular, 'backward' characteristics of the country, including nationalism, and believed that the rest of the population needed guidance on the road to Western development (Gagyi 2016).

The *'nationalist–populist'*, bloc on the other hand, propagated the protection of 'national' wealth from Western capital and its local allies, and strove to build a strong national bourgeoisie. In ideological terms, this bloc relied on the symbolic nationalism of the anti-Communist interwar bourgeoisie. It argued that the country's position in the global hierarchy should be improved by overcoming the internal and external enemies of national development (Gagyi 2016). In the 1990s, the Conservative bloc was represented by the Hungarian Democratic Forum (MDF), but from 1998 onward, the Federation of Young Democrats (Fidesz) became its main political representative. Fidesz has established a strategic alliance with the small Christian Democratic People's Party (KDNP) since 1998, which is presently its coalition partner in government.[2]

In this dual, polarized political landscape, the interests of the working class did not gain powerful political representation (Gagyi 2016). As the capitalist integration of the early 1990s boosted labour insecurity and unemployment rates and required the elimination of socialist welfare institutions, the interests of proletarized workers were undermined. The political discourses of the nationalist–populist bloc veiled conflicting interests of the national capitalist class and the proletariat by employing emotionally tuned references to the 'national interest' and through the criticism of external economic dependence, while the antipopulist–Westernist bloc silenced economic complaints by claiming the mission of protecting the democratic establishment (Gagyi 2016).[3]

Between 1990 and 2010, Hungarian governments, irrespective of their current ideological standpoints, took a strong Westernist, pro-EU stance which cherished the 'free-market' version of Western capitalism and strongly associated 'true' democratization, modernization and the promise of economic prosperity with Europe and the European Union (Böröcz 2012: 25). The EU accession in 2004 was narrated by the ruling Socialist–liberal coalition as a long-awaited historical opportunity for 'catching up' and symbolically reintegrating to the culturally and economically superior 'West'. At the same time, Hungary's economic

---

[2] The concepts of 'democratic antipopulism' and 'antidemocratic-populist' were coined by Gagyi (2016).

[3] The liberals, vindicating the moral legacy of the former dissidents, claimed exclusive authorship in defining 'democracy'. This version of democracy prioritized superior Western-type institutions of market and democracy, and less so the requirements of participation and popular control. The Socialist–liberal alliance was forged in the mid-1990s on the foundations of dissociating itself from the Conservative definition of 'national interest' and substantiated its legitimacy as the defender of democratic progress from the threat of anti-Semitic nationalist–populist claims associated to the nationalist–populist bloc.

dependence was aggravated by the EU accession, as the country's economy had become greatly dependent on EU transfers and credits. From an EU perspective, the 2004 and 2006 accession not only offered investment opportunities but also provided a new workforce asset in terms of Eastern European labour migration to Western Europe on the one hand and relatively cheap local labour force for expanding Western European companies on the other (Gagyi et al. 2016). The incoming EU transfers had effectively counterbalanced the profits extracted from Hungary by transnational companies which had arrived since the regime change and after the EU accession.

How did these elite identification struggles leave their mark on education policy-making? Across Eastern Europe, the 'West' or 'Europe' was viewed as an embodiment of progress and a model for emulation (Silova and Eklof 2013), and democracy had been a fundamental driver for post-Socialist education policy-making. In Hungary, the decentralization of school maintenance and operation in the early 1990s was an illustrative example of the adoption of Western models. Citing the decentralized English education system as a model of true democratic governance, expert groups tied to the liberal party argued that placing social, healthcare and educational services under municipal oversight is the viable, liberal alternative to the rigidity of centralized socialist planning and close bureaucratic control (Kovai and Neumann 2015). It soon became evident that the 1991 Municipal Act had generated major redistributive inequalities in the social and educational provision. The introduction of free school choice in 1985 and the decentralization of school governance in 1991 paved the way for the creation of one of the most unequal, socially and ethnically segregated public education systems in the world.[4] Referring to the same democratic ideal, the 'antipopulist–Westernist' expert group urged giving schools wide professional autonomies. In the early 1990s, school staff were entrusted with the right to devise their local curriculum and school principals were granted autonomy in professional, organizational and practical matters.

For two decades after the regime change, Hungarian education policy-making was dominated by the contrasting narratives of the failure of the old (Eastern, Socialist, centralized, 'Prussian-style', chalk and talk, teacher-centred, rigid) and the promise of progress (Western, capitalist, decentralized, market-led,

---

[4] In the primary sector, early selection (entrance exams to specialized primary school classes) exacerbated within and between school social differences, and accelerated the institutional segregation of Roma children. In the secondary sector, the establishment of new elite educational tracks (eight- and six-year *gymnasia* alongside the old four-year *gymnasia*) created a further refined system of secondary pathways, while it also sucked out the most able children from upper primary schools.

innovative, child-centred, playful). In the early 2000s, the PISA survey revealed that the Hungarian education system was significantly underperforming and was among the least equitable education systems within the participating countries. This provided further legitimacy for the pro-EU, Westernist Socialist–liberal coalition to renew the problem space of education policy-making by pushing the low quality and equity of the public education system onto the policy agenda (Bajomi et al. 2009). The Socialist–liberal coalition in power between 2002 and 2010 launched a comprehensive initiative to desegregate public schools as well as vast projects to introduce skills and competence-based instruction in the teaching and curriculum of primary, secondary and vocational schools, with the aim of attenuating the dominance of the 'whole-class method' and teacher-centred instruction. Overwhelmingly financed from the European Structural Fund and the European Social Fund between 2004 and 2013, public education initiatives were rhetorically framed as essential elements for the 'modernization of education' and 'catching up with Europe'.

The conceptualization of the school desegregation initiative succinctly illustrates how ideological struggles between elite fractions translate into policy initiatives. As the nationalist–populist elites vindicated the nationalist symbolic universe, antipopulist–Westernist elites, citing the directives of the EU social model, forged their own version of solidarity and aimed to represent minority groups outside the boundaries of the nation carved by nationalist ideology, such as Roma, Jews, women and LGBTQ (Gagyi 2016). The ideal of democratic inclusion according to this political bloc concentrated on the recognition of minorities and on the ideology of antiracism. Hence, the criticism raised by PISA about the inequity of the Hungarian education system was translated into a policy which considered the racial desegregation of Hungarian schools as its primary objective and oversaw the links between intersecting forms of deprivation, oppression and educational disadvantage (e.g. the underperformance of the working class, intersecting gender inequalities).

The financial crisis and the political rearrangements at the end of the 2000s

By 2006, following two decades of market-liberalization policies, Hungary accumulated a high budget deficit (9.3 per cent of the gross domestic product [GDP], OECD 2012) and it became the country most indebted to international banks in the region. Eastern Europe was hit especially hard by the financial crisis due to these countries' small and liberalized economies, and internal social and economic tensions following EU accession. In 2006, a political crisis shook the ruling coalition and prompted a series of demonstrations. The 2008 financial crisis, which had instigated a major – public and private – debt crisis and shook the Hungarian economy fundamentally, questioned the political legitimacy of the above-discussed post-socialist integration. The popularity of the far-right party, Jobbik, was considerably strengthened by the political crisis and the party has successfully channelled the economic losses of the former working class into a radical populist and protectionist ideology, and gained 17 per cent of the votes in the 2010 elections (on the ideological differences between Jobbik and Fidesz see Bozóki and Ádám 2016). After decades of austerity which fuelled disillusionment with the ideology of cathcing up and led to the legitimacy crisis of the Socialist–liberal bloc, the eight year period of governing of the antipopulist–Westernist bloc ended. With the support of the lower social classes alienated by the multiple crises since 2006 and its traditional conservative middle-class base, the 2010 elections brought the sweeping political victory of the nationalist–populist bloc led by Viktor Orbán (Éber 2018). This victory brought about a significant rearrangement in the ideological orientations of public policies.

The post-2010 ideological field in Hungarian politics is marked by the symbolic division between the 'freedom fighter' rhetoric, enacted by the right-wing nationalist–populist Orbán government and its vision of developing an 'illiberal democracy',[5] and the pro-European rhetoric voiced by the antipopulist–Westernist opposition which conceives Europe as a potential saviour of Hungarian democracy. The Orbán government has constructed a Eurosceptic political rhetoric which portrays a freedom fighter government that confronts the European Union – served by the antipopulist–Westernist bloc – to defend the country's sovereignty (Gyurgyák 2017: 57–8; Bozóki and Ádám 2016).[6] After 2010, the antipopulist–Westernist opposition had become extremely fragmented and has not been able to re-establish its political legitimacy since.

---

[5]   Using its two-third supermajority in parliament, the Orbán government altered the constitutional system and changed electoral laws and other fundamental laws which gave significant control over the judiciary, media and the banks to the ruling party, Fidesz. The PM first explicated his vision of 'building an illiberal state based on national foundations' citing Russia and China as examples in 2014. After the 2018 election victory, when the European People's Party threatened to marginalize Orbán, he distanced himself from the notion of illiberalism and declared to build an 'old-style Christian democracy' in Hungary.

[6]   This performative political strategy was most evident in Orbán's reaction to the refugee crisis and the stance he took on the refugee quota negotiations. At the internal political agenda, preparing a 'national consultation' about the refugee quota in 2017, the EU negotiations were thematized by an intensive media campaign and an infamous government-funded billboard campaign spreading the slogan 'Let's stop Brussels!'

The development of Orbán's illiberal democracy has prompted several protest waves since 2010, but these Budapest-centred middle-class movements typically concentrated on the curtailing of the democratic establishment and did not recognize nor represent the economic challenges of day-to-day subsistence for the lower social classes (Éber 2018).[7]

Importantly, despite the incompatible ideological differences, in terms of their economic strategy, both elite fractions continue to strive to 'catch-up' with the core capitalist countries and to integrate Hungary into the post-crisis world order. In contrast to the antipopulist–Westernist faction which had, for two decades, prioritized foreign investment and credit, the nationalist–populist bloc aims to enact a model of capitalist integration which benefits the interest of the national bourgeoisie[8] (Gagyi et al. 2016), and developed an extremely centralized oligarchic and clientelist economic and ideological system. Orbán's double-faceted economic policies alter according to economic sectors: while they favour national capital interests on non-tradable markets and transfers, in export-oriented sectors, policies support transnational investments (most importantly south German industrial interests) and on this basis the government launched a programme of reindustrialization. Therefore, while at the level of the political rhetoric, the 'freedom-fighter' government's illiberal, anti-democratic ideology openly confronts the values of the European Union, on the economic level, the country has continued to play the role of the dependent ally of capitalist factions (Gagyi et al. 2016).

The economic strategy of 'national development' has marginalized social expenditures. Examining Hungary's social policy between 2010 and 2014, Szikra (2014) and Ferge (2017a) argue that the government reacted to the financial crisis with paradigmatic and distinctive reforms which equally featured neoliberal, étatist and neoconservative elements. The government introduced the idea of the work-based society. In this new workfare framework, unemployment benefits were tied to a vast new public work scheme, social benefits are bound to one's active labour market status, and the 'undeserving' poor, who are unemployed or not employed legally, are made responsible for their situation and are deprived

---

[7] For example, curbing the consultation system, the new Code of Labour considerably impaired workers' rights and labour union competences and led to the decrease of unemployment benefits from nine to three months.

[8] The government introduced protectionist policies and new economic opportunities for the domestic economic elite which had previously been marginalized from the globalized segments of the economy. While the greatest winners of this strategy were clearly the oligarchs closely tied to Fidesz, but corruption-centred theories are alone weak in explaining new processes of class formation.

of basic social rights.[9] The Orbán government's social policy measures, its flat tax system and tax credits that target better off families, its family benefits system, the severe austerity measures in the social sector and the decreasing central redistribution in general have further enhanced class differences by depriving the 'undeserving poor' of welfare provisions and greatly benefiting those in stable employment (Szikra 2014, 2018; Ferge 2017a).

The steady decrease in the educational budget traversed political cycles. In the post-Socialist period, state expenditure on public education peaked in 2003 (5.7 per cent of the GDP) when a general teacher salary rise was implemented. Although the educational budget has decreased continuously since 2003, neither before nor after the financial crisis have governments framed their policies as austerity measures. Between 2001 and 2011, educational expenditure compared to national GDP decreased by 0.5 per cent; and in this period, the level of educational expenditures was around half of the EU average. According to Balogh (2015), there were two distinctive periods in the 2000s: before 2006, national GDP was growing, as was the overall spending on public education. While national GDP drastically dropped in 2009 due to the financial crisis, educational expenditures stagnated nominally, although their actual value decreased. In that period, in response to budget cuts, municipal school managements were constrained to rationalize their institutional structures, which led to school mergers and school closures across the country (Balogh 2015: 96). According to OECD statistics (OECD 2016), state expenditure on public education decreased by 25 per cent between 2008 and 2012. The period between 2010 and 2012 was marked by severe budgetary austerity, for example, spending on primary schools decreased by 10 per cent on average (Balogh 2015: 100–1). In 2013, 3.8 per cent of the GDP was spent on public education when the OECD average was 5.2 per cent, which made Hungary the country spending the least on public education among Central-Eastern European countries. Although the student cohort had gradually decreased due to negative demographic trends, budget cuts had significantly exceeded the rate of population decrease (OECD 2015). Budget calculations indicate that following the dip of 2012–13, educational spending has started to increase slightly. However, as it will be explicated below, educational expenditures have been disproportionately redistributed in the favour of church-maintained schools.

---

[9] Approximately 200,000–300,000 citizens in need are denied any social benefits. This responsibilizing and penalizing policy logic first penetrated the education sector when family benefits were withdrawn from the parents of persistent absentees in 2012.

As with its social policies, the Orbán government's education reforms fit into a broader étatist and neoconservative turn which also embraces certain neoliberal policy instruments and discourses. The following section explicates the cornerstones of the unfolding education policy regime, paying special attention to its consequences for access to education and social mobility. Attending to some specific but characteristic features and trends, we closely scrutinize changes in two areas: the centralization of school governance and the expansion of the non-state sector. Finally, turning back to our initial theme of positionality, we will discuss the relations between Hungary and the European education space.

The new education policy paradigm: Étatism and neoconservativism

One important caveat that must be remembered in advance is that education policy has not been a key area where political positionings have been elaborated in the election debates or after the elections since 2010. It is indicative of the lesser status of the sector that education ceased to be governed by an independent ministry and, alongside other areas, was grouped under a super-ministry of Human Resources. While major legislative and institutional restructurings have taken place in the sector, especially between 2010 and 2014, the legislation was produced at an accelerated pace and without any consultation, resulting in policy goals and instruments that were often contradictory (Ferge 2017b; Bajomi and Csákó 2017).

Educational philosophy and historical context

In terms of the rhetorical and problem space of policy-making, the government between 2010 and 2014 was passionately engaged in symbolically dissociating itself from the education policies of the Socialist–liberal educational administration of the 2000s. This political rhetoric, which blamed the previous antipopulist–Westernist government for placing too much emphasis on children's rights and too few on their responsibilities, and which reclaimed the authority of teachers, bore strong connections to the English Conservative education policy rhetoric of the time (Bailey and Ball 2016). Symbolic initiatives of the 'liberal' administration, such as the replacement of numerical grading by written evaluations and abolishing grade repetition in lower primary schools, were instantaneously wiped out after the elections.

The Christian Democratic People's Party, Fidesz's politically insignificant coalition partner,[10] played an important role in forging the alliance between the government and traditional churches, and in the ideological tuning of policies, with special regard to family and birth policies and the promotion of a patriarchal, traditional family model (Darvas and Szikra 2017). Between 2010 and 2014, the Christian Democratic People's Party provided the secretary of education, Rózsa Hoffmann. As a significant initial act of rebranding, the government prepared and ratified the new Act on National Public Upbringing (Törvény a Nemzeti Köznevelésről) in 2011, which replaced the 1993 Act on Public Education (Közoktatási Törvény). Hoffmann explained her vision in her opening speech in the parliamentary debate about the law:

> We consider public upbringing a public service and not a provision. ... The education system shares the tasks of upbringing with the parents and the carers of the child, this baseline originates from the law of nature, it is ancient wisdom. ... One of the root problems is that the public upbringing system used to be considered a market actor, and thus it became vulnerable to a sphere which was indifferent about the Hungarian national interest. As I stated, we think that the public upbringing system is not a market provision, it is a public service whose provision is the right, the task and the duty of the Hungarian state, and, since there is a clear social demand for them, this involves non-state, that is, church and private institutions – and we must give an adequate response to these demands.

In the framing of *public upbringing*, the state shares the responsibilities of education with the family. From a typical neoconservative perspective, the educational government views education as a sector key to the 'national interest' and a great emphasis was placed on reclaiming 'traditional values' and knowledge. The 'national interest' is in contradiction with the interests of the market, yet this criticism never targeted neoliberal market forces explicitly.

Conceptualizing the teaching profession as a 'service to the families, to the nation, and to future generations' (speech of Zoltán Balog, Minister of Human Resources 2014), neoconservative ideology broke away from the concept of the autonomous professional and represented teachers as public servants. School principals' autonomy was severely curtailed, and their decision-making capacities in human resource management were eliminated. Since the nationalist–populist

[10] Since 2006, the Christian Democratic People's Party has participated in the election on a shared party list with Fidesz which ensured that its major figures entered the Parliament; the party, however, does not have a significant electoral supporter base.

bloc historically has a strong anti-Communist identity, these changes were never associated with the Communist centralized governance.

Drawing harsh criticism from teacher unions, the government established the National Teacher Chamber (Nemzeti Pedagógus Kar) in 2013 which in effect replaced the function of labour unions in collective negotiations. All teachers employed in state schools automatically became members of the Chamber. Its ethical code, which meticulously describes the proper countenance and behaviour of teachers, prompted widespread criticism from professional organizations and labour unions which saw it as an instrument of curbing teachers' professional and personal autonomy and as evidence of the government's mistrust in the profession. The new educational inspectorate, established in September 2014, is another instrument for enforcing central control on what is 'correct knowledge' and how it should be taught (Apple 2006). The market for textbooks was nationalized in 2014, and concurrently teachers' autonomy in choosing textbooks was seriously curtailed. The latter has been criticized by unions and professional organizations as a critical expansion of central control and command over the definition of 'correct' knowledge and values. Breaking away from the unquestioned principle of separating the state and the church during the 2014–15 school year, religious education was integrated into the curriculum and parents were offered a compulsory choice between the subjects of religious or moral education.

We will shortly turn to discuss the fundamental structural transformations which led to the production of new lines of class and ethnic segmentation in the Hungarian educational landscape. We will first attend to how the neoconservative étatist strategy has transformed the institutional landscape.

Continuity and hybridization

While the government has been keen to rhetorically dissociate itself from the 'past eight years', there is remarkable continuity in the professional discourse and expertise shaping the guidelines of daily professional practice. The professional and policy discourse of the 2000s has fully endorsed the neoliberal policies mediated by the European education space. The development of competitive skills and competences, as well as the framing in which schooling is an instrument to raise the country's international competitiveness has become a central driver of educational reforms. Unlike the Anglo-American school accountability systems, the Hungarian system of annual national competence assessments which has been in use since the early 2000s, accountability measures.

Educational policy debates replicate the polarized ideological landscape. While the politicians and experts of the nationalist–populist bloc are generally reluctant to make public appearances and comment on initiatives, they are confronted by a populous and united, pro-European Union, antipopulist–Westernist educational expert alliance, who are the former and currently dismissed advisers of the Socialist–liberal coalition. These experts consider their views incompatible with the current policy direction and their propositions are predominantly oriented to restorative demands (Erőss 2017). Although the nationalist–populist government has completely replaced the pool of policy-making expertise with practising teachers coming from elite and church schools, and experts from the main Catholic university, the neoliberal discursive framework continues to guide the content of strategic documents. This is partly due to the continuity of expertise: while the educational government rhetorically dissociates itself from the Socialist–liberal era, most experts underwent professional socialization by developing and implementing EU-funded projects in the 2000s. For instance, the inspection framework developed by the new inspectorate body has endorsed the vocabulary, indicators and instruments of the European Union's competence and skills agenda.

Policies related to teacher professionalism and curricular content exemplify the hybridization of neoconservative and neoliberal ideologies. Between 1990 and 2012, key aspects of the National Core Curriculum have been shaped in accordance with European regulations and have enacted a neoliberal policy discourse emphasizing life-long learning, competence development and transferable skills. In the most recent National Core Curriculum adopted in 2012, these elements are complemented with an emphasis on more traditional knowledge-based curricular contents and conservative values (a focus on national identity, patriotism, moral and character education). Furthermore, the new curriculum is more prescriptive and expects teachers to cover an extensive amount of taught material making it especially challenging to find lesson time for skills-development and cross-curricular competencies such as critical thinking.

Referencing the practice of ten European countries, but not the EU explicitly, the conservative administration implemented the so-called teacher career model which regulates the promotion and salaries of the teachers. Teachers are expected to produce portfolios which provide the basis of inspection and their promotion. This post-bureaucratic regulation instrument, adopted under the influence of EU expertise, which follows the neoliberal policy logic of soft surveillance and enacts its power through the subject-moulding power of self-evaluation, soon became an excessive bureaucratic burden triggering criticism and defiance among teachers.

New étatism and the involvement of the church

Since 2010, two major, previously inconceivable changes have taken place regarding school maintenance: the centralization of the operation of public schools and the steady rise of church-maintained primary schools.

The centralization of school maintenance and operation

Breaking away from the symbolic heritage of the decentralized system, the government launched a programme of dual power concentration in education: the centralization of school governance and the impairment of professional autonomies (Szalai and Kende 2014). Alongside health and social care institutions, local self-governments' licences, which enabled them to make education policy (school governance and professional oversight including the regulation of school admissions and catchment zones, budgetary management, decisions about school profiles and principal appointments) were transferred to a newly founded school maintenance centre on 1 January 2013. The centralization provoked professional debates within the government and seriously clashed with the interests of municipal leaderships. Eventually, the prime minister had to intervene directly to push the process forward. The central authority consisted of 19 regional and 198 micro-regional offices. It was argued that centralization would increase the efficiency and equity of the public educational system and improve policy delivery (Györgyi 2015; Ferge 2017a). Yet, in retrospect, there is little evidence that the offices moved beyond executing central orders. Furthermore, hopes about financial efficacy remained unfulfilled, first and foremost due to the underfunding of the state education system in general, and because authorities had neither been incentivized nor had been assisted in efficient budget planning.[11] Due to alarming signs of institutional and budgetary

---

[11]   The per capita financing of schools was replaced by a 'task financing' system in 2013. Teacher salaries are directly financed from the state budget and infrastructural expenditures are distributed by the central authority.

inefficacy, the central authority was reorganized by 2017: the number of regional offices was decreased to fifty-nine and each was given more budgetary and decision-making independence.

While the earlier governance system had been profoundly determined by the financial inequalities between local municipalities, centralization has resulted in a more balanced minimum funding system for state-operated schools. However, since – with the generous support of the state – the church has become a major actor in school operation and maintenance, educational inequalities have been greatly aggravated by funding disparities across sectors.

Church schools and the exacerbation of between-school segregation

> Our goal is to provide a Christian upbringing to as many children as possible, so that they can absorb the values on which Europe and Hungary have been built. (Dr Rózsa Hoffmann at the school year opening of the Metropolitan Archdiocese of Eger in the Basilica, August 2011)

The traditional churches have become important allies of the Conservative coalition. In exchange for providing ideological resources, political support and legitimacy to nationalist populism, historical churches administer a growing share of publicly financed services in health, social care and education (Ádám and Bozóki 2016). While before 2010, the separation of the state and the church was considered a cornerstone of the democratic establishment, post-2010 education policy decisively turned away from this principle. It is indicative of this unfolding alliance that between 2012 and 2018, the Ministry of Human Resources, a super-ministry overseeing social, cultural, sport, church and minority, family and youth, health and education, was led by a former Calvinist priest. It also shows the symbolic recognition of the church that the national school year opening ceremonies have taken place in church schools three times since 2010 (2012, 2013, 2017). Beyond the symbolic recognition of the political 'alliance of the state and the church', traditional churches have been strongly incentivized to take over social and educational institutions since 2012. While church-run institutions are entitled to the same funding as state schools and kindergartens for teacher salaries,[12] churches receive additional complementary financing for institutional maintenance and they can retrieve targeted state funding for other expenses such as infrastructural development. Independent

---

[12] Teacher salaries are paid from the state budget, but in contrast to state schools, the principals of church schools can allocate supplementary wage benefits to top up teacher incomes.

research conducted by the Fiscal Responsibility Institute Budapest concluded that for material expenses, church schools could receive 2.6 times more funding than their state-operated counterparts.

The number of church-maintained schools has rapidly risen since 2010. This process was aggravated by the fact that before 2013, financially struggling and indebted smaller school authorities were keen to hand over their schools to the church hoping that they could get away with the financial responsibilities of school maintenance. While the share of church and private schools remained as low as 5–6 per cent until the early 2000s, the number of church-maintained schools rose by 64 per cent between 2010 and 2014. In the primary sector, the percentage of students attending church-maintained schools rose from 3.8 per cent in 2001 to 13.5 per cent by 2015. While in 2001, 4.2 per cent of the primary schools were maintained by the church, this number rose to 8.6 per cent by 2010, and to 15 per cent by 2015. The number of academically oriented secondary schools (gimnázium) maintained by the church rose by 150 per cent between 2010 and 2015 (Hagymási and Könyvesi 2017).

The expansion of the church-maintained sector has fundamentally redrawn local educational markets in towns and villages. While all state-maintained primary schools have assigned catchment zones, church-run schools do not have compulsory catchment zones, unless the church school is the only school available in the settlement. Therefore, most church-run primary schools are endowed with complete freedom in selecting among their applicants. With the expansion of the church school system, the social polarization and ethnic segregation of primary schools has been further exacerbated since 2010. Although church-maintained institutions are overrepresented in deprived regions, socially disadvantaged, Roma and SEND students are underrepresented in these schools (Ferge 2017b). Church-maintained schools typically offer an ethnically homogeneous alternative to underfunded state schools for the rural white middle class and lower middle class, with the notable exception of the Greek Catholic and the Methodist church which characteristically took over segregated schools in Eastern Hungary and, in many cases, engaged in pastoral work with Roma communities. These schools however typically follow a segregating model.[13] The Catholic and the Calvinist churches have typically taken

---

[13] This practice was infamously propagated as 'caring segregation' (*szeretetteljes szegregáció*) by Minister Zoltán Balog in a hearing at a desegregation litigation case filed against the Ministry of Human Resources in 2013. Criticizing the 'forced' desegregation practice of the Socialist–liberal coalition, Zoltán Balog infamously argued for the segregated, small-class instruction and 'caring catch-up instruction' of Roma pupils. Details on the *actio popularis* claim about the ghetto school

over schools which have acquired high prestige within local school systems and enforced a strict and exclusive system of ability and faith-based selection.

Resistance: Trade unionism and grass-root organizations

The forms of expressing criticism about education policies have fundamentally changed since 2010. Traditional consultative bodies in education were either dissolved or became invisible after 2010 (Bajomi and Csákó 2017). Even though they had limited representative legitimacy and actual political influence, trade unions previously vindicated the representation of teachers, but they have since completely lost their efficacy in organizing resistant forces. Instead, newly created grass-root movements gathered critical voices and organized demonstrations against the government's education policies. In 2012–13, a series of student protests organized by the Student Network (Haha), later accompanied by the Teacher Network (OHA), took place against the planned changes of the Higher Education Act. Their main demands focused on the planned curbing of university autonomies, the decreasing number of state-financed higher education seats, higher education budget cuts, student contracts which obliged scholarship holders to work in Hungary for some years, and at a later point, they complemented these with a demand about widening participation (Éber 2018).

While in the first cycle these movements tended to criticize the process of legislations (lack of consultations) and focused on single issues, ensuing movements have grown and tended to formulate broader, systemic demands (Bajomi and Csákó 2017). In 2016, a series of bottom-up organized teacher demonstrations took place putting forward demands in relation to the rapid reorganization of vocational education and the baccalaureate exams, high working hours, transparent negotiations with stakeholders about education reforms, educational desegregation and SEN support, teachers' autonomy to select textbooks, and other employment-related issues. The movement reached its peak when over 10,000 supporters turned up in a demonstration at March 2016, but it lost the impetus by 2017 without achieving a real breakthrough.[14] Since January 2018, the Independent Student Parliament has successfully mobilized secondary school students and a broad pool of sympathizers and organized a

reopened by the Greek Catholic church in Nyíregyháza can be accessed at http://www.cfcf.hu/node/129

[14] It is difficult to assess the outcome of the demonstrations. In response to the demands, the government quietly and partially retreated from some controversial actions and plans (i.e. expanded the autonomies of principals) or adopted some proposals. The government's tactic is, however, not to communicate such decisions as compromises but to keep quiet about that they had ever existed.

student strike and three large-scale demonstrations centring on demands for an education system which prepares students to 'life' on the labour market, instead of overwhelming them with factual content. While these movements dissociate themselves from parliamentary parties and the trade unions, their claims about wider professional autonomies, instruction oriented to skills valuable at the labour market and which is responsive to the challenges of 'modern life' clearly echo the earlier policies and modernization discourse of the antipopulist– Westernist elite bloc, and fit into the broader symbolic demands of opposition movements about 'European values'.

A new class policy of social (im)mobility

Alongside the above-mentioned changes, the government has developed an overarching class policy which has completely abandoned previous social justice initiatives as well as disrupting the steady trend of educational expansion and growing access to education of the previous decades. From the perspective of social (im)mobility, the education policies of the Orbán government are based on two fundamental cornerstones: creating an environment which fosters the expansion of the church and private sector predominantly offering services for the middle classes, and aligning the institutional structure of vocational secondary education to industrial interests and the economic strategy of reindustrialization.

Streaming out the middle class from state education: Loyalty, exit and the mushrooming of private schools

Like other policy areas, the recent reorganization of the education system has exacerbated existing processes of social polarization and prompted new boundaries of class-based separation. While the middle class in rural areas and small towns has increasingly been concentrated in church-run schools, in urban settings, fee-paying, private primary schools are mushrooming. The exodus of the 'Westernist' urban middle class from the state sector is fuelled by a profound distrust in the underfunded and over-controlled school system widely regarded as teacher-centred, rigid and outdated. While so-called alternative private schools established in the late 1980s and early 1990s teach from accredited curricula (Steiner and Rogers schools, etc.), one of the most popular and hyped school network established by the Hungarian start-up business, Prezi, in 2015 proposes an alternative model of private education. Here, students are enrolled in state schools as 'private learners',[15] where they take end-of-year exams, while they attend the fee-paying private school in day-to-day life. These schools advertise themselves by progressive teaching methods and their child-centred atmosphere, and concurrently employ a neoliberal argument explicating the ways in which 'progressive methods' enhance learners' labour market competitiveness. Alongside fee-paying schools, as a form of homeschooling, so-called learning circles have recently been established in a growing number, typically by the parents of lower primary-age children.

Tertiary education

In 2012, the prime minister announced the vision of self-sustaining tertiary education. Parallel to the funding trends of public education, the state funding of tertiary education reached a low point in 2013. State-funded university places in sixteen courses including law and economics were decreased with the aim of driving students to the field of engineering and natural sciences. Furthermore, to raise standards, the minimum threshold that must be achieved at the entry exam was raised and the advanced baccalaureate was made a compulsory requirement for entering certain courses. Consequently, between 2010 and 2015, university enrolment numbers have decreased by more than 20 per cent while the cohort's population decrease only accounted for 4–5 per cent decrease (Berács et al. 2015). The reduction of state-funded places has not been counterbalanced by widening participation measures and incentives; hence the ratio of socio-economically disadvantaged students has further decreased in tertiary education (Berács et al. 2015; Berlinger and Megyeri 2015).

Tertiary education reforms and the general disillusionment with state education have initiated an unprecedented increase in tertiary mobility to foreign universities. Tertiary educational migration towards Austria, Germany and the UK has become extremely popular in elite secondary schools (Nyírő 2017). These trends have also triggered an instantaneous private sector response; a growing number of private institutions offer courses and targeted support for

---

[15] The private learner status was originally created for the needs of professional athletes and permanently ill children. However, studies extensively documented that schools tended to employ this category to exclude students struggling with mental, emotional and behavioural difficulties as well as pregnant girls and young mothers from daily school attendance (Csepregi 2014). National educational statistics do not provide detailed data on private learners participating in homeschooling or other alternative forms of schooling.

secondary school students who consider applying to Western–European and US universities.

In conclusion, neoconservative education reforms have introduced new, sector-based social stratification within the education system. While the education system that unfolded in the 1990s was already extremely unequal and ethnically segregated, the unprecedented expansion of the non-state sector and the reluctance of the state to invest in state education further exacerbated inequalities of access and social polarization. The school choices of the middle class follow the binary segmentation of the political–ideological field: while parents loyal to the nationalist–populist government benefit from the privileged opportunities and resources allocated to church-maintained schools, the Westernist, 'progressive' urban middle class tends to opt out to private institutions. However, regarding tertiary educational choices, the upper-middle class seems to be unanimous in orienting it offspring abroad and investing in their futures in the international tertiary education market.

The end of the expansion of secondary education: Vocational education aligned to the strategy of reindustrialization

The Orbán government announced the target of raising the share of industrial production above 30 per cent, and alongside the automotive industry, which has been a long-standing priority of industrial development, to develop other branches of machinery industries.[16] Concurrently, in close cooperation with the Commercial and Industrial Chamber, the government took decisive steps towards restructuring the vocational education system[17] with an aim to align it to the needs of the government's industrial partners and to enter young people into apprenticeship schemes at an earlier age. In 2015, the whole vocational secondary sector was detached from the educational administration and moved under the direction of the Ministry of National Economy, and since then, the

---

[16] A grand-scale nuclear plant expansion is planned involving Russian contractors and state loans as well (Mellár 2017).

[17] Following the German model of secondary education, upon completing the eight-year primary school, Hungarian students sit the national secondary entrance exam and enter the hierarchically arranged three-tiered secondary sector at the age of fourteen. The highest achievers are accepted to the academically oriented gimnázium and the lowest achievers enter to vocational colleges. The middle ground is the vocational secondary school where students learn specialized polytechnic subjects but also prepare for the general academic baccalaureate.

Commercial and Industrial Chamber have exerted the actual decision-making power in the sector (Ferge 2017b).

> This logic shared by everybody or many families that the only road to successful
> life is through the [academically oriented] *gymnasia* or some sort of university
> is false. We don't want to support this miscalculation; such thinking is outdated.
> The road to successful life is through a vocational degree. (Prime minister in his
> regular radio interview in October 2014)

In 2011, citing Danish, German, Swiss and Austrian examples, the so-called dual vocational training system[18] which allocates much higher lesson time to work-based training was introduced. While the emphasis on practical skills invokes the European Union's apprenticeship policies, policy-makers refrain from referring to related EU policies directly. The time of obtaining a vocational qualification was reduced from four[19] to three years. With an emphasis on the importance of practical skills and 'the honour of manual work' (a term often used by the head of the industrial chamber and Viktor Orbán himself), lesson time spent on practical lessons was doubled while academically oriented subjects aiming to strengthen basic numeracy and literacy skills had their lesson time reduced by 33 per cent.

Under the decisive influence of the Commercial and Industrial Chamber which lobbied for channelling 'more able' students into vocational tracks, the government also proposed to centrally steer secondary entrance quotas and to introduce a threshold for entry to the academically oriented *gymnasia*. The government presented this proposal as an incentive to raise standards and to make *gymnasia* 'truly elite' institutions. The idea that more than 50 per cent of a cohort should be directed to vocational colleges was first announced in 2015 and triggered professional and academic criticism (Horn et al. 2015). Although the *gymnasia*-quota has been on the government agenda for years, perhaps due to conflicts with middle-class interests, it has been repeatedly postponed. It is presently scheduled to be introduced from 2019 onwards.

With the early introduction of vocational lessons, the vocational tracks have become much less flexible, allowing limited opportunities for learners to correct their secondary vocational choices by changing tracks or school types.

---

[18] In the dual vocational training system, the theoretical training takes place in vocational schools while the practical training takes place at factories. The collaboration between schools and factories is coordinated and overseen by the industrial chamber.
[19] Vocational colleges were extended from three to four years in 1995 when the so-called 2+2 years system was introduced. Here, students continued to learn mostly academic subjects in year nine and ten and specialized on vocational professions at the age of sixteen, for the subsequent two years.

Underpaid, company-based apprenticeships pushed down average wages (Gerőcs and Pinkasz 2018).

One of the most controversial elements of the government's programme was the decrease of the compulsory schooling age from eighteen to sixteen in 2012. The minister argued that in most European states, fifteen or sixteen is the compulsory schooling age and stated that some young people who do not like to learn could still become 'decent craftsmen'; therefore, they should be given the choice to enter the world of labour. Critics argued that this was essentially an austerity measure serving the decrease of educational expenditures.

As a direct result of the decrease of the compulsory schooling age, the level of early school leaving has been rising steadily, reaching 11.6 per cent in 2015. Estimates claim that about half of the early school leavers come from Roma background. Although dropout rates have constantly been high in vocational schools, the estimated proportion of dropouts rose to 30 per cent in the relevant cohorts (G. Tóth 2016). A significant proportion of early school leavers ended up in the government's public work scheme: by 2015, every sixth public worker was under twenty-five. In 2017, the government decided to exclude under twenty-fives from the public work scheme and to reorient them into a new, EU-funded labour market integration programme targeted at young people. Arguably, the vast surplus population of un-, semi- or low-skilled labourers fulfils the cheap labour needs of auto-manufacturers (Gerőcs and Pinkasz 2018). The concept of the work-based society enacts a binary opposition – both morally and in terms of direct economic interests – between we and they, worthy and unworthy, the law-abiding, hardworking and deserving citizens and those who are not motivated and choose not to study, and therefore undeserving and not entitled for social support (Apple 2006; Szikra 2018).

Hungary in the European education policy space

The country's position within the European education policy space is inextricable from the broader developments in the relations between the European Union and Hungary since 2010. On the one hand, the government forges a close, dependent alliance with German industrial capital, which requires working relations with the European Union. On the other hand, the government deflects symbolic EU expectations about how democracy, social justice and human rights issues should be treated, presuming that beyond symbolic actions, such as adopting resolutions and producing reports on Hungarian political developments, the

European Union lacks sufficient instruments and mechanisms to tackle right-wing populism and the 'illiberal' legislation established in Hungary. In the few cases when the European Commission has been effective in enforcing its agenda on the Hungarian government, it had specific financial and legal 'disciplinary' instruments at hand (Bíró-Nagy 2017). For example, in the domain of education, the EC launched an infringement procedure on the discriminatory educational segregation of Roma children in 2016 and another one on the modification of the higher education law regarding the status of the Central European University in 2017, but so far the legislation has not been changed in either cases. The prime minister regularly explicates his vision on the European stage, yet these performances of the 'freedom fighter government' typically target the domestic audience and aim to position the PM within the domestic political field (Feledy 2017: 112).

While prior to 2010 Hungarian education policy aimed to align itself with the vocabulary and policies of the European Union, a more complex relationship to EU policies has unfolded of late. Szalai and Kende (2014: 27) found that apart from mandatory reporting, the communication between EU education policy bodies and Hungarian educational governance ceased after 2010. While strategic documents densely cite EU priorities, domestic policy-making with a relevance to social reproduction and class policy go against EU equity and social justice priorities.

Analysing the response of the United Kingdom to the European Union's open method of coordination, Alexiadou and Lange (2013) argue that English education policy-making has deflected EU influence. The Hungarian government has aimed to maximize EU funding, and for that reason, has presented strategic documents aligned to the EU policy discourse while, concurrently putting policies that had contradictory effects in place. For instance, localities or micro-regions, as part of the application process for EU development tenders, must produce action plans to enforce equity and desegregation in housing and education. However, having been successful in the tenders, they are rarely made accountable for the enforcement of their anti-segregation plans. The government launched showcase pilot projects which abide by the European Union's social justice priorities; for instance, a project was launched for the comprehensive institutional development of the 171 most underperforming primary schools. Thus, policy documents use a double register, the European goals and vocabulary are documented in strategic documents, while they disappear from the legislation and interventions which regulate and effectively shape daily practice (Ferge 2017b). The concepts of 'equal opportunity', 'inclusion', 'Roma' and 'educational integration' have been erased or omitted from the new legislation and replaced by aims which individualize learning problems and needs such as 'the prevention of lagging behind' and 'the catch-up and compensation of socially disadvantaged children' (Ferge 2017b).

A prime example of the complex and ambiguous relationship between Hungary and the European Union is the adoption of the target to reduce early school leaving.[20] Until 2016, the concept of 'early school leaving' was almost entirely missing from domestic policy-making documents; in professional discourse the term 'dropout' was commonly used instead (Szalai and Kende 2014). Szalai and Kende, contributing to an EU-funded comparative project on ESL, argued that neither the target groups nor the policy solutions have been harmonized between the European and the national level in Hungary (Szalai and Kende 2014).

Experts mostly positioning themselves as critical and sceptical opponents of the current educational administration[21] were convened by the government to produce the ESL strategy of Hungary until 2014. In 2016, a country report for the European Commission noted that the execution of the strategy had not started. Finally, on the basis of the document, the National Action Plan for Young People Leaving Education without Qualification was ratified by the Parliament in 2016. While the government had produced and endorsed the requested strategic documents, the educational administration launched such comprehensive structural changes that fundamentally compromised the goals set in the EU recommendations. The EU Commission warned Hungary that its system-wide education policies are non-compliant with the EU 2020 objectives and that Hungary's education system has become less inclusive and flexible (EC 2015). Decreasing the compulsory schooling age and the restructuring of the vocational sector have resulted an unprecedented increase in ESL, reaching 12 per cent in 2015. Finally, in October 2016, the Ministry of Human Resources announced that 27 billion HUF would be made available for ESL-related projects between 2017 and 2020 in the framework of Hungary's midterm ESL strategy. In 2017, relying on EU funding, teacher-training-focused pilot projects were launched in selected secondary schools.

---

[20] Reducing early school leaving below 10 per cent is one of the headline targets of the EU 2020 strategy.

[21] While some experts abstained from policy-making after 2010, the continuity of expertise is due to the other typical expert standpoint which collaborated in strategic documents in the hope to produce effective instruments which can reach schools even if they are rebranded by the government rhetoric.

Table 1 The chronology of the remaking of the Hungarian educational landscape since 2010

2010	Legislation: reintroduction of grading and grade repetition in lower primary school (modification of the Public Education Act).
2011	Legislation: CXC. Act on National Public Upbringing; CCIV Act on National Higher Education (studentship holders are obliged to work in Hungary for a certain period of time; closer ministerial control over universities); Curricular changes: 2011–13. Introducing the 'dual vocational education' model, lesson time for work-based practice raised by 50 per cent.
2012	Legislation: family benefits are withdrawn from the parents of persistent absentees (modification of the 1998 LXXXIV Act on Family Support 15§) Curricular changes: National Core Curriculum, decreasing the share of academic subject in vocational education (110/2012 Gov. decree); drastic decrease of state-funded places at legal and economic university courses; Representation: 2012–13. Student Network (Haha): student movement against the tertiary education reform.
2013	Legislation: reducing the compulsory schooling age from eighteen to sixteen; new performance-centred Teacher Career Model (326/2013. decree); Institutional changes: primary and secondary schools are operated by the KLIK central maintenance centre; gradual implementation of the Frame Curricula. Employment: scholarship for students participating in teacher education (especially natural sciences); National Teacher Chamber (National Public Upbringing Act 63/A–63/L.§).
2014	Strategic documents: Early School Leaving Midterm Strategy; Public Education Strategy Curricular changes: Religious education integrated into the curriculum; launch of the Bridge-programme for overaged pupils in public education; Institutional changes: Educational Inspectorate.
2015	Strategic documents: Vocational Education Serving Economy Concept Paper; raising the age of participation in full-time vocational studies to twenty-five years; Institutional changes: vocational sector becomes independent from the KLIK centre and the 303 vocational institutions are merged into 44 vocational centres; Curricular changes: obtaining a second qualification becomes free of charge; work-based practice-oriented dual-model courses start in higher education.
2016	Strategic documents: Action Plan: Tackling Leaving School Without Qualifications 2014–20; Gear-change in Tertiary Education: Midterm Policy Strategy; Institutional changes: reorganizing and renaming vocational institutions (2015 LXV Act);

Curricular changes: 3+2 years long vocational schools (+2 years is optional and leads up to the baccalaureate exam) and 4+1 years long vocational secondary school (students following the baccalaureate can obtain an optional technician qualification in one year); New vocational frame curricula and exam system (2015 LXVI Act);

Representation: teacher demonstrations, the establishment of the Civic Public Education Platform.

2017   Legislation: 'Lex CEU' – modification of the Higher Education Act.

Institutional changes: January: the KLIK maintenance centre is reorganized and deconcentrated into fifty-nine independently governed educational districts;

Employment: teacher pay rise.

Representation: Protests against the planned closing of the Central European University.

2018   Representation: student demonstrations.

Conclusion

Developing an argument for 'spatializing the sociology of education', Susan Robertson (2009: 15) urged education researchers to apply a critical spatial lens to trace 'the ways in which space is deeply implicated in power, production and social relations'. The geospatial approach proved to be insightful in analysing the broader ideological context of educational policy-making. On the ideological level, post-2010 education policy-making has been shaped by the ideological framing of the nationalist–populist elite bloc. This neoconservative and étatist framework has created increasing control and dependence in the public sector. The emphasis on 'traditional' knowledge and Christian values, the closely-knit alliance with the church and the shift from the ideal of the autonomous professional to the vision of obedient public servants align these policies to neoconservative education policy trends across the globe. While sustaining a bureaucratically controlling state apparatus, the state has also limited its role in educational provision. However, in contrast to Western European trends of forming public-private partnerships, the end of the era of state education and the emergence of a deeply segmented educational landscape (Ball 2011) have taken shape on the foundations of the alliance between the church and the state. To explain some current processes, the personal histories and ties of powerful actors and the processes of political bargaining in the context of power centralization seem equally important.

We have been particularly interested in the ways in which the country's dependent economic relations and the structural adjustments in the wake of the financial crisis have shaped education policies. The geospatial approach has provided us with an invaluable tool for raising such questions, which, even when we could not respond to them satisfactorily, opened up new perspectives in understanding the current restructuring of Hungarian education. Within a specific local constellation of semi-peripheral positionality, neoconservativism and centralization have become instruments of a state-based programme for national capital development. Similar to the social sector, education reforms have further exacerbated and solidified societal polarization and generated new class ruptures. The secondary vocational sector, and to some extent tertiary education, have been directly subordinated to national and transnational industrial interests. State support has been channelled into church-run schools and thus to the building of the national–populist middle class, while Westernist, urban liberal groups gradually opted out from state education and invested in the private educational sector.

Relations with the European Union are as dual-faceted as the country's economic policy strategy. The government ceased to respond to soft pressures designed to trigger policy convergence in the area of social justice and deflected the European Union's expectations. The educational administration has reluctantly built a Potemkin village of strategic documents and pilot projects to pretend convergence with EU priorities, while the sweeping reform of secondary education has completely extinguished such initiatives. The window of opportunity to develop this dual political and economic strategy has opened wide in the current context of disintegration across the European Union.

References

Ádám, Z. and Bozóki, A. (2016) State and faith: Right-wing populism and nationalized religion in Hungary, *Intersections EEJSP*, 2 (1): 98–122.

Alexiadou, N., and Lange, B. (2013) Deflecting European Union influence on national education policy-making: The case of the United Kingdom, *Journal of European Integration*, 35 (1): 37–52.

Apple, Michael W. (2006) Understanding and Interrupting Neoliberalism and Neoconservatism in Education, *Pedagogies: An International Journal*, 1 (1): 21–6.

Bailey, Patrick L. J. and Ball, Stephen J. (2016) The Coalition Government, the general election and the policy ratchet in education: A reflection on the 'ghosts' of policy past, present and yet to come, in Hugh Bochel and Martin Powell (eds), *The Coalition Government and Social Policy: Restructuring the Welfare State*, 127–51, Bristol: Policy Press.

Bajomi, I., Berényi, E., Neumann, E. and Vida, J. (2009) The reception of PISA in Hungary, Research report. https://www.knowandpol.eu/IMG/pdf/pisa.wp12.hungary.pdf, accessed 21 December 2017.

Bajomi, I. and Csákó, M. (2017) Fórumok és tiltakozómozgalmak a közoktatásban [Forums and Resistance Movements in Public Education], *Educatio*, 26 (4): 528–39.

Ball, Stephen J. (2011) The *reluctant* state and the beginning of the end of state education, *Journal of Educational Administration and History*, 44 (2): 89–103.

Balogh, M. (2015) A hazai közoktatás finanszírozása az ezredfordulót követően [The funding of public education after the millennium], in Zoltán Győri, Mária Simon and Viola Vadász (eds), *Szerep és funkcióváltások a közoktatás világában* [Role and Functional Shifts in Public Education], 93–114, Budapest: Oktatáskutató és Fejlesztő Intézet.

Berács, J., Derényi, A., Kováts, G., Polónyi, I. and Temesi, J. (2015) *Magyar felsőoktatás 2014, Stratégiai helyzetértékelés* [Hungarian higher education 2014. Strategic analysis], Budapest: Budapesti Corvinus Egyetem. Available at: http://unipub.lib.uni-corvinus.hu/1849/1/MF2014_strat.pdf, Retrieved on 12 January 2019.

Berlinger, E. and Megyeri, K. (2015) Mélyszegénységből a felsőoktatásba [The Road from Extreme Poverty to Tertiary Education], *Közgazdasági Szemle*, 62 (6): 674–99.

Bíró-Nagy, A. (2017) Illiberal democracy in Hungary: The social background and practical steps of building an illiberal state, in Pol Morillas (ed.), *Illiberal Democracies in the EU: The Visegrad Group and the Risk of Disintegration*, 31–44, Cidob: Barcelona.

Böröcz, J. (2012) Hungary in the European Union: 'catching up' forever, *Economic and Political Weekly*, 47 (23): 22–5.

Csepregi, E. (2014) *A magántanulóvá nyilvánítással kapcsolatos eljárás szakmai ellenőrzése* [The inspection of the private student declaration procedure], Budapest: Education Office.

Darvas, Á. and Szikra, D. (2017) Családi ellátások és szolgáltatások [Subsidies and Provision for Families], in Zs. Ferge (ed.), *Társadalom és szociálpolitika. Magyarország 1990–2015* [Social policy in Hungary 1990–2015.], 215–54, Budapest: Osiris.

Éber, Márk Á. (2018) A jéghegy csúcsa: Középosztályi tiltakozások a 2010 utáni Magyarországon globális összefüggésben, a Hallgatói Hálózat példáján [The Tip of the Iceberg: Middle Class Protests in Hungary after 2010 in a Global Context, on the Example of the Student Network], in A. Antal (ed.), *Mozgalmi társadalom* [Movement Society], 220–42, Budapest: Noran Libro.

Erőss, G. (2017) Ki tud többet az iskoláról? [Who knows more about the school?], *Új Pedagógiai Szemle*, 67 (1–2): 95–107.

European Commission (2015) *Country Report Hungary 2015. Including an In-Depth Review on the Prevention and Correction of Macroeconomic Imbalances.* http://ec.europa.eu/economy_finance/publications/occasional_paper/2015/pdf/ocp220_en.pdf, accessed 21 December 2017.

Feledy, B. (2017) Feltárhatatlan fekete doboz? Egy hiperpragmatikus külpolitika kockázatai [Unlockable black box? The risks of a hyperpragmatic foreign policy], in A. Jakab and L. Urbán (ed.), *Hegymenet. Társadalmi és Politikai Kihívások Magyarországon*. [Uphill. Social and Political Challenges in Hungary], 111–29, Budapest: Osiris.

Ferge, Zs. (2017a) A magyar szociálpolitika 25 éve madártávlatból - némi történelmi előzményekkel [25 years of Hungarian social policy from a bird's eye view - complemented with some historical antecedents], in Zs. Ferge (ed.), *Társadalom és szociálpolitika. Magyarország 1990–2015* [Social policy in Hungary 1990–2015], 91–124, Budapest: Osiris.

Ferge, Zs. (2017b) Iskola és esélyek [Educational chances], in Zs. Ferge (ed.), *Társadalom és szociálpolitika. Magyarország 1990–2015* [Social policy in Hungary 1990–2015], 188–214, Budapest: Osiris.

Gagyi, Á. (2016) 'Coloniality of power' in East Central Europe: External penetration as internal force in post-socialist Hungarian politics, *Journal of World-Systems Research*, 22 (2): 349–72.

Gagyi, Á., Gerőcs, T., Szabó, L. and Szarvas, M. (2016) Beyond moral interpretations of the EU 'migration crisis': Hungary and the global economic division of labour. http://www.criticatac.ro/lefteast/beyond-moral-interpretations-of-hu-eu-migration-crisis, accessed 21 December 2017.

Gerőcs, T. and Pinkasz, A. (2018) Debt-Ridden Development on Europe's Eastern Periphery, in Manuela Boatcă, Andrea Komlosy and Hans-Heinrich Nolte (eds), *Global Inequalities in World-Systems Perspective: Theoretical Debates and Methodological Innovations,* 131–53. New York: Routledge Publishing.

Györgyi, Z. (2015) Iskolafenntartás helyi szinten – előzmények és tapasztalatok [School maintainance at the local level – Antecedents and lessons], in Zoltán Győri, Mária Simon and Viola Vadász (eds), *Szerep és funkcióváltások a közoktatás világában*, [Role and Function Shifts in Public Education], 18–44, Budapest: Oktatáskutató és Fejlesztő Intézet.

Gyurgyák, J. (2017) Uralja-e a jövőt, aki a múltat uralja? [Does someone who rule the past rule the future too?], in A. Jakab and L. Urbán (eds), *Hegymenet. Társadalmi és Politikai Kihívások Magyarországon* [Uphill. Social and Political Challenges in Hungary], 51–73, Budapest: Osiris.

G. Tóth, I. (2016) Rögtön a születésnap után eltünedeznek a kölykök, *HVG*, 9 January 2016.

Hagymási, T. and Könyvesi, T. (2017) *Statistical Yearbook of Public Education 2015/2016*, Budapest: The Ministry of Human Capacities.

Horn, D., Hajdú, T., Hermann, Z., Kertesi, G., Kézdi, G., Köllő, J. and Varga, J. (2015) Az érettségi védelmében [In defense of the maturity exam], *Budapest Working Paper Series* 2015/1. http://www.econ.core.hu/file/download/bwp/bwp1501.pdf, accessed 21 December 2017.

Kovai, M. and Neumann, E. (2015) Hová lett az egyenlősítő közoktatás? [Where has comprehensive education policy gone?], *Educatio*, 24 (4): 65–78.

Mellár, T. (2017) Nincsenek bombabiztos receptek, Gazdaságpolitikai alternatívák a modernizációra [There aren't bulletproof solutions – Economic policy alternatives for modernisation], in A. Jakab and L. Urbán (eds), *Hegymenet. Társadalmi és Politikai Kihívások Magyarországon* [Uphill. Social and Political Challenges in Hungary], 251–64, Budapest: Osiris.

Minister of Human Resources (2014) Speech of Zoltán Balog, 4 October 2014. Available at: http://www.balogzoltan.hu/balog-zoltan-az-oktatas-nem-szolgaltatas-hanem-szolgalat/, Retrieved on 12 January 2019.

Nyírő, Z. (2017) *Külföldi Továbbtanulás a Legjobb Hazai Gimnáziumok Körében – 2017* [Student Mobility from the Best High Schools in Hungary to Foreign Universities – 2017]. http://gvi.hu/research_details/514/student_mobility_from_the_best_high_schools_in_hungary_to_foreign_universities_2017

Organisation for Economic Co-operation and Development (OECD) (2012) *Economic Surveys: Hungary 2012*, Paris: OECD.

Organisation for Economic Co-operation and Development (OECD) (2015) *Education at a Glance 2015*, OECD Indicators, OECD Publishing.

Organisation for Economic Co-operation and Development (OECD) (2016) *Education at a Glance 2016*, OECD Indicators, OECD Publishing.

Robertson, Susan L. (2009) Spatialising' the sociology of education: Stand-points, entry-points, vantage-points, in S. Ball, M. Apple and L. Gandin (eds), *Handbook of Sociology of Education*, 15–26, London and New York: Routledge.

Silova, I. and Eklof, B. (2013) Education in Eastern and Central Europe: Re-thinking post-socialism in the context of globalization, in R. F. Arnove and C. A. Torres (eds), *Comparative Education: The Dialectic between the Global and the Local*, 4th edn, 379–402, New York: Rowman and Littlefield Publishers.

Szalai, J. and Kende, Á. (2014) *Early School Leaving in the Context of Policy-making in Hungary*. CEU Working Paper. http://www.cps.ceu.hu/sites/default/files/publications/cps-working-paper-resleu-wp2-esl-in-context-of-hu-policy-making-2014.pdf, accessed 21 December 2017.

Szikra, D. (2014) Democracy and welfare in hard times: The social policy of the Orbán Government in Hungary between 2010 and 2014, *Journal of European Social Policy*, 24 (5): 486–500.

Szikra, D. (2018) Távolodás az Európai Szociális Modelltől – A szegénység társadalompolitikája. [Drifting moving away from the European Social Model. The social policy of poverty], *Magyar Tudomány*, 179 (6): 858–71.

7

Greece: Towards 'Europeanization'?

Anna Traianou

Like many other European countries, Greece has a long tradition of 'borrowing' institutional structures, curricular policies and pedagogical ideologies. However, recent globalizing trends have increased the pressure on Greek governments to reform the education system in the light of what is going on in other countries. With the full entry of Greece into the European Union (in 1981), along with a gradual shift on the part of successive governments in the direction of neoliberalism, 'modernization' or 'Europeanization' has been linked with ideas about the marketization of education and efforts to make the Greek education system more 'effective' by introducing structures and forms of accountability similar to those that operate within business organizations. At the same time, the distinctive features of the Greek education system, stemming from its socio-historical and cultural context, have continued to play a crucial role, not least in shaping the ways in which it has responded to pressures for modernization.

In this chapter I will begin by discussing some of these features, especially those relating to the nature of the Greek economic and political system and the role of education within it. I will examine the major changes that have taken place in the system since the 1960s in order to set the context for analysing the post-2008 education reforms. I am particularly interested in examining education reform after the 2015 general election, which resulted in the formation of a new government made up of a coalition of the radical left party SYRIZA and the right-wing party ANEL ('Independent Greeks'). My aim is to highlight some of the tensions and controversies generated within the system as the integrative vision of the European education space, expressed through EU policies and the OECD, interacted with local contexts and diverse interests.

Socio-historical and cultural features of the Greek education system

Since the establishment of the modern Greek state in the 1830s, education and political 'clientelism' have been the core mechanisms through which the state has been able to legitimize its power, and structure society more generally (see Mavrogordatos 1997; Bratsis 2010). For a large part of the twentieth century, clientelism, the use of state power to provide special favours in return for political support, helped to strengthen party loyalties and the power of the party in government. Since capitalism in Greece developed initially with a low level of industrialization (and thus fewer opportunities for managers and entrepreneurs) though with a strong merchant/transport and shipping sector, in a very different fashion from most of the rest of Europe, the political party in power served as the main mechanism for the accumulation and distribution of wealth by offering well-paid jobs in the public sector (see Mouzelis 1978). Greek society thus operated on the basis of state patronage, with a bureaucracy that paid its officials well. It has been pointed out, for example, that the combined salary of its government officials in the 1880s was greater than the yearly profits of the largest capitalist enterprise in Greece at that time (Tsoukalas 1981). At the same time, recruitment to public sector posts was on the basis of academic qualifications, and this gave the education system central importance.

After the Second World War, Greek industry kept pace with its Balkan neighbours' fast industrial growth by means of direct investment from foreign capital. This created a manufacturing sector that operated largely independently of the rest of the Greek economy, which retained its traditional – agricultural and artisanal – character, rather than undergoing development of the kind typical of the core Western economies from which the investment had come (see Mouzelis 1978). At the same time, the growth of the construction and manufacturing sectors, the influx of peasants into the large cities and the erosion of local economies after the end of the Civil War (1946–9) led to calls for a more skilled and diversified labour force. Discussions around the country's application (8 June 1959) for association with the European Common Market (ECM) suggested that a radical restructuring of the Greek economy and of its education system was a requirement for the full entry of Greece into the Community (in 1981). Subsequently, under increased pressure from the ECM and the World Bank, the 'modernization' of the education system became a government priority and was interpreted as implying the need to promote tertiary (especially vocational) education and to lengthen the period of compulsory education.

Until the early 1960s only primary education was compulsory: there was selection at the end of primary school, and fees were charged for attendance at state secondary schools and higher education institutions. According to the 1961 census only 1.5 per cent of the population had a university degree and 7.5 per cent had a secondary school qualification. Illiteracy was at 37.5 per cent and attrition during secondary education remained around 50 per cent (see Frangoudaki 2015). Thus it cannot be said that in this period Greece had a functioning system of mass education. 'Free education for all' at all levels became one of the achievements of the student movement in the short-lived liberal government's 1964 Education Act. Framed by the principle of 'equality of opportunity' the Act also abolished the entrance examination from primary to secondary education, updated the school curricula, introduced pre-school education and teacher training courses, divided secondary education into technical and academic streams of supposedly equal status, made *Demotike*[1] the official language of teaching and increased the years of compulsory education to nine – reduced to six again during the military dictatorship (1967–74). The 1964 reform was passed by Parliament but never implemented.

In the 1960s the number of University students started to rise but this expansion was not accompanied by an increase in funding and it generated much discontent in the student population. In 1969, the Junta created a network of higher technical schools for medium-level and supervisory technical personnel, claiming that it would enable Greece to keep pace with the educational systems of the more advanced capitalist countries in Europe (Bouzakis 1986). Vocational schools attracted students mostly from low socio-economic classes, and they were considered of a lower status compared to universities; there was high unemployment among their graduates. In the early 1970s student protests demanding better education provision turned into mass actions against the oppressive character of the regime. The student uprising in November 1973 at the Athens Polytechnic for 'bread, education, liberty' was instrumental in the destabilization of the dictatorship.

---

[1] Until 1976 education reforms primarily revolved around the form of the Greek language that should be taught in schools ('the language question'). This issue arose from the existence of two distinct written forms of modern Greek: *Kathareousa*, the 'purified' language, and *Demotike*, the 'common' language. The former was developed by some influential scholars and the Church, and was designed to 'purify' the Greek language of its non-Hellenic features, which had been acquired over the centuries. It is often argued that *Kathareousa* prevented pupils from lower socio-economic classes from continuing their studies into secondary and higher education.

At the time of the fall of the Junta in 1974 compulsory education was limited to six years; there were financial barriers to accessing secondary education, an inadequate technical education and a growing but underfunded university sector. Illiteracy (at over fourteen years of age) was at 22.2 per cent and the high attrition rate from secondary education resulted in around 60 per cent of the population entering the labour market with only primary education qualifications (Frangoudaki 2015). Lacking legitimacy in a Weberian sense, the post-war state exercised political and ideological control of the younger generation through appointing loyalists to key posts in the education system (school inspectorate and university professors). The cleansing of all public administration from those who had served the dictatorship became an imperative.

Education in Metapolitefsi

The November 1973 student uprising produced a powerful generation of political activists which opposed traditional patterns of authority and institutional structures, focusing instead on new political issues and on the youth population as a 'social accelerator' (Kassimeris 2005: 750). In the first years of the transition to multiparty democracy, known to the Greeks as *Metapolitefsi*, the university, whose function was guided since its establishment by Humboldtian principles, came to be regarded as site for the exchange of progressive ideas about education and society and for political action. Indeed, it was home to significant levels of Leftist radicalism post-1974 (Sotiris 2013).

Some of this activity resulted in the Article 16 of the 1976 Greek Constitution which protects academic freedom and makes free education provision a responsibility of the state. It also influenced the 1976 education reform which attempted to re-establish the main elements of the 1964 reform. The Act reintroduced pre-school education, a nine-year compulsory education, abolished the entrance examination from primary to secondary school and made *Dimoteke* the official language of teaching. Despite efforts to promote technical–vocational education most secondary school students continued to opt for the University route. In post-1974 Greece, university qualifications became the main mechanism for social mobility. Students from working-class backgrounds were increasingly able to find a permanent post in the public sector or a relatively secure job in the still small private sector, if they possessed a university degree (Tsakoglou and Cholezas 2005). It is not surprising, therefore, that the university became a core institution for the satisfaction of 'social expectations' and the backbone of Greek society. Yet, with the exception of universities, the social foundations of the old order (e.g. the State bureaucracy and the police) remained largely unchallenged under the centre-right New Democracy (ND) party in the 1970s. For many Greeks this produced a growing disillusionment with democracy.

Along with Article 16 came a centrally controlled school system aimed at ensuring equality of opportunity in education. This has been important for maintaining the legitimacy of the post-1974 State. Right up to the present day, the formulation and implementation of legislation, the administration of financial support to all sectors of school education, the approval of primary and secondary school curricula and textbooks, the appointment of teaching staff and the coordination and evaluation of regional educational services have all been controlled by the Ministry of Education. There are state-prescribed textbooks for each school subject appropriate to each year group, which are distributed free to all pupils. Although there have been a few calls to abandon the one-textbook rule, since it is regarded by some as restricting teachers' autonomy to adapt their teaching to the individual needs of the children in their schools, this policy is considered by others to be one of the most positive features of the Greek education system because it enables all pupils who attend school to have 'equal' access to the same learning materials (Traianou 2013). Here, 'equality' is interpreted in terms of equal input (common schools, common curriculum, etc.); 'an equality achieved by educational rather than social measures' (Persianis 1978: 55).[2]

In the school curriculum there has been a strong bias towards the humanities with religion continuing to influence structure and content. This bias is not unrelated to the perceived need at the time of the establishment of the modern Greek state to build and maintain a national identity by drawing on the ancient 'glorious past' and on the Orthodox Church, which played a key role in maintaining the Greek language during the years of the Ottoman occupation. There is an important sense, then, in which the majority of schools in Greece are faith schools, with only one faith being represented: that of the Orthodox Church (Traianou 2009).[3] It is also necessary to emphasize that the project of

---

[2] To understand this persistence with 'equality', it is important to discuss the role of private education in post-1974 processes of social reproduction of upper- and middle-class groups. Around 6 per cent of the student population attends these schools, most of which are concentrated in Athens and Thessaloniki and they are differentiated according to the socio-economic background of their students. There are 'elite' private schools with a long history and tradition known for their strategic inculcation of an international culture in their students and for 'bypassing' the Greek examination system through the adoption of the International Baccalaureate. Their students usually study abroad and accessing the 'field of power' in Greece by taking up prestigious posts in the Greek and global labour market (Valasi 2014).

[3] A small number of state Muslim schools exist for the minority population of Northern Thrace.

developing a national identity was initially aimed at differentiating Greeks from both their Balkan and their Turkish neighbours, and this aspect of cultural politics continues to be significant.

Assenting to the European Economic Community

Soon after the fall of the dictatorship in 1974 the procedures for the full integration of Greece into the European Economic Community (which had initially got under way in 1959) were accelerated. For much of the Greek population, the cooperative spirit of 'Europe' symbolized an end to poverty, unemployment, emigration and precariousness. It also promised political stability and democracy. It meant being part of the 'West' in a different way from that of the US-imposed post-civil war regime. Joining the Euro seemed to be the logical end of this process.

The Greek Left was extremely sceptical about the EEC project. From the left's perspective, it was impossible for Greece to create an infrastructure which would enable the country to follow the Western trajectory of capitalist development. At that time, Andreas Papandreou's socialist party advocated a developmental path outside the EEC and NATO. Greece, Papandreou said in 1979, would become a 'provincial backwater' if it did not cut ties to both these organizations (Papandreou 1979). The Greek Communist Party also opposed the European integration project on the grounds that the transfer of powers to supranational institutions would limit the country's national sovereignty, whereas the Communist Party of Interior (similar to the Italian CP) opted for a pro-European strategy of democratic socialism within the Common Market.

To understand Greece's attitude to the EEC it is also important to note the dominant role of the Greek centralized state in the country's socio-economic life. At the time of Greece's entry into the EEC the state was regarded as the largest investor and employer. It had nationalized businesses (e.g. Olympic Airways) and banks (e.g. Commercial Bank), set up its own enterprises and controlled the banking system through extensive regulation. This expansion, was based on patron-client relationships. As Featherstone and Kazamias (2001:76) point out, 'The huge economic state interventions driven by clientelistic political motives gave rise to a paternalistic, regulatory model clearly at odds with the economic logic of the EU.' Because of this peculiar state-society situation the 'Europeanization' process seems to have had 'more consequences in Greece than elsewhere' (79).

Greece joined the EEC officially in January 1981, and a few months later Papandreou's Panhellenic Socialist Movement (PASOK) came to power.[4] PASOK gradually accepted EEC membership, though later this turned into a sharp tension between a commitment to an expansion of state provision and a commitment to a European economic order which was moving towards neoliberalization.

Under the pressure of the class struggles of the previous decades, PASOK increased the salaries of public sector employees, social welfare benefits and pensions. But the main element of radicalism in PASOK's political agenda had to do with institutional democracy. It introduced progressive institutional changes in education, in health care and in industry and its policies provided the necessary legal support. Greece was thus moving in a social democratic direction in the 1980s when many other European countries were making a neoliberal turn at least in their economic policies.

Socialist transformations and education

Influenced by the recent struggles of the student movement, early PASOK's policies for education aimed at democratizing the education system and increasing the number of students in compulsory and post-compulsory tertiary education. The latter was also a precondition for Greece participating in the process of European economic unification (Prokou 2003). In terms of democracy, PASOK institutionalized the participation of parents and representatives of the local community in the so-called local committees, whose main aim was to facilitate the operation of the school and to improve the communication between schools and local authorities. PASOK's policies gradually led to the abolition of selection at 16+ and of the school inspectorate. In relation to tertiary education, PASOK established new university departments and new technological institutions throughout Greece. Although its policies were successful in increasing the number of students studying at secondary level and in vocational schools, most secondary students continued to opt for the university route; there was a dramatic increase in the number of students studying at university from 26.7 per cent in 1993 to 58 per cent in 2005 (GMNERA 2005).

---

[4] Greece ratified the European Social Charter on 6 June 1984 and the Additional Protocol to the European Social Charter on 18 June 1998. It ratified the Revised Social Charter on 18 March 2016, accepting ninety-six of the ninety-eight paragraphs.

In higher education, PASOK introduced stronger forms of institutional democracy which included an extensive participation of students and members of academic staff in the administration of universities (Parliamentary Act No 1268/1982 amended thereafter). Rectors, Vice-Rectors and Heads of Department were appointed by an electoral body in which the votes of the student representatives from the youth sections of the political parties were given almost equal weighting to those of academic staff (40 per cent, see Gouvias 2012). The wide participation of students also shaped decisions made by the general assemblies of individual departments and the Senate, which controlled, among other things, the content and structure of studies. University space was protected from intervention by the police through the right of university asylum. However, financial autonomy was limited, the reverse of what neoliberal marketization would require. Budget allocation remained the responsibility of the state (under the control of the Ministries of Education and of National Economy) with the spending of each department being controlled by an independent auditory mechanism, subordinated to the Ministry of Justice. Initiatives to attract funding from private sources were infrequent, partly because of state control over funding but also because such initiatives were considered a threat to its Humboldtian principles (Zmas 2015). The tensions between these principles and the assumed role of the state in safeguarding them, and the Europeanization agenda, reached breaking point in the late 1990s.

PASOK's policies did not change significantly what Mouzelis (1978) refers to as the 'Greek capitalist mode of development'. The Greek economy continued to be based on locally produced low-cost products, and imports (especially in the areas of technology and car manufacturing). Small Medium Enterprises run as family businesses, not particularly orientated to knowledge-intensive activities. Almost 75 per cent of those who graduated in the 1980s were employed in the public sector in the 1990s (OECD 1997). As a result of these policies, the public debt rose from 22.9 per cent of the GPD in 1980 to 57.8 per cent in 1985 – though taxation of private capital was not increased and tax evasion was, in effect, permitted to continue. The low increase in productivity in comparison to wages during the 1980s forced the PASOK governments to change direction. In 1985, Greece sought the assistance of the European Union in order to deal with its growing debt. The EUs stability programme required the Greek government to initiate an austerity programme aimed at reducing public sector spending, beginning in effect the dismantling of the short-lived welfare state (Tsoukalas 1986). Although this programme was abandoned in 1987 under mounting social pressure the increase in public employment waned in the 1990s and unemployment rates started to rise up to 11.3 per cent (ELIAMER 2006: 13–15), especially among university graduates, including graduates from teacher education courses. Austerity continued under the centre-right Nea Democratia (ND), which won the 1989 general elections and remained in power until 1993. The public debt rose to 79.6 per cent in the 1990s. In the name of avoiding a fiscal crisis, state expenditure on education as a proportion of the GNP remained at low levels, between 3.5 per cent and 4 per cent, one of the lowest in OECD countries (OECD 2002).

Throughout the 1980s and 1990s, 'clientelism' continued to operate in multifaceted ways, creating new networks between the state and selected corporate interests, or maintaining existing ones (Lyrintzis, Nikolakopoulos and Sotiropoulos 1996): decisions to establish new higher education institutions, for instance, were often made in order to serve local interests. In addition, the number of places in higher education offered was used by both PASOK and ND as a means to attract voters (Pshacharopoulos 2003). Within this kind of state-society transaction, 'familialism' – family and individual networks – maintained their role as 'guarantors of trust and solidarity' (see Zambeta and Kolofousi 2014: 6).

Moreover, new problems emerged as a result of large-scale immigration, primarily from countries of the former socialist Eastern Europe. These new problems exacerbated perennial concerns with maintaining Greek national ideologies, with preserving the strong presence of the Greek Orthodox Church in political and social life and with the management of relations with neighbouring countries. Political conflict with Turkey continued over the occupation of Nothern Cyprus, and, following the break-up of Yugoslavia, there developed a dispute over the constitutional name of FYROM (Former Yugoslavian Republic of Macedonia) in which matters of territory and identity were again in question (see Kouvelakis 2018).

Neoliberal aspirations: Universities and schools

From 1996 onwards both PASOK and ND governments endorsed further the European integration project. It was among the member states which supported the idea of a European Constitution and the European Union's efforts towards a greater degree of economic and social convergence. At the same time, as with France, Spain and Portugal, the notion of transformative change was dropped. After the 1996 elections PASOK's policies were aimed at reducing the national debt, and inflation, in order to bring the country in line with the necessary convergence criteria so as to enable it to join, in 2001, the Economic and Monetary Union. This led to a considerable reduction in state economic activities and a transformation of the tightly state controlled regulatory pattern of the Greek economy into one closer to the European Union's regulatory regime. PASOK's policies included measures for financial deregulation, lowering labour costs and sell-offs which boosted the Athens stock market to unprecedentedly high levels, thereby 'creating a new financialised elite' (Kouvelakis 2011: 21). The need to 'accelerate modernization and the rate of economic growth' (PASOK 2000: 3) persuaded much of the Greek population that a better political, as well as economic and social, future was in the offing, giving PASOK the mandate to promote it further (in the 2000 general elections).

Likewise, in education, PASOK's policy constituted a break with the policies of the post-1974 period. Its discourse shifted from a commitment to 'equality of opportunity' towards an emphasis on an education of 'high standards' adjusted to the needs of the market. Drawing on human capital theory as expressed in EU documentation (European Commission 1993), knowledge was presented as the key to economic growth and to fighting social inequalities: 'The investment in knowledge is the decisive factor for combating unemployment, the confrontation of economic competition, the strengthening of social cohesion and fighting social exclusion' (PASOK 2000: 74).

In the compulsory education sector PASOK's Europeanization agenda were reflected in the 1997 Education Act (modified in 2001). The Act instituted a new type of academically orientated upper-secondary school and a new technical–vocational school which was classified as post-compulsory. Compulsory school education became more intensive both in terms of the amount of subject knowledge to be covered but also in the number of subjects taken in the school-leaving examinations for entry to university (Koustourakis 2007). By contrast, the school-leaving exams for entry to vocational institutions were easier. The number of students studying at vocational schools rose to just below 20 per cent but this rise was the result of necessity not of choice – around 90 per cent of students would still opt for the university route. The patterns of separation (academic/vocational institutions of different prestige and status) established in the 1960s were being continued. Moreover, without a vibrant labour market and with only weak links with existing firms there were few opportunities for graduate employment. At the same time by strengthening even further central control over what was to be taught and how, the government deepened the separation of high-achieving students from average- or low-achieving ones, channelling the latter into vocational education and producing in this way an even more hierarchized labour force.

The 1997 Act (and the subsequent 2002 Education Act) also presented teacher and school evaluation as an important element of administrative practice. Whereas in the 1980s, school advisers operated in an advisory role, with the 2002 Act they became responsible for working collaboratively with the head teacher and the regional administrative director to detect weak practice and ensure that it was improved. While these moves were postponed under pressure from teachers and teachers' trade unions (drawing on the legacy of the school inspectorate), the idea was not abandoned. Both Acts were significant because they introduced the concepts of evaluation and accountability onto the educational agenda 'creating conditions for negotiations over its meaning and scope' (Tsatsaroni, Sifakakis and Sarakinioti 2015: 514). They presaged a further shift in the definition of teachers' professional identities: making them accountable for their outcomes of their work according to extrinsic values – competencies and standards.

Teachers' working conditions

Until 1997, university graduates who wished to become school teachers were appointed automatically through a directory of seniority, a system which appeared impermeable to clientelism. As in Italy, this system led to an over-production of teachers who would often join a waiting list which could last up to fourteen years. This changed with the 1997 Education Act, which introduced a points system for the hiring of school teachers, so that the system became competitive: appointment depended (and still depends) on the number of qualifications a teacher possesses (e.g. postgraduate qualifications, knowledge of foreign languages, knowledge of information and communication technologies (ICT)) and the results obtained in national examinations concerned with subject knowledge, pedagogy and lesson planning. This change in the appointment process seems to signal the beginning of an era where 'lifelong training' and 'precarity' would be legitimized through an ideology of meritocracy based on performance in public examinations. The introduction of the new system reduced the relative value of the simple possession of a degree in favour of an individualized record of performance.

Many of the unemployed teachers found jobs in the private tuition sector (*parapaideia*) as private tutors or as teachers in private preparatory schools (*frontistiria*) for those students who planned to take the national higher education entrance examination. This private support sector constitutes an extensive and powerful education network. Over 90 per cent of students from state and private schools including high achievers and low achievers seem to receive extra tuition (OECD 2018). The need for this is associated with the competitive nature of the examination system, and distrust in the capacity of formal schooling to adequately prepare students for university entrance examinations. Over the years the private tuition sector has expanded its services to include private lessons in foreign languages, art education, extra-curricular activities and so on. The financial burden on families is one of the highest in Europe. Many of the prestigious preparatory schools charge fees unaffordable for students from low socio-economic backgrounds contributing in this way to the deepening of education inequalities (see Sianou-Kyrgiou 2008). 'Elite' departments (such as Medicine, Law, Engineering, Architecture) and 'elite' universities (e.g. University of Athens and the University of Thessaloniki) continue to attract students from middle socio-economic backgrounds (see Maloutas 2016). How to tackle a system which enables the success of socially advantaged students has been a perennial topic of negotiations between parents' associations, teachers' unions and Ministers of Education, with the former asking for an increase in spending on education – so that more teachers are employed in order to offer within schools the necessary support to students – and for a reform of the examination system.

Changes in tertiary education

When ND came to power in 2004, it attempted to push the neoliberal agenda further by focusing particularly on the privatization/marketization of tertiary education and on promoting accountability at all educational levels. European Union policies especially support for the Bologna process (1999), the Lisbon strategy (2000) have played a crucial role in this project. As Alexiadou and Jones discuss in Chapter 2, EU policies began to be disseminated to member states through the Open Method of Coordination and they gradually infiltrated the Greek higher education system with a discourse of 'evaluation', 'accountability', 'quality', 'efficiency' and 'transparency' (see Zmas 2015).

When EU Cohesion Policy Funds for growth, jobs and innovation became available on Greek state schools and universities, the Greek government attempted to link the management and operation of vocational schools and higher technological institutions with the market, and to establish new university departments in areas such as finance, business and technology ('Operational Programme for Education and Initial Vocational Training', 2000–06). The private sector also began to get involved in the construction and maintenance of school buildings and in teachers' training.

Of political importance in this context has been the campaign since the 1990s for the amendment of the Article 16 of the Greek constitution, to make way for the introduction of tuition fees in higher education institutions and for the establishment of private universities. A few research-intensive technological universities which had been successful in making links with industry, using European research funding, began to call openly for a more entrepreneurial university, responsive to the needs of the market (Milios 1994). Up until now this campaign has not been successful. Over the years there has been a tremendous resistance from the Left – including teacher trade unions, University Rectors and the student movement – to the perceived privatization of higher education. Students blocked reform attempts in 1991, 1992, 1995, 1998 and 2002 (*Times Higher Education Supplement* 2006).

However, drawing on European Union legislation on labour mobility and qualification recognition (see directive 2005/36/EC on the recognition of professional qualifications) the 2005 Parliamentary Act allows recognition of degrees by private institutions which act as franchises of foreign universities, the argument being that graduates from such colleges should have the same job opportunities as those available to candidates from Greek public universities. This aims to introduce competition between state and private higher education institutions along neoliberal lines – a project which continued to be resisted.

A second wave of protests started at the beginning of the new academic year in 2006. It was accompanied by a series of school building occupations by secondary school students, and coincided with strikes of primary and secondary school teachers over pay. Fearing that a wider social movement was developing against the government, the parliamentary debate on HE reform was rescheduled initially from November 2006 to January 2007. It finally came to Parliament in 2011; the deal highlights the difficulty of reform.

The right to 'free education for all', one of the most important positive features of the Greek education system, has been a crucial mechanism for maintaining the legitimacy of the post-1974 state. Partly because of this, both PASOK and ND governments were very reluctant to push forward too far their privatization agenda, fearing that any challenge to the electorate's belief in their children's entitlement to free education could jeopardize re-election. The pressures to delay were compounded by frequent changes of Ministers of Education even within the same government and a tendency for each new minister to amend the work of their predecessors, partly as a response to pressures from protesters but also because education goals are often dictated by loyalty networks. As Minister of Education George Papandreou said, 'One of the major obstacles to the success of educational reform in Greece has been the discontinuity brought about because of political changes, including changes of Ministers of Education even within the same government' (Papandreou 1997). As a result, the implementation of laws is, generally speaking, a very slow process.

But in the 2000–8 period demands to reform educational provision were mounting. Critics pointed to a number of well-established problems, such as under-resourced schools; an over-burdened curriculum; a secondary school system which functioned primarily as a preparatory level for higher education; the continuation of the key role of over-crowded private schools and private preparatory schools that and the high level of unemployment among higher education graduates. New types of political and ideological conflicts emerged between those who regarded the European Union as the major driver for change and those who resisted the adaptation of Greece's political and socio-economic life to the rationality and requirements of European integration. For Featherstone and Kazamias (2001: 79) these conflicts cut 'cross political parties'. Alongside these critiques and ideological conflicts came a new intensity of protest. The secondary school students' resistance in 2006–7 was also an expression of their accumulated discontent with the intensification of studies and the experience of precarious and devalued labour. As Greece was entering recession in 2008 and youth unemployment levels were rising (24.3 per cent in September 2008), the killing by the police of a fifteen-year-old student, Alexis Grigoropoulos, on 6 December 2008, prompted a new wave of social unrest (Karamichas 2009).

The crisis years 2008–present

Up until 2008, Greece – like Spain, Italy, Portugal and Ireland – was regarded as a Eurozone 'success story'; its shipping industry was booming and its banks had expanded their businesses into Romania and Bulgaria. Growth rates remained high during the Euro bubble years, mainly through credit provided by French and

German banks, which fuelled a lending boom to Greek consumers. As Greece entered recession in 2008, the public debt rose to 127 per cent of the GDP, drawing on both domestic and above all foreign loans, the latter comprising two-thirds of the total (Eurostat 2010). This level of debt was soon seen as unsustainable though many commentators argued that at that stage a structured default would have been a manageable procedure (Landon 2011; Kouvelakis 2011). Instead in 2010, George Papandreou's government decided to roll over the debt by signing the first bailout agreement with the European Union, the International Monetary Fund and the European Central Bank known as the 'troika'.

The bailout agreements insisted – through the mechanism of the 'memoranda of understanding on financial assistance to the Hellenic Republic' – on structural reforms, especially of the labour market, the argument being that a reduction of social provision and more flexible employment conditions would result in lower wages, enabling Greece (and other peripheral countries such as Ireland and Portugal) to become competitive within European and global markets. As a result of the reforms, Greece entered an extended period of economic stagnation. Between 2009, when the crisis erupted, and 2014, the net worth of Greek households fell by 40 per cent, with the unemployment rate going up to 27.9 per cent in 2013, and youth unemployment reaching 60 per cent in March 2013 (Eurostat 2018).

The Greek crisis was framed as a crisis of the European periphery, a consequence of excessive public debt and spending. In this way, it sustained neoliberal discourses and legitimated the imposition of austerity policies across Europe. It diverted attention from the crucial role of financial liberalization in bringing about the crisis in the first place, from the culpability of the private banking system, and of course from the central role that European monetary integration has played in the affair (see, for example, Guilen 2012; Streeck, 2016; Coakley 2016). The representation of the European banking crisis as a Greek sovereign debt crisis enabled the ECB and the core states to re-finance their major banks very quickly. Various studies of the beneficiaries of the rescue programmes to Greece all arrive at the same conclusion: over 95 per cent of the money found its way back to the original creditors and very little remained in Greece (see Rocholl and Stahmer 2016). As Traianou and Jones discuss in Chapter 1 the arguments which supported austerity policies were presented in 'moral' terms: Greece had sinned by overspending and it should therefore be punished by paying back what it owed. As Angela Merkel told a group of Christian Democratic Union-supporting business leaders: 'The question of whether Greece carries out its programme is not just a question of whether the programme succeeds or not, but rather of whether obligations will be observed in Europe in future' (KeeptalkingGreece 2012).

The anger and despair of the Greek population, not only at the austerity measures but also at the political system as a whole, was expressed through general strikes, mass rallies and street clashes. The forms of political representation and political loyalties shaped in the post-Junta period came under severe question. The 2010 parliamentary debate on the first Memorandum prompted a wave of strikes and mobilizations starting on 5 May 2010, reaching its peak in May 2011 with the occupation of Syntagma Square (the 'movement of the squares'). In June 2011, as the Parliament was about to vote through another set of austerity measures, a massive demonstration of 300,000 people in the centre of Athens was fiercely repressed by the police. The Greek radical left, including the coalition party SYRIZA, had a significant presence in these mobilizations, strengthening as a result its position in the electoral landscape.

The political crisis reached its peak in the election results of 2012, when the mainstream parties struggled to form a PASOK-ND coalition government and the extreme-right Golden Dawn party emerged as a political force. A second 'Memorandum of Understanding' had been signed earlier that year, on 1 March 2012, and the general consensus was that it was only a matter of time before SYRIZA took office. As Sotiris (2015) points out, 'The Greek crisis opened a historical rift that traversed Greek society and created the conditions for a new bloc.' Indeed, a new educational formation, a new set of directive forces was created after 2010 but, as I discuss in the next sections, not the kind of bloc which Sotiris anticipated.

Education in the crisis

As we have seen, the Europeanization process has been taking shape for some time now, albeit implemented only in part. However, in conditions of state decomposition/recomposition the neoliberal aspirations of the post-1996 governments were close to being actualized. For the European Union, the crisis created the right environment for an acceleration of the enforcement of its education agenda. The release of each financial instalment to the Hellenic Republic was subject to a satisfactory review by the European Union of the progress of the implementation of the adjustment programme. The Troika employed the OECD as its 'independent evaluator' of the success of its programme in relation to education. The 2011 OECD report for Greece (OECD 2011) has undoubtedly played a crucial role in shaping the direction of post-2008 Greek education policy. The report insisted that Greece must take action 'in order to address the unsustainable cost-structure of the system and the inefficiencies that are inherent in an outdated, ineffective centralized education structure' (OECD 2011: 4). Its immediate policy recommendations for the compulsory education sector fell into four strands: (a) 'development and use of human resources' by, for example, increasing teachers' workload and 'lay-offs of supply teachers'; (b) 'the rationalization of the school network' (e.g. by the merging of schools and classes); (c) 'evaluation and assessment' to include the establishment of mechanisms for the external evaluations of schools and teaching and for external assessments of student learning based on standardized national tests (d) 'governance and management' to devolve budget responsibilities from the ministry to schools and regional education offices (OECD 2011: 20).

The OECD policy recommendations permeated the Greek education system through the 'New School: The Student First', programme introduced by the socialist government in December 2009 (Ministry of Education 2012). The programme was modelled on the Bush administration's 'No Child Left Behind' Act in the United States (see Gounari and Grollios 2012); it focused on restructuring the administrative framework of primary and secondary education, and on reforming the school curriculum so that the emphasis would be on the improvement of student performance in literacy, mathematics, physics, foreign languages and ICT. These changes were deemed necessary in order to align national educational goals with PISA competencies and to improve in this way the relatively low position of Greece in the results of the 2009 competition (Breakspear 2012). A year later, the 2010 Education Act (Law 3848/2010) specified key competencies for teachers and leaders in education, and introduced evaluation and quality assurance mechanisms for primary and secondary teachers and schools (Sarakinioti and Tsatsaroni 2015). The government presented these changes as radical, as a 'paradigm shift' in Greek education: a necessary response to the need for modernization, for transforming education according to European standards, objectives and forms of accountability (Hellenic Pedagogic Institute 2009). What was involved here was a regulatory system that purported to mimic 'the rigour of the market' (see Ball 1998; Gerwitz, Dickson and Power 2004; Tsatsaroni, Sifakakis and Sarakinioti 2015).

Interlinked with these changes in regulation and management, there were (since 2010) rapid changes in the working conditions of teachers, including changes in their contract. Between 2010 and 2013 teachers' salaries were cut by up to 30 per cent, and a number of schools, mainly secondary, merged or closed. At the same time, the government increased maximum class sizes (up to thirty pupils), 'froze' the appointment of new teachers and closed a number of local primary and secondary education authorities in order to 'release' teachers and relocate them in schools where there was a perceived shortage of teaching staff. As in the French situation, analysed by Guy Dreux in Chapter 4, the 'proletarianization' of teachers was intensified: 'to an ever greater extent they are being dispossessed of the meaning and the content of their work (see Dreux 2013: 32).

The depth of the difficulties experienced by young people on the labour market was used by politicians to justify further education reform, even though the changes proposed were unlikely to stem the growth of a precariat (Standing 2011; see also Innes 2013). In August 2013, as part of the 'New School – The Student First' programme, a reform of the vocational upper-secondary school (ΕΠΑΛ) introduced an optional fourth year apprenticeship route which aimed to strengthen the links between the school and the local labour market.

The 'autonomous' university

In 2011, two-thirds of the Greek Parliament voted in favour of the Framework Act for Higher Education. Following the 2011 OECD report, this Act challenged the high degree of autonomy traditionally enjoyed by Greek universities, by introducing changes to their management, including the participation of members from outside the academic community, modification of the structure of departments and degrees, and changes in accreditation and quality control procedures. While the Greek state continued to assume a regulatory role in terms of 'structures' and 'legal frameworks', it withdrew partially from its obligations to provide financial support to HE, and as a consequence from its role in safeguarding constitutionally free HE provision. Equally significant in this process was the government's retreat from the principle of democratic participation by shifting decision-making from the members of academic communities, including student representatives, to 'outside experts' (i.e. academics from other HE institutions in Greece and abroad and/or representatives of professional associations and local businesses).

Much of the emphasis in the 2011 Act, however, was on the funding system. Income should be generated as much as possible through external funding, tuition for postgraduate studies, sponsorships, donations and market-oriented research. This change signified a break with the historic principles of Greek higher education. More significantly, for the first time, state funding was clearly linked to performance. In this, the Hellenic National Quality Assurance Agency for Higher Education (HQAA) would take over many of the functions of the Ministry of Education, was given new responsibilities. These included allocating funding, according to a list of indicators of 'quality' such as the number of graduates per year, the number of students who graduate within the time limits for their courses, the amount of research funding attracted by each school, the number of doctorates awarded and so on. The setting up of quality assurance processes has, of course, increasingly dominated the European agenda of intergovernmental cooperation, and similar funding systems have recently appeared in many EU countries such as Germany and Finland (see Gouvias 2012, 2007).

Alongside these changes in the types of degree and the fear of privatization in the still-public HE sector, another important element of legislation was the stress on 'individual differences' and 'needs'. Higher Education Institutions were asked to set up life-long learning programmes which would be offered at school level, aiming to attract students from a 'wider social strata and age groups' (GMNERA 2010 in Gouvias 2012: 296). The emphasis in the government's rhetoric here is on 'the flexibility of the content and the mobility of student/learners, so that the skills acquired will meet the demands of the market economy' (ibid.). As Traianou and Jones discuss in Chapter 1 a simplistic version of human capital theory underpins this agenda. Individuals are induced to invest 'in their future well-being by accumulating credits, learning units and so on in order to survive in a world of economic uncertainty' (Gouvias 2012: 300). It also signals a change in the character of the 'student', from being a member of a collective group to a 'customer' who caters for his/her own needs.

Finally, several aspects of the 2011 Act aim at disciplining political activity within universities, including on the part of students. Of particular significance in this process was the redefinition of Academic Sanctuary, which was linked with Article 15 (1) of the 'Charter of Fundamental Rights of the European Union' on the protection of the 'right to work'. With the new Act, strikes of academic and non-academic staff, and student occupations, which are seen to violate the right of university employees to enter into work, can be repressed by the police without the consent of university senates. Under the new legislation, not only would students find it more difficult to protest but demonstrations would be subject to police intervention.

Not surprisingly the 2011 Act (and that of 2012) generated stormy reactions from rectors and students. However, the economic pressures the country was facing helped to spur universities to adopt the changes as a means of survival (see Kanellopoulos 2018). During the period 2009–13, funding for HEI was reduced by 31.74 per cent, though the real reduction rate was significantly higher (GMERRA 2017). Several universities, including the University of Crete and the Athens Polytechnic, reached the verge of financial collapse. Their Rectors urged the government to increase its funding.

The 'People's Austerity': Post-2015 Greece

SYRIZA came into power in January 2015, forming a coalition government with the Independent Greeks (ANEL), a right-wing political party. SYRIZA had invested hugely in the movement against austerity. It nurtured the hope of changing things for the better. Its rhetoric was anti-austerity; its programme emphasized the need for national sovereignty.

Between January and June 2015 the government embarked in tough negotiations with the Troika aimed at achieving a better deal over the management of the Greek debt – negotiations which ended in the capitulation of the government to the Troika's demands (see Kouvelakis 2016; Lapavitsas 2018). The measures in the third memorandum of understanding – which the prime minister, Alexis Tripras, signed in June 2015 – included further pension reforms and taxation; the recapitalization, and in practice privatization, of the Greek banks; and structural changes to the Greek state, dismantling in effect a large part of what was left of its national sovereignty. Commenting on the events of 2015, Kouvelakis (2018: 20) says the following: 'In order to impose a course of "shock therapy", overwhelmingly and consistently rejected by the Greek public, it was necessary to destroy democratic accountability, even in its limited, class-loaded and highly problematic representative form.' Some members of the government, adhering to the 'Left Platform' resigned in protest against the government's decision to remain within the Eurozone. But the government's policies were approved by the electorate again on 20 September 2015, giving the coalition the mandate to 'do the best it could under the circumstances'.

Critics from the Left argued that the government managed politically the post-2015 situation by delaying the implementation of measures which would directly affect people's income, such as pension reforms, concentrating instead on changes such as the privatization of banks which did not affect people's income in a direct manner, but which would have significant long-term consequences (Kouvelakis 2016). By contrast, Tsipras defended his government's programme and actions on moral grounds. Its members, he argued during an interview in *The Guardian*, have escaped criticisms of corruption and his government is determined to 'bring about a moral revolution that will profoundly change the way Greece is governed: "I will manage to take the country out of the bog in which it had been led by those who bankrupted it … and move ahead with a programme of deep reform"' (Tsipras 2017). Unlike neoliberal discourses mobilized by the centre-right political forces in Greece and in Europe, the government's 'deep reform' rhetoric is both pro-European and social democratic; the purpose of Tsipras's moral revolution is to 'restore' the welfare state and to address social inequalities. Between 2015 and the next general elections planned for 2019, the prime minister argued, it will be possible to apply a social justice agenda, close to the liberal values of his coalition. To this end, 'laws aimed at alleviating hardship, starting with reconstruction of the welfare state, are in the pipeline' (Tsipras 2017).

Tsipras's argument presents a tall order for his government. As a result of relentless austerity, the country's economic and social situation continues to deteriorate. Greece's debt was at 180 per cent of its GDP. In 2018, more than 1 million Greeks (22.2 per cent of workers) were unemployed (down from 27.9 per cent in 2013) with youth unemployment at 43.6 per cent (EUROSTAT 2018). Since 2009 more than 427,000 Greeks have left the country to seek jobs abroad. Fifty-five per cent of new contracts are part-time and there has been a sharp deterioration in the working conditions of both private and public sectors employees (see European Trade Union Institute 2018). For example, during 2008–17, the percentage of secondary school teachers in full-time employment was reduced by 35.8 per cent. By contrast the employment of supplementary teachers on temporary contracts was raised to 11 per cent in 2017–18. The port of Piraeus has been sold to a Chinese company, fourteen airports have been sold to the German company Fraport, and most of the coastline will be heavily privatized. Public services including health and education are suffering. The basis for an education system expressing historical aspirations for an expansion of state provision and for 'equality of opportunity' is being eroded. At the same time, the system remains underfunded and its perennial problems continue to be reproduced.

Post-2015 Greek education policies

In SYRIZA's 2015 election campaign, its education proposals were anti-neoliberal and anti-OECD. The party claimed that it was impossible to promote a democratic education system within a neoliberal system (SYRIZA political manifesto 2014) and it supported the resistance of teachers, students and academics to the 2011 Education Act. However, by signing the third memorandum of understanding, the government also agreed to comply with the recommendations of the troika and the OECD: 'The Memorandum of Understanding concluded in August 2015 under the third economic adjustment programme ... considers education as part of a future national growth strategy. ... It calls for the OECD to undertake a review of the Greek education system by the third quarter of 2016' (European Commission 2016: 4). As discussed in Chapter 1 in their memorandums on Greece, the European Union expresses in the clearest form its vision of education, including its strong links to the labour market, and its framing within human capital theory. In their 2018 compliance report the European Commission stressed that 'the expansion of vocational education and training (VET) is a key element to support growth and job creation' (European Commission 2018: 21). The OECD has strengthened further its role as a regulatory body. The relationship between external institutions and the making of national education policy has become much more direct. The OECD's recommendations are 'set to constitute a further basis for the necessary legislative and regulatory changes to be carried out by the Greek authorities and a new education action plan for 2016-2018' (ibid.).

Since 2015 the OECD has visited Greece twice to inspect the progress of the implementation of its 2011 programme (OECD 2017, 2018). As with the 2011 OECD report, both reports highlighted the continuing centralized character of the Greek education system and, drawing on the relatively low position of Greece in the 2015 PISA league table, and on discourses about the impact of the austerity measures on the Greek public sector as a whole, pointed to six areas which once addressed 'can contribute to raising the quality and equity of education in Greece ... [and] help Greece to restore prosperity' (OECD 2018: 5). The OECD's 2017 immediate 'policy options' included (a) the reintroduction of mechanisms for teacher and school self-evaluation whose results could be used to (b) 'rationalize' expenses so that funds are directed to the neediest schools and (c) to pre-school education and care; (d) to develop educational leadership by creating professional development opportunities for existing and future school leaders; (e) to further develop all-day primary schools and improve the quality of the training of primary school teachers. In tertiary education, emphasis was placed on improving the links between post-secondary provision with labour market opportunities in order to ease the transition of students from compulsory to tertiary education and eventually to the labour market. Explicit in the reports is the need for an improvement of the learning outcomes of all students in the key areas of mathematics, literacy and ICT, and the need to develop mechanisms for making better use of data for evaluation purposes. The latter is used to justify the introduction of national assessments of student learning which would eventually replace the university entrance examination system and tackle the private tuition system. The strong similarity to the organization's 2011 recommendations is an indicator of the extent of resistance to the redrawing of boundaries between state and society.

The government's direction of education policy is unclear both in relation to European education policy and in terms of its past promises to create a more democratic education system. This may reflect the unavoidability of compromise. It is not surprising that the first visit of the supranational organization in 2016 was initially kept secret from the public until February 2017, when some of the intentions of the government's forthcoming education reform had been announced as necessary for the 'productive reconstruction of the country'. The July 2017 Education Act, while it modified some parts of the 2011 Education Act, especially those related to the individual evaluation of teachers' work and to the management of Universities, did not alter significantly its content and meaning. In the compulsory sector, the Act introduced twelve year compulsory schooling with emphasis on pre-school education and promoted further the apprenticeship model in vocational education as a positive way of equipping students with the necessary skills for entering the labour market. The policy ambitions of the 1970s are reiterated in a stronger, neoliberal form. The Act reintroduced school self-evaluation (internal evaluation) as the essential means for improving the quality of teaching, and it endorsed the role of 'The Greek Independent Authority for Quality Assurance in Primary and Secondary Education' (Α.ΔΙ.Π.Π.Δ.Ε) in overseeing the evaluation process (see Kalimeridis 2018). Other parts of the 2017 Act are about the professional development of school leaders and the probation of newly appointed teachers according to certain 'pedagogical competencies'. A process which started in the 1990s to 'normalize' practices with the 'best' of Europe seems near completion. The findings of a recent study, which included interviews with education administrators (Tsatsaroni, Sifakakis and Sarakinioti 2015: 523), suggest 'a managerial attitude permeating the educational administration apparatus', also evident in the 'emerging modes of control of the entire public sector.' More importantly, the findings of this study point to the emergence of a new school ethos among a new generation of teachers 'a disposition [among education leaders] to neutralize, depoliticize and de-specialise educational issues'.

The situation in the tertiary education sector is complex. Most academic departments have established accountability mechanisms for internal and external evaluation, their position in international league tables is improving and they offer fee-paid postgraduate courses (up to 12,000 Euros). They also seek funding from private sources. The 2017 Education Act strengthened further these structures and created another layer, the so-called unified higher education framework, to include both universities and higher technological institutions in order to offer more education options to students from vocational routes. With the 2017 Act, universities are asked to develop not only more short life-long learning courses but also two-year degrees suitable to the needs of graduates from secondary vocational schools. What seems to be at issue here is the role of university education and ultimately the meaning of academic freedom. A campaign in the centre-right and centre-left media promotes the need to reduce and simplify the content of the higher education courses and to make them suitable to the needs of the students and to the labour market – a cross-European agenda.

Nevertheless, the government appears still to be committed to protecting the free character of state education provision and to the principle of academic freedom in the humanities, social sciences and sciences. Kostas Gavroglou, Minister of Education, Research and Religious Affairs has repeatedly stressed his government's opposition to the privatization of higher education. The 2017 Act partly restores the power of an academic senate to make decisions about university matters and it gives back to the students the right to participate in the elections of university administrators. It also reinstates, in a peculiar way, the University Sanctuary, which can now be suspended by the police without the agreement of the relevant University Senate only in cases of crimes and crimes of life (e.g. murder). However, the government relies heavily on European funding to sustain the tertiary education system. For the period 2016–20, financial support to higher education institutions will be covered by loans of 550 million Euros from the European Investment Bank (with the national funding at 235 million Euros), which raises questions about how funding priorities will be negotiated. Moreover, the conditions of repayment of these loans are unclear. It is possible that, by mortgaging state Higher Education Institutions to sustain their function, the government has taken a huge risk, paving the way for the introduction of tuition fees for undergraduate studies in the future (see Kargas 2017).

Greece 'returned to the markets' in 2018 and both centre-right and centre-left Greek political forces are pressurizing the government to complete the 'Europeanization' education project. The Left argues that it is impossible to oppose austerity and neoliberalism within the existing monetary union and perhaps within the European Union; 'a rupture is indispensable' (Kouvelakis 2016: 25). Questions about the purpose of higher education and its relation to the labour market, the content of the school curriculum and examination system and the education of teachers remained unresolved.

Conclusion

To a large extent, Greece remains a traditional society, both in economic and in social terms. The reforms proposed by the European Union and the OECD are an attempt to resolve an organic crisis of the Greek education system through external intervention. As we have seen, while these reforms have faced considerable resistance, overt and covert, the centralized Greek education system – with its precious Article 16, its emphasis on academic qualification and insistence on engagement in independent research and scholarship – is gradually being eroded. What are being challenged are both the commitments to the more politically radical conception of the university and an education system for 'equality of opportunity' that prevailed during the *Metapolitefsi*. In post-1974 Greece, the 2011 education reform has been the most coherent, and decisive attempt to modernize its education system according to European policies and standards. The post-2015 reforms have not changed the direction of travel.

Yet, in many ways despite this critical attitude to the reforming commitments of the past, education in Greece is more equitable than it was in 1974. The number of years students spend in formal education has increased; they gain ever greater numbers of qualifications. But the connection between educational success and secure, well-paid employment has weakened especially post-2008 and there are increasing incidents of gender discrimination.

Furthermore, principles of equality do not extend very far into questions of race. Although immigration over the past twenty years has altered Greece's traditional perspectives on race and ethnicity, anti-racist policies remain relatively weak. Racist incidents increased post-2008 putting obstacles in the education of migrant children in mainstream schools.

At present, unlike some of the political parties and formations discussed in the next chapter, the Left does not seem to have a coherent alternative education policy agenda, one which takes into account the country's current socio-economic circumstances and its position in Europe. It may well be true that the all-pervasive desire to 'catch-up' with the rest of Europe, which underpins much of the rhetoric of recent education reforms, including that of a section of the left, is an illusion. As Greece is struggling to reconfigure its position in the post-2008 EU core and periphery (peripheries) division, fresh thinking and the will to try out new ways of tackling the country's education (and social) problems, may be required.

References

Ball, S. J. (1998) Big policies/small world: An introduction to international perspectives in education policy, *Comparative Education*, 34 (2): 119–30.

Bouzakis, S. (1986) *Modern Greek Education*, Athens: Gutenberg (in Greek).

Bratsis, P. (2010) Legitimation Crisis and the Greek Explosion, *International Journal of Urban and Regional Research*, 34 (1): 190–6.

Breakspear, S. (2012) *The Policy Impact of PISA An Exploration of the Normative Effects of International Benchmarking in School System Performance*, OECD Education Working Papers, No. 71, Paris: OECD Publishing.

Coakley, M. (2016) Ireland, Europe and the Global Crisis, *Journal of World- Systems Research*, 23 (1): 177–201.

Dreux, G. (2013) On not addressing the crisis: Neo-liberal reform and the new capitalist school, in K. Jones (ed.), *Education and Europe: The Politics of Austerity*, 19–38, London: Radicaled Books.

ELIAMEP (2006) *The Transition of Greek Universities Graduates in the Labour Market*, Athens: ELIAMEP (in Greek).

European Commission (2016) *Education and Training Monitor 2016, Greece*. Available at: https://ec.europa.eu/education/sites/education/files/monitor2016-el_en.pdf

European Commission (2018) *Compliance Report ESM Stability Support Programme for Greece*, Fourth Review. Available at: http://www.consilium.europa.eu/media/36299/compliance_report_4r_2018-06-20-docx.pdf

Eurostat (2018) *Statistics explained*. Available at: https://ec.europa.eu/eurostat/statistics-explained/index.php/Unemployment_statistics#Youth_unemployment

Featherstone, K. and Kazamias, G. (eds) (2001) *Europeanization and the Southern Periphery*, London: Routledge.

Frangoudaki, A. (1981) The impasse of educational reform in Greece: An introduction, *Journal of the Hellenic Diaspora*, 8: 7–18.

Frangoudaki, A. (2015) Education and social reproduction in post-war Greece, *Athens Social Atlas*. Available at: http://www.athenssocialatlas.gr/en/article/postwar-education/

Gewirtz, S., Dickson, M. and Power, S. (2004) Unravelling a 'spun' policy: A case study of the constitutive role of 'spin' in the education policy process, *Journal of Education Policy*, 19 (3): 321–42.

GMNERA (2005) *Implementation of Lifelong Learning and Other Provisions* (L. 3369/2005), Athens: Governmental Official Journal (in Greek).

Gounari, P. and Grollios, G. (2012) Educational reform in Greece: Central concepts and a critique, *Journal of Pedagogy*, 3 (2): 303–18.

Gouvias, D. (2007) The response of the Greek state to global trends of educational policy making, *European Educational Research Journal*, 6 (1): 25–38.

Gouvias, D. (2012) The post-modern rhetoric of recent reforms in Greek Higher Education, *The Journal for Critical Education Policy Studies*, 10 (2): 282–313.

Guillén, A. (2012) Europe: The crisis within a crisis, *International Journal of Political Economy*, 41 (3): 41–68.

Innes, R. (2013) Italian education: Between reform and restoration, in K. Jones (ed.), *Education and Europe: The Politics of Austerity*, London: Radicaled Books.

Kalimeridis, G. (2018) On the culture of school and teacher evaluation: A critique (in Greek), *Selidodeiktis* 4, 20 August 2018. Available at: https://selidodeiktis.edu.gr/

Kanellopoulos, N. (2018) *Analysing discourses in Greek HE reform during the financial crisis: Discourse analysis as an approach to critical policy studies*, Paper Presented at the 5th Patras International Conference of Graduate Students in Linguistics (PICGL5), University of Patras, 29 May 2018.

Karamichas, J. (2009) The December 2008 Riots in Greece, *Social Movement Studies*, 8 (3): 289–93.

Kargas, G. (2017) Greek national strategy for higher education, *Selidodeiktis*, 1: 79–80, in Greek.

Kassimeris, G. (2005) Junta by another name? The 1974 metapolitefsi and the Greek extra-parliamentary left, *Journal of Contemporary History*, 40 (4): 745–62.

Koustourakis, G. (2007) The new educational policy for the reform of the curriculum and the change of school knowledge in the case of Greek compulsory education, *International Studies in Sociology of Education*, 17 (1/2): 131–46.

Kouvelakis, S. (2011) The Greek cauldron, *New Left Review*, 72: 17–32.

Kouvelakis, S. (2016) SYRIZA's rise and fall, *New Left Review*, 97: 45–70.

Kouvelakis, S. (2018) BORDERLAND Greece and the EU's southern question, *New Left Review*, 110: 5–32.

Landon, T. (2011) The denials that trapped Greece, *New York Times*, 7 November.

Lapavitsas, C. (2018) *The Left Case Against the EU*, London: Polity Press.

Lyrintzis, C., Nikolakopoulos, E. and Sotiropoulos, D. (eds) (1996) *Society and Politics: Aspects of the Third Hellenic Republic*, Athens: Themelio (in Greek).

Maloutas, T. (2016) Intergenerational social mobility: Social inequality in the access of young people to education and occupation during the 2000s, *Athens Social Atlas*. Available at: http://www.athenssocialatlas.gr/en/article/intergenerational-mobility/

Mavrogordatos, G. (1997) From traditional clientelism to machine politics: The impact of PASOK populism in Greece, *South European Society and Politics*, 2 (3): 1–26.

Milios, G. (1994). From the 'shift to technical education' to the 'generalization of the continuing training' [in Greek], *Theseis*, 47: 25–47.

Ministry of Education (2012) From today to the new school putting the student first. Retrieved 15 January 2019, from http://www.minedu.gov.gr/apo-to-simerasto-neo-sxoleio-me-prota-ton-mathiti/όλες-οι-σελίδες.html

Mouzelis, N. (1978) *Modern Greece- Facets of Underdevelopment*, London: Macmillan.

OECD (1997) *Measuring Public Employment in OECD Countries: Sources, Methods and Results*, France: OECD.

OECD (2002) *Education at A Glance. Paris*. Available at: http://www.oecd.org/education/skills-beyond-school/educationataglance2002-home.htm

OECD (2011) *Strong Performers and Successful Reformers: Education Policy Advice for Greece*. Available at: www.oecd.org/greece/48407731.pdf

OECD (2017) *Education Policy in Greece: A Preliminary Assessment*. Available at: http://www.oecd.org/education/educationpolicyingreeceapreliminaryassessment.htm

OECD (2018) Education for a bright future in Greece, 19 April 2018. Available at: http://www.oecd.org/education/education-for-a-bright-future-in-greece-9789264298750-en.htm

Papandreou, A. (1979) Greece Becomes 10th Member of Common Market, *New York Times*, 29 May. Available at: http://www.nytimes.com/1979/05/29/archives/greece-becomes-10th-member-of-common-market-integration-in-effect.html, accessed 4 December 2017.

Persianis, K. P. (1978) Values underlying the 1976–1977 educational reform in Greece, *Comparative Education Review*, 22 (1): 51–9.

Prokou, E. (2003) International influences on educational policy – with special reference to the technological sector of higher education – in Greece as a European semi-periphery, *Compare*, 33 (3): 301–13.

Pshacharopoulos, D. (2003) The Social cost of an outdated law: Article 16 of the Greek Constitution, *European Journal of Law and Economics*, 16 (2): 123–37.

Rocholl, J. and Stahmer, A. (2016) *Where Did the Greek Bailout Money Go?* Working Paper 16-02, European School of Management and Technology, Berlin.

Sarakinioti, A. and Tsatsaroni, A. (2015) European education policy initiatives and teacher education curriculum reforms in Greece, *Education Inquiry* (EDUI), 6 (3): 259–88.

Sotiris, P. (2013) *Neoliberalism and Higher Education in Greece*. Available at http://leftunity.org/neoliberalism-and-higher-education-in-greece/, accessed 5 September 2018.

Sotiris, P. (2015) The Future is Now, *Jacobin*, 13 July. Available at: https://www.jacobinmag.com/2015/07/tsipras-debt-eurozone-bailout-deal-germany/, accessed 4 December 2017.

Standing, G. (2011) *The Precariat: The New Dangerous Class*, London: Bloomsbury Academic.

Streeck, W. (2016) *How Will Capitalism End?* London: Verso.

SYRIZA (2014) *Political Manifesto for Education*. Available at: https://left.gr/news/programmatiko-keimeno-toy-syriza-gia-tin-paideia

Traianou, A. (2009) The uncertain character of recent educational reform in Greece, *Forum*, 51 (2): 131–42.

Traianou, A. (2013) Greek education reform: Resistance and despair, in K. Jones (ed.), *Education and Europe: The Politics of Austerity*, 86–112, London: Radicaledbooks.

Tsakoglou, P. and Cholezas, I. (2005) *Education and Inequality in Greece*, IZA Discussion Papers No. 1582 Institute for the Study of Labor (IZA). Available at: http://ftp.iza.org/dp1582.pdf

Tsatsaroni, A. Sifakakis, P. and Sarakinioti, A. (2015) Transformations in the field of symbolic control and their implications for the Greek educational administration, *European Educational Research Journal*, 14 (6): 508–30.

Tsipras, A. (2017) The worst is clearly behind us, *The Guardian*, 24 July. Available at: https://www.theguardian.com/world/2017/jul/24/alexis-tsipras-the-worst-is-clearly-behind-u

Tsoukalas, K. (1981) *Social Development and the State: The Formation of the Public Sector in Greece*, Athens: Themelio (in Greek).

Tsoukalas, K. (1986) *State, Society, Work in Postwar Greece*, Athens: Themelio (in Greek).

Valassi, D. (2014) Elite private secondary education in Greece: Class strategies and educational advantages, *Culture & Education*, 92 (6): 22–41.

Zambeta, E. and Kolofousi, A. (2014) Education and social solidarity in times of crisis: The case of voluntary shadow education in Greece, *Education Inquiry*, 5 (1): 69–88.

Zmas, A. (2015) Financial crisis and higher education policies in Greece: Between intra- and supranational pressures, *Higher Education,* 69 (3): 495–508.

8

Conclusion: The Contested European Educational Space

Ken Jones and Anna Traianou

Previous chapters have tracked policy developments in national states and in the European Union. In this chapter, we review and summarize these developments in order to address questions which are central to the future of education policy and practice in Europe:

- What is the current meaning of 'Europe'? What policy choices does it embody? Towards what goals does it seek to travel?
- What have been the long-term effects of '2008' – of crisis and austerity – on European societies and their education systems, and on the activity of the European Union?
- What kinds of political challenge to EU orthodoxies are in play within member states?
- How, in these circumstances, have the politics of education been remade?

To these questions, a long period of economic crisis and political upheaval has added a particular sharpness. It is over thirty years since European states began a process of conversion to neoliberalism. The policy framework of the European Union is one aspect of this process, and is not the cause of it. Nevertheless, the policy directions agreed by the European Council have had an increasing influence on the resources available to national policy-makers and the constraints experienced by them. The leading idea of Europe 2020 was 'growth', defined mainly in terms of GDP increase, with other aspects of policy being viewed in terms of the contribution they might make to it (Daly 2012). Since growth was assumed to depend upon the balancing of budgets, the financial objectives of stability and convergence took precedence over the social dimension and were pursued through the mechanism of the European Semester with a new rigour, not effectively mitigated by a concern for a coherent approach to social rights (Pochet 2017). The European Union thus moved away from prioritizing social policy issues, and 'privileged the economic route as the main engine of European integration' (Bouin 2017: 11; Pochet 2017).

The emphasis on economic priorities, with these priorities defined in terms of neoliberal orthodoxy, was replicated in the 'top lines' of EU thinking about education. The making of an integrated European educational space was to occur around a particular conception of educational purpose. 'To be competitive in the global market,' stated the European Council, 'Europe must ... have education and training systems that respond to the demands of the labour market and learners. Effective and adequate training gives employers the best chance of hiring qualified people to be successful in their business.' Therefore, the Council concluded, the skill and aptitude level of young people and adults must be attuned to the 'evolving needs of the economy and the labour market' (European Council 2012a, 2012b). This orientation should be universal – every sector of the future workforce needed to acquire transversal skills – and its implementation was a matter of urgency. As policy reviewers for the OECD continually pointed out, education systems were slow to meet new economic needs (Froy, Giguère and Meghnani 2012).

These social and educational emphases were familiar features of EU policy discourse before the credit crunch, and if anything they have become more prominent since then. In the new economic situation created by '2008', they have been put to a severe test. Prioritizing the economic route to integration entailed continuing the option for austerity, and the labour market conditions which it had created. Nearly ten years after 2008, the European Union's Foundation for the Improvement of Living and Working Conditions noted that the 'Great Recession' continued to have 'significant and lasting effects on European labour markets, with a big drop in employment levels'. The employment structure had been significantly changed, generalizing 'a pattern of job polarisation across Europe, in which employment in mid-paid jobs declined more than in jobs at the top' (Eurofound 2017). In peripheral countries the labour market impact of recession was particularly acute. Historically, countries of the European periphery had sought competitiveness by keeping input costs low. They had used 'second rate technology and a high proportion of low qualified labour' (Etxezarreta et al. 2011). This was the model of industrialization throughout the European South – a model which the rise of low-cost production in developing countries outside Europe put seriously at risk: 'secure' low-skilled jobs decreased in number. When growth occurred it tended to be in high skill sectors, or in those where precarity was the norm. For this reason, the pursuit of aggregate growth and skills acquisition have proved to be far from unequivocal paths to more social cohesion: they by-pass many parts of the population (Leschke, Theodoropoulou and Watt 2015). The situation was made worse by the focus on deficit reduction, which reduced the availability of public sector employment, at the same time as it weakened social provision.

Thus, there was no functioning model of economic growth to which social policies, including education, could easily be related. There was a tension between the aims of educational modernization set out by governments and international organizations and actually existing socio-economic conditions. It was one thing to define new social and educational objectives, but quite another to root them in the deindustrializing, recession-hit, poverty-ridden economies and societies of many European states, where funding levels were falling and the conditions in which many learners lived were inimical to success at school and college. The priority given to 'employability' as a policy goal (Seijo and Seijo 2016) served more as a lever to dismantle established educational programmes, and to prepare individuals, families and societies to adapt to various threatening transformations, than as a realistic means of addressing the needs of European populations.

Post-2008 educational formations

In these conditions, of social turbulence and policy failure, new kinds of political challenge to policy orthodoxies have developed within member states. None of the countries discussed in Chapters 3–7 of this book has retained or developed an alternative model to that of the European Union. In all of them, problems of social and educational inequality are deepening, and precarity is a central feature of working life. Educational institutions are steered towards a human capital approach to education's objectives and those who work in education are pressured, by means of systems of accountability, to provide answers – in the form of better test and exam results – to problems that are not amenable to solution at school or college level.

The broad uniformity is not a simple creation of the European Union, whose norms, procedures and regulations are just one factor in a policy matrix that is also, and sometimes more powerfully, shaped by the commitment of national governments to neoliberalism. The preceding chapters have outlined the various policy assemblages which result from the combination of elements from global, European and national policy repertoires – a process which is influenced by what Neumann and Mészáros call the positionality of national states in relation to a global political economy, by the path dependencies created by national histories, and by the social and political struggles that go on in and around national education systems. As Traianou and Jones argue, in Chapter 1, an adequate and concrete analysis of neoliberalism in education needs always to take account of neoliberalism's embeddedness within particular national situations – what they refer to as 'educational formations'.

Educational development, then, does not proceed evenly across European societies. The long period of neoliberalization charted in this book is punctuated, at national level, by policy turns and accelerations, by challenges and by periods of stasis. The contrasts here, between different 'educational formations', are striking. The election in Hungary of a national–populist bloc led to a rapid reorientation of education policy towards nation-centred themes, and formalized inequalities of access; the elements of equity and social justice retained in EU policy were rejected by the Hungarian state. As Neumann and Mészáros provocatively suggest, the parallels with English education are not difficult to detect – a neoliberal orientation articulated with the characteristic preoccupations of neoconservatism enjoying a second wind. In this ensemble, old themes and old policy actors make a reappearance, alongside an emergent array of private sector organizations, in the context of a long-term adherence to policies of austerity.

In Greece, by contrast, as Traianou shows, the main drivers of change are external. Though it has its supporters in the Greek policy elite, neoliberalism appears not as a native product, but as an intrusive force, imposing a European 'normality' on an education system in which equal opportunity and a certain kind of institutional autonomy had been long-established reference points; and demanding from Greek society the most drastic austerity experienced in its history. More severely even than in Portugal and Spain, a combination of austerity measures and recession, high levels of household debt, collapsing savings rates, cuts in wages and pensions, tax increases, unemployment, under-employment and job insecurity, and the deterioration of core services of the welfare state has formed a 'perfect storm' (Papadopoulos and Rampakis 2018). However hostile they were initially to the emergence of this catastrophe, Greek political actors – including the left-led Syriza-ANEL government – found their field of action circumscribed by economic – and educational – policies devised at a distance by EU and OECD experts. As Traianou suggests, whether the shock doctrine applied to Greece produces a new cadre of policy-makers committed to neoliberal reconstruction is an open question.

To this situation, France and Sweden stand as antitheses, as countries in which educational contestation remains a matter largely for decision-making at a national level, with the European Union's influence being peripheral and Sweden's economic strength keeping Troika-like interventions at bay. In Sweden the European Union's influence is not immediate. In some senses, the country has a school system which is more neoliberalized than others – if the level of privatization is to be taken as the main indicator of neoliberalization. In other senses, as Alexiadou and Rönnberg show, historic national concerns for social equality influence policy-making more strongly than in many states, to the point where the effects of neoliberal reforms are called into question. In France, under the presidency of Emmanuel Macron, EU policy recommendations function as a useful alibi for policy changes which have long been discussed among the governing elite. Macron's government is attempting to accomplish a policy turn which was in part challenged and blocked in the previous decade (Maroy, Pons and Dupuy 2017). In the context of measures to increase the extent of privatization in the French economy, and to weaken the position of labour, the government, as Dreux shows, aims at a comprehensive 'economization' of education, in which student aspiration is intended to be closely linked to an occupational destination determined at an early point, with the educational system being explicitly restratified to enable the steering of students onto appropriate educational pathways. These changes are intended to be achieved within the fiscal constraints of EU agreements, but they owe little to any specific EU blueprint.

Analysing the five countries addressed in this book bears out the claim of Alexiadou and Rönnberg that 'the global flows of education ideas, purposes and governance mechanisms have become embedded in national contexts in very different ways'. In none of our countries, however, are these differences strong enough to suggest that any education stands outside neoliberal orthodoxy. The same can also be said of another set of influences charted in earlier chapters, that relate to issues of race, nationalism and migration. The new, racialized salience of migration as a political issue contributed in part to the election of the Fidesz government in Hungary, to the elevation of the Lega to a place in the coalition government of Italy in 2018 and to the success of Brexit in the 2016 UK referendum on EU membership. Combined with the precarizing effects of an unresisted austerity, it has served to loosen the political hold of established social democratic parties on working-class constituencies in several countries. It is a permanent presence in the education politics of France – where the question of the veil acts as a symbolic condensation of the relationship between 'republican' tradition and new French populations. It has an increasing influence in Denmark, Austria and Germany, not simply as a 'background noise' to the work of educational institutions, but as a set of legal stipulations which materially affect educational practice – from the regulation of clothing in France, to the introduction of the concept of 'ghetto' to social and educational policy in Denmark, and to the elaborate framework of 'Prevent' legislation in Britain (see Chapter 1).

The eclipse of social democracy

Ongoing austerity, linked to the effects of migration, has contributed to a crisis of legitimacy, both for the European Union and for national governments. The crisis tended to reinforce the progressive narrowing of programmatic differences among mainstream parties in national party systems (Streeck 2011), drawing historic parties of the left further into the management of crisis, and leaving them susceptible to a process of rapid outflanking, in which 'a diverse array of popular constituencies – many of them outside the ranks of organised labour – regained a capacity to mobilise resistance to market orthodoxy' (Roberts 2017).

The depth of this distrust was not fully realized by EU policy-makers on the centre-left. In 2018, European Finance Commissioner Pierre Moscovici visited Athens to celebrate the government's achievement in balancing its books through the imposition of enormous cuts in salaries and pensions, and the privatization of large parts of Greek public goods. 'This is not an ordinary moment', he said, 'this is a magnificent moment'. We're talking about eight years of efforts coming to a close for Greece, and it is an important moment for the Eurozone, too. We're seeing an end to a crisis that had threatened our common strategy' (Psaropoulos 2018). That a Socialist politician like Moscovici could not appreciate Europe's crisis in terms of its impact on the lives of populations said much for legitimacy problems of the European Union: prioritizing 'convergence' above issues of social sustainability and national democracy indicated the extent to which commitment to the 'economic route' had become a non-negotiable part of EU thinking.

This kind of commitment was a feature not just of EU policy-making but of the politics of the centre-left across Europe. The German SPD agreed to the European Union's Fiscal Pact (Busch et al. 2013). The Hollande presidency did not honour its pre-election pledges to French voters that it would renegotiate the Pact. In Southern Europe, governments of the left agreed to cuts on a very large scale. In 2009–13, public investment was cut back by 58 per cent in Spain, 55 per cent in Greece and 48 per cent in Portugal; spending on education was a particular target, falling by 19 per cent in Spain, 18 per cent in Greece, 13 per cent in Portugal (Perez and Matsaganis 2017). At the same time as implementing austerity, the centre-left sometimes committed itself to education reform which matched the priorities of international organizations but which was disliked at home. Thus in 2015, the Italian government approved a comprehensive set of new education measures, La Buona Scuola, which, in the approving words of the OECD, had the objective of 'radically transforming the Italian education system by addressing several of the long-standing issues that are at the core of the low level and quality of Italy's skills pool'. Performance pay for teachers, greater autonomy for school managements and an extensive programme of workplace experience for secondary students all featured in the reforms (OECD 2017). Dislike for the programme was widespread and contributed to the defeat of Prime Minister Renzi's proposals for the reform of the Italian constitution, in a referendum which had a strong 'social accent': over 81 per cent of 18- to 34-year-olds voted against the government (Pasquino and Valbruzzi 2017).

Oppositions

The EU president, Jean-Claude Juncker, devoted his first State of the Union speech to the same theme: 'Our European Union is not in a good state. There is not enough Europe in this Union. And there is not enough Union in this Union. We have to change this. And we have to change this now' (Juncker 2015).

However, in the absence of a persuasive set of policies to address Juncker's concerns, the most coherent alternative response is that of social democracy's challengers to the left. Karl Polanyi (1944) suggested that societies have a tendency to push back against market innovations which worsen social protection, and in the process to evoke lost solidarities as alternatives to present depredations. In conditions of 'crisis neoliberalism' (Mulvey and Davidson

2018), this counter-movement has found two outlets – social movements of protest and new parties of the left.

Social movements opposed to neoliberalism have been a feature of European politics since the French movement against the Juppé cuts to wages and pensions in 1995 (Bourdieu 2003), and education has frequently been at their centre – hence the ubiquity of the slogan, 'Education is Not for Sale.' Between 2002 and 2008, the European Social Forum sought to bring together different constituencies of protest, including trade unions and new social movements. Large-scale protests in France (2005) among youth of the banlieue and the lycées, in Italy (2008) among students and Spain (2011), against the effects of austerity indicated both the extent of support for counter-movements and the range of their concerns. Silova et al. in their account of student protests in Eastern Europe analyse further the terms of the movement's discourse. It is based on 'opposition to an ongoing decimation of public services, commodification of knowledge and education, institutionalization of competitive individualism, and resulting social inequality' (Silova et al. 2014: 76). Drawing on the

> metaphors of death, degradation, and danger, youth protesters strongly oppose neoliberal reforms by arguing that these reforms are killing education, converting intellectual humans into primitive beings, and degrading culture, while at the same time increasing poverty and social inequality. Equating reforms with genocide, social hell, or nightmare, youth protesters express deep concern over the gradual transformation of education into a paid-for service. (2014: 76)

The new parties of the left have come into being because of recent social upheavals, but though they owe much to the new social movements of the past two decades, they are also deeply shaped, in their education policies, by the histories of contestation in their national states. To this extent, they are products of particular, distinct educational formations; their policies react to a recent neoliberalism, but are also influenced by the paths of conflict and development taken by education policy over the past fifty years and more. The very different positions of the French and the English left illustrate this point. In contrast with the classical liberalism of Britain and the United States, France (Van der Pijl 2006) established a developmental state, in which governments had a strong role in economic planning and social provision. After the defeat of fascism, popular movements pushed such development further, inflecting the social order, at many levels, in democratic and socially inclusive directions (Canfora 2006): the influence of the CNR (National Council of the Resistance) on French education, through the Langevin-Wallon plan of 1944 is a case in point (Jones et al. 2008).

It is this process – obviously uneven and incomplete, but capable nonetheless both of shaping the character of the state apparatus and of commanding a certain popular – which market-orientated policies have put into reverse. Educational struggles are overdetermined by the terms of this general conflict. They are seen as reactions to processes, both of disenfranchisement through which key prerogatives of national parliaments have been displaced onto European structures, and of social dispossession and regression, in which historic commitments to equality are diluted, and goods once held in common are privatized, in a move typical of the accumulation strategy of neoliberalism (Harvey 2005).

In this context, opposition to government reforms in the 1990s and after became a symbol of the defence of a particular social model against the reform project advanced by transnational elites, and by a national political class that has accepted the global policy orthodoxy. The 2017 education programme of La France insoumise (whose candidate J.-L. Melenchon came 2 per cent behind Macron in the first round of the 2017 presidential elections) reflects this historical dynamic, presenting neoliberalism as the antithesis of French republican/ socialist traditions, and as an existential threat to a model of education that embodies the gains of past struggles (La France insoumise 2017).

In the narrative presented by La France insoumise, the enemy is clear. It is neoliberalism which bears responsibility for national educational decline. In the period of austerity, under the presidencies of Sarkozy and Hollande, 80,000 teaching jobs were lost and the quality of teachers' work was degraded. The 'educational offer' to students was reduced, especially in the schools of the banlieue. Neoliberalism has turned education into a marketplace, threatening the republican principles of liberty, equality and laicité – laicité, the programme stresses, requires the exclusion of all vested interests, business-orientated as well as religious, from the process of education. The 'socle commun' – the core curriculum introduced under Sarkozy and retained by Hollande's governments – should also be rejected, since it reduced education to a minimal and utilitarian set of competences. The goals of education had been turned inside out. Instead of developing free and autonomous learners, the system focused on the production of employable workers, adapted to market demands. The European Union was heavily implicated in these changes: its guidelines and target-setting promoted the subordination of the French education system to the demands of the 'knowledge economy'.

Against these measures, La France insoumise proposes what is both a return to, and an extension of, the republican model of the school. The programme envisages a common school, with a culture of sociability and cooperation; selection would be minimized and inclusive principles extended, including to undocumented migrants (sans papiers). Teachers would have pedagogic freedom, within a system of national, rather than localized regulations. The purpose of schooling would be to 'transmit knowledge', and traditional academic disciplines would be restored to their place at the centre of the curriculum.

France offers the clearest example of the ways in which historic practices and beliefs are 'remobilized', and linked to a programme of anti-austerity. New oppositional movements in Spain and Italy follow a similar, though less robustly argued, set of principles. The positions of the left in Spain were shaped by the struggle against Franco and a centralized reactionary state which promoted the influence of the Church. Under the first PSOE governments (1982–96) the left made gains in democratizing the management of schools (through the election of heads, for instance), in promoting special education, and in devolving control of education to autonomous communities. Podemos, the party established in 2014 out of the experience of the *indignados* movement of 2011 and two years of direct action against cuts and evictions, distanced itself from the PSOE's support for austerity. In other ways it returned to the historic programme of the Spanish left – forsaken by PSOE – so that its opposition to neoliberalism is combined with an attempt to democratize the Spanish state. It aims to increase educational spending, to strengthen the role of local authorities in shaping the school system, and at the same time to lessen the influence of the central state over the educational policies of the autonomous communities (Andalusia, Catalonia, etc.). It emphasizes the adverse effects of the *concertados* – state-funded, privately controlled, often religious schools – on working-class and migrant children, and proposes cautious reforms to integrate them into democratized local systems. It wants to return to a tradition of democratic management of schools; it wants to restore 'critical pedagogy' to teacher education; it criticizes 'education for the market', from a perspective which defends 'social and humanistic education'. It fervently supports inclusive education (Podemos 2017).

In Italy, following the 2018 elections, the Five Star Movement became the largest party in parliament, much larger than parties with roots in the Italian left. The M5S, though claiming many radical positions, was a more ambiguous formation than either La France insoumise or Podemos. Whereas Podemos responded to of local autonomy, framed Spain as a 'nation of nations' and defended the rights of migrants and refugees; the M5S employed a more nationalist discourse, as expressed in tirades by party leaders against migrants and refugees, and in the movement's entry into government alongside the right-wing Lega (Gerbaudo and Screti 2017). A poll for the Corriere della Sera (27 January 2018) indicated that M5S had the support of around one-third of Italian teachers. Its programme, determined by the electronic vote of party supporters, had a strong focus on education; it reflected perspectives of the forces which had opposed the educational programme of the Berlusconi and Democratic Party (PD) governments of the first fifteen years of the century – the Gelmini legislation of 2008, which increased teacher insecurity and increased class sizes, and the PD's Bona Scuola reforms. In their place, the M5S programme proposed an increase in education spending, measures to deal with teacher shortage, and to improve the quality of teaching – with the accent on new methodologies, interdisciplinarity, innovation and inclusivity (Micocci 2018). The private sector would be better regulated, especially in relation to the scandal-ridden vocational education sector (Innes 2013), and subsidies to private schools would be ended. Notably, the M5S programme, perhaps for reasons to do with the collapse of the organized left and its role in preserving historical memory, did not refer back to the educational struggles of the twentieth century: its curriculum emphasis was on 'innovative' research-based pedagogy, not the struggle for democratization and equality; unlike Podemos and La France insoumise its educational programme did not mention migrants.

In Greece, Syriza, before it adapted many of its policies in order to comply with EU demands, had developed a similar framework. Neoliberalism was not securely implanted in Greek society, and the party was able to relate to many issues and struggles where the challenge to neoliberalism was strong and ongoing, rather than exhausted and in need of revival. Its programme for the 2015 elections, from which it emerged as part of the governing coalition, was opposed to neoliberalism, pledged to make increases in funding, opposed to managerial pressures on teachers, committed to historic national principles of free education and aiming to bring about open access to higher education. For Syriza, this was not only a national programme, but one which the party imagined could be argued for at European level.

Across the four countries can be discerned the shape of opposition: a demand for greater public spending, a concern about inequalities and privilege; an objection to a narrow and market-focused curriculum, in which the results of superficial kinds of assessment are used as accountability measures to steer the work of schools. There is an explicit commitment to break with what are seen as neoliberal policies – a break which relates not only to questions of spending but to the market orientation of the school system, and to its departure from what are seen as core principles of education.

In England, the situation is different. England's pattern of educational reform was fragmentary, incomplete, reliant on decentralized local initiative. Beyond the idea of the comprehensive school, decades of reform left no potent legacy that might serve as a reference point for opposition. England, moreover, is the country where neoliberalism has been established the longest, and where the ideological attacks of the right have left their deepest mark, casting the whole project of reform as a road to educational disaster – an analysis which was accepted and elaborated by successive Labour governments. These experiences have deeply affected the character of opposition – especially in schools, where large parts of the neoliberal agenda have become embedded and routinized (assessment practices, market-orientated management).

In other countries, social democracy, seen as complicit in neoliberalism, has been weakened since 2008, and in consequence new organizations of the left have developed, beyond its political scope. In England, that has not been the case – it is through a change in the leadership and to some extent in the policies of the Labour Party that opposition to neoliberalism has been most centrally expressed – with electoral support for Labour increasing as a result. However, the Labour Party remains an ambivalent formation. It does not, at the time of writing, possess a programme which has broken from neoliberal arrangements. Although committed to spending increases and to some headline policies that address issues of fairness and equality (cutting tax relief for private schools, reintroducing free higher education), it has not developed an alternative set of policies as far-reaching as those of new Southern European oppositions. It remains overshadowed not simply by neoliberal arguments about the relationship between education and the economy, but by the weight of a Conservatism that has made certain educational questions – notably around 'standards' – very difficult to answer for a party that has not fully rethought its educational position.

Challenges at EU level

Although the challenge to national forms of neoliberalism has been increasingly sharp, transnational coordination within Europe, of a sort which might offer an alternative to the line of development followed by the European Union, remains weak, to the point where it is difficult to speak of a Europe-wide field of contestation. The European Trade Union Confederation (ETUC) has been consistently criticized for pursuing a narrowly circumscribed role within processes of European integration, distanced from broader social movements (Bieler and Martin 2004), and committed to a 'social partnership' approach, which in broad terms accepted objectives of 'monetary stability, market flexibility and employability at both European and enterprise level' (Taylor and Mathers 2002: 49). The most significant alternative project of the last two decades, the European Social Forum, ambitiously sought to bring together the established organizations of the European labour movement – including trade unions – and new social movements. Successful in mobilizing against the war on Iraq (2002/3), it could not maintain this momentum and ran out of steam precisely at the point where Europe fell into political and economic crisis, without having stimulated a change in labour movement policy.

The prolonged crisis since 2008 has led to some changes in attitude, visible in the policy statements of the European Trade Union Committee for Education. Its response to the ongoing development of the 2020 strategy is still wrapped in a language of 'social partnership' and makes the implausible claim that 'the social partners in the education sector are key partners in designing EU level policy on education' (ETUCE 2018). In other respects, its tone is more critical and its comments accurate. It notes the EU tendency to define educational objectives in terms of labour market needs; it comments on the absence of equality-oriented educational goals from the 2020 strategy; it evokes at length a deterioration in teachers' conditions of work. Yet it is not possible to say that the organization has taken the full measure of the problems of European education, nor of the depth of social crisis which persists around them; it remains within the symbolic field set by the institutions whose partnership it seeks.

Unresolvable problems: Disrupted convergence?

Neoliberalism is both a commanding orthodoxy and a field of contestation. Endeavouring to create a new hegemony in which the beliefs and policy programmes of labour were driven to the margins, it has produced instead a situation in which its doctrines continue to be accepted by policy elites, while their consequences are opposed to the point of social and political destabilization both by old ('dispossessed') and new ('precarious') sections of the working, retired or unemployed population. Education is one of the hubs around which discontent with the social and economic trajectories of national states gathers. As our various chapters show, the problems of national education systems have been several decades in the making. Over these decades, neoliberal policies have become embedded in routine educational practice. At the same time, however, their inability to address the deep-seated problems highlighted by austerity is increasingly clear; education seems to consolidate social inequalities rather than to provide a resource for challenging them.

EU policy is not able to rescue these problems of the national state. An orientation towards human capital objectives in education has become normalized, but a continuing emphasis on educating for labour market requirements, when those requirements themselves do not offer security, leaves European education policy awkwardly placed. Moreover, the European Union's broader policy framework, especially around questions of economic and financial policy, tends to work against its educational promises. In many national states, 'equity' and 'employability' are undermined by the realities of youth unemployment on a massive scale, and what looks like a programmatic hostility towards welfare and labour rights. The creation of a smooth space of European policy-making, which seemed a credible prospect in 2000, now looks much less possible. Post-2008, EU institutions have been organized on the basis of a readiness to intervene in cases where states – particularly smaller and more peripheral states – adopted policies which were not in line with EU decisions on central questions of finance and economics. In the 1980s, the principle of 'subsidiarity' had been invoked to guarantee that the European Union would not involve itself in policy fields which were seen as areas of national prerogative. By 2017, 'subsidiarity' had been turned inside out, so that it signified not a means of protection against centralized power, but rather defined the conditions of legitimate intervention, in which it was 'preferable for action to be taken by the Union, rather than the Member States'. In some cases, notably Greece, this was a provision that was taken to justify specific guidance and intervention (European Parliament 2018). Thus, though convergence remains a goal of the European Union, and though the Council of Ministers has endorsed policies which work towards this goal, the processes through which convergence is sought are attended by conflict: it is more appropriate to speak of a 'disrupted convergence' than a steady and consensual process.

We began this chapter by asking about the contemporary meanings of 'Europe' – the policy choices they embody and the arguments and conflicts that accompany them. The meaning of Europe has never been stable, and the idea of a European union has been configured in many ways, which imagine different kinds of balance between the political, economic and social dimensions of a European project. Altiero Spinelli's Ventotene Manifesto of 1941 emphasized political federalism; Jacques Delors's 'Social Europe' of the 1980s attempted to increase the importance of issues of inclusion and social protection. Since Delors, we can see that Europe has acquired a different inflection, in which the social dimension has been overshadowed by an emphasis on growth and competitiveness, and then by what the Commission and the Council of Ministers saw as the fiscal imperatives arising from the deep global crisis of 2008 (Daly 2012). In this chapter, we have tried to summarize both the problems associated with this inflection and the challenges that it is now facing. These contests are important both in a broad socio-economic sense and in an educational one. In many countries, in the later part of the twentieth century, educational change formed part of a wider programme of social reform which promised greater security and prosperity to the mass of the population. That wider programme has been severely damaged by the policy orientations of national governments and of the European Union. In its absence education in Europe has been asked to face a future in which it functions for some as a possible escape from insecurity, for others as a compromised and inadequate preparation for an uncertain working life.

It is around the terms of a response to this historical shift, and the new expectations which arose from it, that the politics of European education will be constructed. We have tried to show in this chapter both the depth of existing problems and the stirrings of an alternative to them.

References

Bieler, A. and Morton, A. D. (2004) Another Europe is possible: Labour and social movements at the European Social Forum, *Globalizations*, 1 (2), December 2004: 305–27.

Bouin, O. (2017) The end of European integration as we know it: A political economy analysis, in M. Castells, O. Bouin, J. Caraca, G. Cardoso, J. Thompson and M. Wieviorka (eds), *Europe's Crisis*, 11–48, London: Polity Press.

Bourdieu, P. (2003) *Counterfire: Against the Tyranny of the Market*, London: Verso.

Busch, K., Hermann, C., Hinrichs, K. and Schulten, T. (2013) *Euro Crisis, Austerity Policy and the European Social Model: How Crisis Policies in Southern Europe Threaten the EU's Social Dimension*, Bonn: Friedrich Ebert Stiftung.

Canfora, L. (2006) *Democracy in Europe: A History of an Ideology*, Oxford: Blackwell.

Daly, M. (2012) Paradigms in EU social policy: A critical account of Europe 2020, *Transfer*, 18 (3): 273–94.

Etxezarreta, M., Navarro, F., Ribera, R. and Soldevila, V. (2011) Boom and (deep) crisis in the Spanish economy: The role of the EU in its evolution, *Communication for 17th Workshop on Alternative Economic Policy in Europe*, Vienna.

Eurofound (2017) *Employment Transitions and Occupational Mobility in Europe: The Impact of the Great Recession*, Publications Office of the European Union, Luxembourg.

European Council (2012a) *Promoting Vocational Education and Training in Europe: The Bruges Communique*, Brussels: European Council.

European Council (2012b) *Council Conclusions of 26th November on Education and Training in the Context of the Europe 2020 Strategy – the Contribution of Education and Training to Economic Recovery, Growth and Jobs*, Brussels: European Council.

European Parliament (2018) *Factsheet: The Principle of Subsidiarity*. Available at: http://www.europarl.europa.eu/factsheets/en/sheet/7/the-principle-of-subsidiarity

European Trade Union Council on Education (2018) *ETUCE Views on Education in Post-2020 Europe*. Available at: https://www.csee-etuce.org/images/attachments/ETUCE-views-on-education-in-post-2020.pdf

Froy, F., Giguère, S. and Meghnani, M. (2012) *Skills for Competitiveness: A Synthesis Report*. Paris: OECD.

Gerbaudo, P. and Screti, F. (2017) Reclaiming popular sovereignty: The vision of the state in the discourse of Podemos and the Movimento 5 Stelle, *Javnost - The Public*, 24 (4): 320–35.

Harvey, D. (2005) *A Brief History of Neoliberalism*, Oxford: Oxford University Press.

Innes, R. (2013) Italian education: Between reform and restoration, in K. Jones (ed.), *Education and Europe: The Politics of Austerity*, 55–85, London: RadicalEd.

Jones, K., Cunchillos, C., Hatcher, R., Hirtt, N., Innes, R., Johsua, S. and Klausenitzer, J. (2008) *Schooling in Western Europe: The New Order and Its Adversaries*, Basingstoke: Palgrave Macmillan.

Juncker, J.-C. (2015) *State of the Union 2015: Time for Honesty, Unity and Solidarity*. Available at: http://europa.eu/rapid/press-release_SPEECH-15-5614_en.htm

La France insoumise (2017) *L'ecole de l'egalite et de l'emancipation 20*, Paris: LFI.

Leschke J., Theodoropoulou, S. and Watt, A. (2015) Towards 'Europe 2020'? Austerity and new economic governance in the EU, in S. Lehndorff (ed.), *Divisive Integration*, 295–330, Brussels: European Trade Union Institute.

Maroy, C., Pons, X. and Dupuy, C. (2017) Vernacular globalisations: Neo-statist accountability policies in France and Quebec, *Journal of Education Policy*, 32 (1): 100–22.

Micocci, S. (2018) Programma Scuola del Movimento Cinque Stelle per le elezioni 2018, 27 February. Available at: https://www.money.it/programma-M5S-scuola

Mulvey, G. and Davison, N. (2018) Between the crises: Migration politics and the three periods of neoliberalism, *Capital & Class*, 1–22. Available at: http://journals.sagepub.com/doi/abs/10.1177/0309816818780652?journalCode=cnca

OECD (2017) *Getting Skills Right: Italy*, Paris: OECD. Available at: https://read.oecd-ilibrary.org/employment/getting-skills-right-italy_9789264278639-en#page82

Papadopolous, T. and Rampakis, A. (2018) Rattling Ordoliberalism's Iron cage: Contesting austerity in Southern Europe, *Critical Social Policy*, 38 (3): 505–26.

Pasquino, G. and Valbruzzi, M. (2017) Italy says no: The 2016 constitutional referendum and its consequences, *Journal of Modern Italian Studies*, 22 (2): 145–62.

Perez, S. and Matsaganis, M. (2017) The political economy of austerity in Southern Europe, *New Political Economy*, 23 (2): 192–207.

Pijl, K. van der (2006) A Lockean Europe, *New Left Review*, II/37: 9–37.

Pochet, P. (2017) *The European Pillar of Social Rights in Historical Perspective*, London School of Economics European Institute blog. Available at: www.blogs.lse.ac.uk/europpblog/2017/11/14/the-european-pillar-of-social-rights-in-historical-perspective/

Podemos political manifesto (2017) Available at: https://podemos.info/derogacion-de-la-lomce-y-apertura-de-un-debate-educativo-para-una-nueva-ley-de-educacion/

Polanyi, K. (1944/2001) *The Great Transformation: The Political and Economic Origins of Our Time*, Boston: Beacon Press.

Psaropoulos, J. (2018) Greece declared fit for markets after eight years of austerity, *Al Jazeera*, 22 June. Available at: https://www.aljazeera.com/news/2018/06/greece-declared-fit-markets-8-years-austerity-180622061601739.html

Roberts, K. (2017) State of the field party politics in hard times: Comparative perspectives on the European and Latin American economic crises, *European Journal of Political Research*, 56: 218–33.

Seijo, M. and Sejio, J. (2016) The road travelled in Europe towards the 2020 European objectives in education. A Spanish perspective, *European Journal of Education Research Development and Policy*, 51 (2): 270–80.

Silova, I., Brezheniuk, V., Kudasova, M., Mun, O. and Artemev, N. (2014) Youth protests against education privatization reforms in Post-Soviet States, *European Education*, 46 (3): 75–99.

Streeck, W. (2011) The crises of democratic capitalism, *New Left Review*, II/71, September–October: 5–30.

Taylor, G. and Mathers, A. (2002) The politics of European integration: A European labour movement in the making? *Capital & Class*, 78: 39–60.

Index